MASTERING BREXITS THROUGH THE AGES

Entrepreneurial Innovators and Small Firms —
The Catalysts for Success

More Praise for *Mastering Brexits through the Ages*

Every generation experiences various challenges and for the current UK generation, Brexit is but one of these challenges. Brexit is a form of transformation and during such transformation road maps seldom exist. There might be more questions than answers, which are often in conflict with one another and the validity of solutions is questioned from a factual or emotional basis. In this regard, Culkin and Simmons utilise historical paradigms to create understanding how the UK can seize the opportunity to build a sustainable and innovative socio-economic environment for the future. They base their debate on a rich basis of literature and provide refreshing discussions on Brexit from a total different perspective.

— Prof Gideon Maas, President Institute of Small Business &
Entrepreneurship (ISBE)

The uncertainty that Brexit has provoked affects the future of investment, trade, innovation and employment, and it will impact on micro, small and medium enterprises. This book seeks to make a novel contribution to the ongoing debate, identifying alternatives based on lessons learned from the past, before offering the reader an action plan for firms to cope with the future challenges. Nobody can say with any degree of certainty whether small firms will win or lose from the process, but it is urgent to ask these questions and prevent fallouts.

— Mdme Fiorina Mugione, Chief Entrepreneurship Section,
Enterprise Branch, UNCTAD (in a personal capacity)

Culkin and Simmons take the opportunity of impending Brexit to remind us that this is not the first time that Britain has tried to sever its ties with Continental Europe or to be plunged into a crisis due to the disruption of foreign alliances. They look at these crises from a business perspective, drawing on a rich literature on how organisations cope with change and disruption. Firms that do adapt in the ways they suggest might reap the benefits.

— Professor Geoff Hodgson, Editor-in-Chief,
Journal of Institutional Economics

MASTERING BREXITS THROUGH THE AGES

Entrepreneurial Innovators and Small Firms — The Catalysts for Success

BY

NIGEL CULKIN
University of Hertfordshire, UK

RICHARD SIMMONS
University of Hertfordshire, UK

United Kingdom − North America − Japan − India − Malaysia − China

Emerald Publishing Limited
Howard House, Wagon Lane, Bingley BD16 1WA, UK

First edition 2018

British Library Cataloguing in Publication Data
A catalogue record for this book is available from the British Library

ISBN: 978-1-78743-897-2 (Print)
ISBN: 978-1-78743-896-5 (Online)
ISBN: 978-1-78754-500-7 (Epub)

ISOQAR certified
Management System,
awarded to Emerald
for adherence to
Environmental
standard
ISO 14001:2004.

Certificate Number 1985
ISO 14001

INVESTOR IN PEOPLE

Contents

About the Authors   *xi*

Foreword   *xiii*

Preface   *1*
Economic Background: Opportunity and Challenge   *3*
The Pace of Change   *3*
Community Fears and Frustrations   *4*
Nostalgia and Radicalism: The Striving for Simple Answers   *5*
Entrepreneurs Drive Success   *5*
Pictures vs. Brushstrokes   *6*
Seizing Opportunity   *7*
The Fourteen Propositions   *8*
Acknowledgements   *8*

Chapter 1   Today's Landscape   *11*
1.1.   Innovation and Productivity   *12*
1.2.   Accelerating Product Innovation and Consumer Expectations   *14*
       1.2.1.   Innovation Comes in Different Forms: All Forms
                Matter   *16*
       1.2.2.   A Perception of Risk: Entrepreneurs vs. Professional
                Managers   *17*
1.3.   Financialisation has Interrupted Business Credit Mechanisms   *17*
1.4.   Capitalism and the Entrepreneur   *18*
       Figure 1.1.   The Innovation and Profit Generation Circle   *19*
1.5.   Historic Events: Our Window to the Future   *21*
1.6.   The United Kingdom Today   *22*
       1.6.1.   Consumers   *22*
       1.6.2.   Balance of Payments   *23*
       1.6.3.   The Regions   *23*
       1.6.4.   Manufacturing   *24*
       1.6.5.   Services   *24*
       1.6.6.   Generational Mismatch   *24*

1.7.	International Dependence	*24*
1.8.	Today's Biggest Challenges?	*25*

Chapter 2   Brexit Paradigms — *27*

2.1.	Brexit No. 1: AD 410	*28*
2.2.	Brexit No. 2: Break with Rome (Again!)	*30*
2.3.	Brexit No. 3: Adjustment and Stabilisation	*36*
	Table 2.1. Brexit Challenges	*40*
	Figure 2.1. Previous Brexits	*42*
2.4.	Summary	*42*

Chapter 3   Smaller Firms: Engines of Innovation — *43*

3.1.	The 'Ambition Gap'	*43*
	3.1.1. Mission-based Innovation Driven by 'Ambitious Firms'	*44*
3.2.	Differing Market Landscapes	*45*
	3.2.1. Conventional Wisdom	*45*
	Table 3.1. MSMEs by Industry (2016 Employee Count Data)	*46*
	Figure 3.1. MSME 2010 Count by Business Stage (after Blackburn, 2012)	*47*
3.3.	MSME Importance to Overall Economy	*47*
	Figure 3.2. SME Employment and Innovation Impact	*49*
	Figure 3.3. SME Employment and Total Factor Productivity Impact	*50*
	Figure 3.4. E-commerce as % Intangible Innovation by Sector 2000–2007	*51*
	Figure 3.5. Innovation Contribution vs. Employees on Low Pay	*52*
	Table 3.2. Sector Pre-tax Operating Profit Adjusted for Leasing and R&D	*53*
3.4.	The Triangle of Opportunity	*54*
	Figure 3.6. The Triangle of Opportunity	*55*
	Figure 3.7. 'Opportunity Triangle' Sectors	*56*
	Figure 3.8. Opportunity Triangle 'Growth' Sectors	*57*
3.5.	Zombies and New Entrants	*58*
3.6.	Complexity Rather than 'One Size Fits All'	*61*
	3.6.1. Group 1: High-growth Potential 'Big' (or Little!) Bang Disrupters	*61*
	3.6.2. Group 2: Complex Supply Chain Players	*66*

3.6.3.   Group 3: Simple Supply Chain Players   *72*
3.6.4.   Group 4: Professional Advice   *73*
3.6.5.   Group 5: Financial Services   *74*
3.6.6.   Group 6: Local Retail and Artisan Products   *75*
Table 3.3.   Number of Tailors Operating in the United
             Kingdom   *76*
3.6.7.   Group 7: Labour-intensive Service MSMEs   *80*
3.6.8.   Group 8: Knowledge-driven Innovators   *82*
3.7.   Diverse Groups Requiring Differing Brexit Outcomes   *85*
3.8.   Summary: Brexit Implications   *85*
Table 3.4.   Potential EU Impacts   *86*
Table 3.5.   MSME Sectors vs. EU Impact   *88*

Chapter 4   Shocks Revisited   *93*

4.1.   Recap from Historical Brexits   *94*
4.2.   Our 'Stones' and 'Ripples'   *94*
Table 4.1.   Lessons from Previous Brexits   *95*
Figure 4.1.   Sterling Effective Purchasing Power   *99*
Table 4.2.   Disruption Events   *103*
4.3.   Shock A: Financial System Disruption
       ('Sudden Stop Events')   *104*
Table 4.3.   Sample Sudden Stop Events   *105*
4.4.   Shock B: Legal and Regulatory Risk   *106*
4.5.   Shock C: Brexit Day Operational Imperatives   *110*
4.6.   Shock D: Continued Market Innovation   *113*
4.7.   Shock E: Regional Execution   *114*
4.8.   Summary   *117*

Chapter 5   Brexit: The Conventional Wisdom   *121*

5.1.   The Optimistic Case   *122*
5.2.   The Mainstream Case   *126*
Table 5.1.   Mainstream Case Examples   *127*
5.3.   Tinkerbell and the Art of Wishful Thinking   *129*
5.3.1.   The Laffer Curve   *129*
5.3.2.   Government Debt, 'Austerity' and Crowding Out   *133*
5.3.3.   Inequality   *133*

Chapter 6   Our Assumptions   *135*

6.1.   Assumptions   *136*
6.2.   Assumptions Basis   *138*

Chapter 7   Coping with a Brexit Shock   *141*

7.1.   Action Points   *144*

    7.1.1.   Proposition 1: Create New 'Family Silver'
(to Sell at a Profit)   *147*

        Figure 7.1.   Basic Invisible Hand Model   *148*

        Figure 7.2.   Basic Invisible Hand Model with
Resources Reinvested in Growing
Sectors   *148*

        Figure 7.3.   Basic Invisible Hand Model with
Financial Sector   *149*

        Figure 7.4.   Proposed MSME Funding
Support Flow   *152*

    7.1.2.   Proposition 2: Link Public Procurement to MSME
Innovation – Example: Use 'Block Chain' to
Establish Event-triggered Payment System for
MSMEs   *153*

    7.1.3.   Proposition 3: Create an MSME Banking
Ombudsman Service   *158*

    7.1.4.   Proposition 4: 'Share the Problem and the Solutions'   *159*

    7.1.5.   Proposition 5: 'Initiate an MSME-focused
Exporting Program'   *160*

    7.1.6.   Proposition 6: Kill Non-viable Firms   *164*

    7.1.7.   Proposition 7: Accept that the Supply Chain Status
Quo Must Change: UK Competitiveness Must Rise
or UK Operations Risk Redundancy   *165*

    7.1.8.   Proposition 8: Publicly Contract MSMEs to
Build Block Chain-based Real-time Certificates of
Origin System   *168*

    7.1.9.   Proposition 9: Follow in the Footsteps of 'Economic
Miracle' Countries to Establish 'Innovation
Contracts' that Blend Public and Private Sectors   *170*

        7.1.9.1.   Fraunhofer and the German Mittlestand   *174*

        7.1.9.2.   DARPA in the United States   *175*

    7.1.10.   Proposition 10: Build the Venture Capital
Exit Chain   *177*

    7.1.11.   Proposition 11: Make it Worthwhile Patenting   *179*

    7.1.12.   Proposition 12: Raise Management Competence   *182*

    7.1.13.   Proposition 13: Give Control of Immigration to
the Market and Up-skill the Indigenous Workforce
through Vocational Training   *184*

    7.1.14.   Proposition 14: New Trade Agreements   *190*

7.2.   How Did They Cope in Previous Brexits?   195
     Table 7.1.   Previous Brexit Experience   196

Chapter 8   Epilogue: Unlocking Our Potential   203

8.1.   Entrepreneurs Must Drive What Support They Need   205
     Table 8.1.   Support Organisations   205
8.2.   MSMEs as Revenue Stream for Some Advisors   207
8.3.   MSME Characteristics   209
8.4.   New Structures Will Be Required Before Brexit Day   212
8.5.   The Real Brexit Challenge   213

Appendix: Simple Glossary   215

Bibliography   219

Index   241

About the Authors

Nigel Culkin is Professor of Enterprise and Entrepreneurial Development at the University of Hertfordshire. He has published widely in the areas of small business leadership, entrepreneurial universities, graduate entrepreneurship and the creative industries, as well as completing projects for UK and overseas government agencies, large multinational organisations and research councils. In 2014, he was elected to the post of President at the Institute for Small Business and Entrepreneurship (ISBE); and, in 2015, was invited to join the prestigious Peer Review College at the Economic and Social Research Council (ESRC). He is a regular attendee at the UNCTAD Expert Meeting on entrepreneurship and building productive capacities, held in Geneva.

Richard Simmons is an Economist with enduring expertise in SMEs as innovation engines. He has a strong belief in market solutions, with interests in growth processes, ethical financing and dynamic (including monetary) equilibrium in an entrepreneurially driven and financially sophisticated world. Formerly holding senior regional and global management roles in various leading-edge high technology and medical device firms, he has lived and worked globally. He now advises a senior global investor based in Riyadh and is a Visiting Lecturer at the University of Hertfordshire.

Foreword

The journey towards this book started with the result of the June 2016 Brexit Referendum and a nagging fear that a 'black swan' or two may be on the horizon. Given, that almost everyone's prognoses differed from the immediate post-Brexit reality, we began looking for some form of reference as to potential outcomes. Could history offer any insights as to what these might be? And from that germ of an idea this book was born. Our manuscript was completed in October 2017.

Having just read the final proofs, it struck us how much about Brexit remains essentially the same as when the manuscript was completed. Every day, the press presents another strand as to what might be, and every day the Article 50 notice clock keeps ticking. Little healing appears to have taken place. What is said to be agreed in one breath seems to be challenged by someone else in the next. And so the arguments go on, but these debates are amongst us in the UK, rather than a genuine negotiation with our European Partners. This narrative often feels like an echo from the discussions of the 1840s and 1850s that culminated in the 1846 Corn Law repeal and the 1860 Cobden Chevalier Treaty. A familiar discourse covering Free Trade, Trade Agreements and with an underlying subtext framed in strategic aims to maintain and expand Empire; or, perhaps as some have more recently suggested, a network of Free Trade Agreements loosely based around the Commonwealth.

Sterling has risen against the US dollar over recent months, but the more business-related "trade weighted" exchange rate index continues to show a sharp decline in the value of Sterling since the 2016 Brexit Referendum. The many European Union – Third Country Treaties that will fall on Brexit Day remain an unresolved issue. And although little is featured in banner headlines, a number of companies and financial institutions seem to be taking steps to quietly move some of their operations into other EU States. It is hardly surprising they are quiet in doing this, as they are acutely aware that just over 50 per cent of the country believes passionately in Brexit as the way forward.

Almost two years after the Referendum, the bitter divisions continue. If anything, it feels like positions have become more entrenched. The 2016 General Election that saw the loss of the Conservative majority in Parliament was also characterised by a higher youth vote than previously registered. The participation of a younger generation in shaping what sort of country they want will, one senses, become a more important feature of the on-going narrative as the story unfolds.

In some sense, we live in a 'social media' framed future, a world in which new groups or 'Tribes' can form and re-form, according to the 'trending' issue of the day. These Tribes are hungry for news that helps confirm their 'Tribal Identity' and disparaging of anything that does not. The traditional print media largely plays to these Tribes to safeguard its own sales in a fast-changing and fast-digitising media landscape. In the sixteenth century, these Tribes would have been defined by religion, today it's more likely to be Leaver or Remainer or perhaps Old or Young, Urban or Rural and forth. The tracts of the Elizabethan or early seventeenth century printing press have morphed into the blogs and social media feeds of today. It's an ironic thought that advanced civilisation is more usually identified with the breaking down of tribal barriers than creating new ones.

Despite the backward-looking feel, we continue to believe that the UK's future well-being will rest upon how it can adapt and embrace emerging technologies and market transformations to leap-frog existing competitors. The winners in this arena will most likely be visionary entrepreneurs who seize the moment to build new, unique and profitable market spaces for themselves. Whilst favourable trade treaties can help, we believe that the 'magic growth dust' will be the entrepreneurs and the firms they build that go on to transform the global markets they operate in. The post-Brexit narrative has not changed this central theme in our book.

So, we are faced with the adage of *plus ça change et pas de change*. So much changing and nothing changing. We believe that history is perhaps the most meaningful window to help us evaluate potential Brexit impacts, in the same way innovation and entrepreneurship will be essential tools to building a new post-Brexit sustainable future. After so many column inches devoted to Brexit, perhaps the past six or so months can be summed up by our definition of Brexit below.

Brexit: *noun*: An act of the people of Britain (sometimes defined as Britannia) exiting foreign (colloquially European) imposed rules and practices.

Historical Precedent	Synonyms
End of Roman Britain (AD410)	*Empire 2.0*
Break With Rome (1529)	*Free Trade 2.0*
Break with Catholic Europe (1560s)	*Sudden Shock Therapy*
	Nostalgic Pipe Dream
	Project Fear
	Falling Sterling and Squeezed Real Wages
	Generational Imbalance and Pensioner Rights
	Bitter Intolerance

As our narrative will demonstrate, entrepreneurs who successfully push technological and market boundaries are key to constant renewal. In summary, entrepreneurs drive the rupture with the sterile, unfruitful or unproductive and build the future, perhaps another way of alluding to "Creative Destruction" in action.

In an echo from another age, we identify 14 points for consideration as the UK comes to establishing the 2019 Brexit Treaty. A treaty that we hope avoids becoming an idiomatic '2nd Treaty of Versailles'.

Brexit can act as a spur to reinvention and will be successful if it enables the support and resources the entrepreneurs, who will build our economic future, need to both attain the quest and surmount challenges they face.

Preface

> *Most people are in favour of progress, it's the changes they
> don't like.*
>
> — Unknown Source

'Taking back control' should unlock the energy of the Greek's immortal
blacksmith Hephaestus (known as Vulcan by the Romans) and harness
the wisdom of Athena to ignite a new age of Entrepreneurial
Opportunity and National Pride according to 'Brexit Believers'. A gift
to all.

> *Then Prometheus, in his perplexity as to what preservation
> he could devise, stole from Hephaestus and Athena wisdom
> in the arts together with fire — since by no means without
> fire could it be acquired or helpfully used by any — and he
> handed it there and then as a gift to man*
>
> (Vlastos, 1956, p. 19)

For the 'Brexit Naysayers' perhaps the journey will be like Icarus, son
of Daedalus, who took the wings made of wax and feathers to escape
with his father from the Minotaur in the Cretan Labyrinth, and soared
too close to the sun with the wings collapsing as the wax melts and the
feathers drop away...

Policy by megaphone is seldom the policy of evidence-based
reason. It too easily becomes the policy of the zealot, and then anyone who disagrees with the zealot becomes an 'enemy of the people'.
A narrative recited repeatedly over the ages, any contrarian opinion
becomes in its mildest form 'fake news' and in its more extreme form
the backdrop to the writing of texts such as Foxe's *Book of Martyrs*
in 1563. Suppressed dissent can bubble over and be conflated with
power battles between different groups and provide the fuel for
events such as the English Civil War, a multi-dimensioned conflict
which was both part secular and part religious. It is for our readers

to take their own view on which was the dominant theme in that conflict.

Reason is lost in hyperbole. Foolishness overtakes wisdom. Wishful thinking replaces reality. 'Snake Oil' becomes 'Miracle Cure'. The cancer of distrust contaminates leaders, representatives and institutions. Experts assert they have the answers without explaining that they only have the answers if their assumptions are correct. Equally, many people, just like Icarus, don't want to listen to the expert, even if it means disaster when reality overtakes hyperbole.

Our book is about stepping away from predetermined views and using historical paradigms to understand future challenges. The 2019 Brexit will not be England's first Brexit, as there have been a number of previous ones. We focus on three of these, the end of Roman Britain, the Henrician Reformation and the Elizabethan Settlement, but there have been others. For example, there is the 10-year Brexit in AD 286 led by Carausius, a Celtic nationalist[1] with distinctly 'pirate' like characteristics (Woolf, 2016). Having risen to Admiral of the fleet and contributing to supressing the Gauls (Franco – English tensions are nothing new), he was found guilty of corruption by Emperor Maximian and so decided his future would be best served by declaring himself 'Emperor of Britannia'. Carausius ignites Celtic nationalism with phrases like 'Liberty' and 'Restorer of Britain' and brings both Army and Navy with him to seize power.

Notably, Carausius having seized power tries to do a deal to make peace with Rome, and fails. He doesn't last long. Seven years later (AD 293) he is murdered by rivals and replaced by his Finance Minister Allectus, who lasts three years until reconquest by the Romans. Rather than creating the first British Empire, Carausius ended up becoming a footnote in history.

---

[1]There is some dispute on Carausius's lineage following a 1911 entry by Chislom in *Encyclopedia Britannica* and copied into Wikipedia that Carausius was a Menapian (a Belgian tribe from north Gaul) of humble origin. Casey in a 1994 book on Carausius and Allectus traces Carausius to be a son of Bonosus who claims royal lineage to Cunobeline King of Ancient Britain from AD 9 to AD 41. Coincidently for lovers of children's rhymes, Cunobeline appears to have had a son called Caractacus. It appears the disputed lineage comes from contrasting sources: Carausius's tomb was a Celtic cairn and the inscription suggests he was a great Celt, the Britannica attribution from Roman historian Sextus Aurelius Victor writing many years after Carausius died.

Economic Background: Opportunity and Challenge

Nostalgic or progressive; traditional or disruptive; whatever our view on the world, a common thread runs through all. A hope and aspiration for a 'better world'. For our narrative 'better' is defined in 'economic' terms, namely defined as rising productivity that drives economic growth and leads to a rise in real living standards, so reversing poor post-2008 living standard growth trends. Machin (2015) tells us how median real wages grew by about 2 per cent per annum from 1980 to the early 2000s, but since the 2008 financial crash median real wages have fallen by around 8–10 per cent corresponding to a 20 per cent relative drop in comparison to the previous trend rate. Ultimately, real wage growth and living standards growth for the whole population depend upon economic growth consequent upon rising Total Factor Productivity (i.e. improved output per unit of labour/capital). In the ten or so years since the 'Credit Crunch' of 2007/2008, economic progress in terms of this Total Factor Productivity and associated real wage growth has been disappointing across the developed world and most especially in the United Kingdom (Haldane, 2017). This disappointment has been against the background of continued and rapid technical change in the products and services in everyday use.

The Pace of Change

We seem to be living in an ever-faster changing world. Illustrating this, many products that are ubiquitous today were figments of consumer imagination just 10 years ago. For example, in January 2007 Facebook did not work on mobile phones and was far from being widely used on PC type devices. In December 2007, there were a mere 58 million active users globally, by December 2016 this had risen to 1.86 billion active Facebook users, many of them (1.15 billion) active on Facebook's mobile platform (Facebook, 2017). The first iPhone, the start of the 'Smart Phone' revolution, was launched in June 2007. Nokia was still the number one mobile phone company globally with over 35% of the market in 2007 (source: Statista) and Android phones were unheard of to the common consumer as their initial commercial launch was not to come until 2008. In this rapidly changing dynamic world, British success has been limited. There have been some winners, for example Dyson, and until its recent acquisition by Soft Bank, ARM Holdings was a UK global technical champion in silicon chip design. More established companies such as Unilever and GSK have also been very successful at driving new products into established markets. Despite the United Kingdom having a number of top global universities – and being one of the world's key finance hubs – it has been unable to create a Google, Amazon or Facebook.

Community Fears and Frustrations

Becker, Pfaff, and Rubin (2016) tell us from a comprehensive study of the Brexit Referendum vote that Vote Leave was more successful where there were lower incomes, high unemployment with less adaptable workforces who are older and have lower qualifications. For many towns and communities located away from London's global finance hub, there has been a steady loss of big name manufacturing. Previous 'greats' such as Rover have disappeared along with their jobs. In their place have come new jobs, mostly in the service sector and many with poorer pay and conditions, including the rise of zero-hours contracts (that do not guarantee a monthly or weekly income) and the fashionable 'gig economy' (something broadly akin to what was known as casual labour). Self-employment has grown relative to salaried employment, particularly in older age groups. Housing has, for many, become more unaffordable, real wages have stagnated and final salary pensions have become, for many, a figment of imagination.

Growth performance and value added per head has substantial variations between regions (Harari, 2016). For example, top in terms of value added per head are the London Borough of Camden and City of London with a Gross Value Added per head in excess of £292,000, against a UK per head average of £25,000 and, a lowest value added per head at under £14,000 per annum (Harari, 2016).

Unease has been heightened by immigration. Culturally, especially Asian and Indian subcontinent immigration has unsettled the indigenous population near areas where these groups have settled. Sometimes integration has been synonymous with fears and phobias of Islamic extremism. European Union (EU) immigration from Eastern EU Accession States has, for some, become a narrative of interlopers taking away well-paid jobs and affordable housing from the native population. For others, especially the old, hearing groups of foreigners speaking an alien tongue conjures up fears for their physical safety. The UK's ageing society has become politically skewed towards protecting the old at the expense of the young, as pensions have their benefits protected, whilst low-pay families are targeted to reduce working tax credits and housing benefit. Measures have been enacted to withhold support for families with more than two children. These generational specific measures are unsurprising given that older people tend to vote more than young ones.

Britain's National Health Service is under a perpetual strain that grows as the population ages, with older people tending to have more medical issues. Equally, strains on health resources have fed back into resentment against immigration as fears are expressed that health service resources are consumed by immigrants. Cuts in Adult Social Care budgets increase the number of old people who cannot be safely discharged as there is no care available, so further increasing strains on hospital services as beds are blocked by people who cannot be discharged for lack of available social care. Such a narrative continues in many other areas of state services, as the government targets reducing public expenditure both to reduce public sector deficits and to reduce the state spending share of Gross National Product, on a belief this will enable the private sector to flourish.

Nostalgia and Radicalism: The Striving for Simple Answers

Facing uncertainty and hoping for the best, humans strive for simple answers. It's a common historical thread. Post-1945 Neo-Keynesian economic stabilisation programmes, 'Monetarism and Liberalisation', the Hayekian narrative of the Thatcher and Reagan years and the Cameron and Osborne world of austerity are examples of simplistic narratives seeking to address complex problems. The real world is more multifarious, a world that needs a supportive and nurturing framework of business to thrive. Look only at the post-1945 economic successes in Japan, South Korea, Taiwan, China and Silicon Valley, to name a few.

Support needs for growing innovating economies, driven by innovating capitalist entrepreneurs, could turn out to be nearly as unsettling as the people disrupting and changing them!

Entrepreneurs Drive Success

> *Someone is sitting in the shade today because someone planted a tree a long time ago.*
> — Warren Buffet (Kilpatrick, 2001)

Products, services and colossal ventures at some point started with an entrepreneur or a group of entrepreneurial thinkers, planting a small acorn. In some cases, the acorn grew into a mighty oak; occasionally, it may have spurted initial growth then withered and died; and often the seed did not even germinate. The Entrepreneur and their associated Micro, Small and Medium Enterprises (MSMEs) are the planters of these acorns. It is these MSMEs that are the heart of our thinking.

Some entrepreneurs are on the receiving end of change (for example, the humble corner shop owner); some entrepreneurs are partners in change (for example the small company providing high technology products to the Automotive or Aerospace industries); and some are crafting the change (the Big Bang Disrupters). The beauty of a smoothly functioning Capitalist System in full flow is that it allocates resources across all types of entrepreneurial activity according to entrepreneurial need. Innovative firms with great products thrive, receive necessary finance and firms with poor products that customers don't want, lose it.

There is nothing new in this. Wicksell (1898) spoke of banks allocating finance to business in line with their productivity and profitability with his *Natural Rate of Interest* giving *dynamic equilibrium* when capital is allocated to its most appropriate uses. Schumpeter (1934) developed further this theme, seeing a process allocating bank credit towards innovative entrepreneurs away from dying entities. Capital flows to businesses consumers want to succeed.

Financial liberalisation and financialisation have reduced financing (especially bank) flows to especially smaller and entrepreneurial SMEs (Krippner, 2005). This is crucial — *'a capitalist system can only function so long as the receipts of entrepreneurs exceed their outlays; in a closed system, and ignoring Government loan expenditure, this will only be the case if entrepreneurial expenditure exceeds workers' savings'* (Kaldor & Kaldor, 1978, p. xvi). Capitalism is about allocating capital to entrepreneurs who drive profitable productive change, not about private vs. public ownership.

Pictures vs. Brushstrokes

If you are a Brexit or Remain Zealot; if you are a Brexit or Remain Bolshevik on the Left or Right; you, as our reader, may be frustrated by our journey and seek to throw Henry Ford's, *History is Bunk*, at us! Can we encourage you to pause, step back and join us to see if using a broad window of history as context can help give form to the picture you are trying to paint?

If you are an expert on any of the events or issues we refer to in our narrative and find yourself in passionate disagreement on some point of detail, we seek your indulgence. Many events we describe are controversial and in many cases the evidence can be patchy. We do not claim solutions to age-old discourses, rather we see these events as brush-strokes in the overall picture we paint. For example, you may radically disagree with our description relating to the speed of events around the end of Roman Britain, or with any suggestion that the subsequent centuries could be labelled, a Dark Age, when scholars such as Bede were at work. Rest assured, we are not seeking to contribute to these debates, rather we are looking to use these as examples to form the detailed brushstrokes in a picture that provides a window into what promises to be an undeniable period of discontinuity and change.

It is these moments of discontinuity, moments of change that are our focus. We anticipate Brexit having the capability to be a similar moment of change. Our pictures from the past are intended to help the reader identify some of the challenges we may face. As the brushstrokes form into pictures, our readers should feel free to add their own examples, their own brushstrokes, not least to help crystallise the picture and strengthen understanding.

Seizing Opportunity

Brexit will be a moment of change, and at such moments throw up significant opportunity. This book is not about 'Leave' or 'Remain', although there may be some cautionary pointers on our journey. In many cases, indeed with most of the issues and proposals we identify, Brexit is not a *necessary condition* to take action, but it will become a condition where it is *necessary to take action*. Even without Brexit many of the proposals could easily be adapted and adopted in other countries and other situations.

Brexit is our trigger event, so necessarily this book will seek to set a road map to make the United Kingdom the number one innovative economy globally in a Brexit context. In some respects, Brexit will help this journey and in some respects, it will hinder it, but that debate is for elsewhere. Our goal is to understand how we can seize the opportunity.

A narrative then, about how to transform the United Kingdom into becoming the next global luminary.

This achievement will not happen by turning back to dreams of Empire, it will not happen by letting ideology drive policy and it will not happen by ignoring reality, by mimicking the actions of King Canute. Brexit is going to disrupt, damage and alter trading relations with our nearest and most important trading partner, the European Union. Brexit is going to lead to the recasting of some international supply chains and it is going to lead to the decline of some industries. Challenge will abound, the question is how to transform this challenge into opportunity.

The Fourteen Propositions

Paradoxically, our narrative identifies 14 propositions (a further echo from 1919); that is, 14 opportunities to change frameworks to drive success. These propositions are derived from looking at past experience from past Brexits and combining this with today's landscape. Our readers will find this analysis to be a cumulative process throughout the book, starting with a highlight of 10 features from previous Brexits, that are then ranked by impact and used to offer solutions.

Our formal narrative finishes at the point where we then close the circle, by contrasting our proposals to what happened in the previous Brexits, in a summary that assesses relative success in each one in their adjustment to the new situation. This is followed by an Epilogue that suggests some implementation and change frameworks. For every reader, the detail may be different, the brushstrokes of different colour and intensity, but the pictures feel consistently familiar.

Rejuvenated Hephaestus and Athena or an Icarus rerun? The keys are in all our hands. Success will come from learning from our past, from the success of others and building frameworks that inspire and support the seizing of the opportunities.

Acknowledgements

This book has been a living and time-consuming organism for many months, so first we would wish to thank our families for their understanding and forbearance.

Additionally, special thanks are due to The Master and Fellows of King's College Cambridge for access to both Lord Kaldor's and J M Keynes's papers; to the archivist at the Hull Historical Centre for helpful guidance through the Hull City Archives; to the archivist at the York Company of the Merchant Adventures for information supplied; to Simon West archaeologist at St Albans for a very illuminating discussion on how Verulamium transitioned from Roman rule; to Professor Ward-Perkins for a very helpful email correspondence and comments on the Europhile nature of the later Saxons; to Michael Simmons for patiently reading and commenting upon many early manuscript drafts and to many others. Thank you.

Chapter 1

Today's Landscape

Extinction is the rule. Survival is the exception.
— Carl Sagan (2007)

It is likely that almost every British citizen has a view on what Brexit will mean for him or her; some will see it as a dreadful end, others a glorious beginning. Whilst expectations may differ, hopes and aspirations are likely to have far more in common, namely to build a better and easier world, a component of which is positive economic development that supports a rise in individual and household living standards. The 'story' as to how all our expectations will translate into reality is yet to be written, but we can be sure that aspiration will remain throughout the writing.

Our narrative is a contribution to this journey; one that starts with the question *'How can we use changes to deliver economic development that helps deliver aspirations?'* Innovation and an associated rise in productivity are the main determinants of economic development. *'From acorns, mighty oaks do grow'* is a simile that justifies our stress on the importance that entrepreneurs and their Micro, Small and Medium Sized Enterprises (MSMEs) play in driving growth. Our part in this unfolding drama will be to seek (with the aid of the window of historical characters and anecdotes) to outline a set of 14 propositions that seek to help enable growth, and minimise negative impacts through learning from the mistakes of previous shocks. Past lessons are combined with today's capacity to innovate to offer suggestive hope as an alternative to the current bout of seemingly existential nihilism.

As of November 2017, there were in excess of 5.7 million MSMEs operating in the United Kingdom with each one at its own individual unique stage of development (BEIS, 2017). MSMEs operate in different markets, develop differently and possess varying capabilities. Additionally, the type of innovation each engages in can be different according to the ambitions of their founding directors. In our context, innovation can be defined as the process of commercialising or bringing into common usage an invention, concept or design for a new or improved device, product or process (Freeman, 1982).

1.1.   Innovation and Productivity

The term *innovation* was first employed at the start of the twentieth century during a time when the field of science was changing beyond recognition. New products were developed for both industrial and consumer markets, which in turn led to a further rapid development of technologies across a wide range of industries, to sustain economic growth, from the 1950s onwards. As markets advanced and became increasingly global in reach, businesses and public research organisations turned to patents to protect the outputs from research and development programmes. However, growth in patenting corresponded to new modes of innovation research practice, which placed more emphasis on knowledge networks and markets than the individual firm as we approached the twenty-first century.

The original definition of innovation was too narrow to reflect the role that patents and knowledge networks play in innovation and economic performance and the OECD was tasked with broadening its scope. The update – announced in 2005 – now asserted that innovation was 'the implementation of a new or significantly improved product (good or service) or process, a new marketing method, or a new organisational method in business practices, workplace organisation or external relations' (OECD/Eurostat, 2005, p. 17). Although the definition above is well understood today, it was Schumpeter who saw innovation very broadly as a product, a process and organisational change that does not necessarily have to arise from new scientific discoveries, but that may combine already existing technologies or their applications in a new context.

Productivity is a main determinant of economic development. Growth in productivity is, therefore, one of the major driving forces behind wealth creation and economic prosperity; and, strong economic growth is behind enhancements in living standards. We can measure productivity growth as the ability to produce more with less or the same overall level of inputs and *inter alia* it is the result of some combination of improved products, services, processes, technologies, organisational structures and ideas. Evaluating how these elements evolve can inform us how efficient an economy is functioning in both a static and dynamic sense. Economists usually distinguish between two main types of efficiency: allocative or productive efficiency, and dynamic efficiency (Hodgson, 1988). The former can be expressed as the Production Function that looks to combine the different factors of production at a given state of technology to drive specific momentary levels of measurable productivity. Conceptually, the latter, dynamic efficiency relates to how the overall relative price system allocates resources across competing needs to arrive at an overall optimal resource allocation or 'General Equilibrium'. This allocation ensures resources are not misallocated into producing products that do not have market demand. Long-run growth rates are determined by changes in the Production Possibilities Frontier that reflect innovation and the pushing forward the technological frontier. Large step changes in technology often require government involvement to investing in new technologies (where risks are too high for the private sector to bear) to encourage firms to innovate and improve (Mazzucato, 2013; see Box 1.1).

Box 1.1. The State as Active Driver

Prior to his inauguration as the 34th president of the United States, Dwight Eisenhower was president of Columbia University (1948–1953), which, in itself, included a sabbatical when Eisenhower became Supreme Commander of NATO. According to Jacobs (2000), Eisenhower's time at Colombia was not without controversy, punctuated as it was by his activity with the Council of Foreign Relations (CFR). His work at the CFR focused on the implications of the Marshall Plan and on the American Assembly; an area that he was particularly keen on and that helped shape his latter position on economic policies. Eisenhower saw the potential for the Council to become a great cultural centre where business and governmental leaders could meet to discuss and reach conclusions concerning problems of a social and political nature (Wiesen Cook, 1981).

Perhaps not as successful an academic administrator as his brother Milton (widely regarded as one of the most successful presidents of John Hopkins University, among others), Dwight Eisenhower did put his Colombia experiences to good use when, in 1958, as a direct response to the Soviet's success in launching Sputnik, he, as American President, funded the Defence Advanced Research Projects Agency (DARPA). Eisenhower was concerned that the United States was in danger of falling behind its Cold War rival in technological achievement, especially in the technologies of war fighting and defence.

DARPA's role was to fund, and coordinate, research programmes carried out by the military, private industry and academia to fulfil its mission of avoiding and creating technological surprise. Today, the agency claims it has spearheaded initiatives that *changed the world* – a phrase frequently heard at DARPA, to ensure a focus on transformative innovation, as opposed to incremental improvements in existing technologies (Mehra, 2013; National Research Council, 2009).

DARPA's achievements have included seminal roles in the development of the Internet from the perspective of both technology and human capital. In her book *The Entrepreneurial State*, Mariana Mazzucato points out that DARPA not only increased the flow of knowledge among research groups, it also engaged in increasing the pool of scientists and engineers available to propel innovations into the market. The agency funded the establishment of computer science departments at universities across the United States, thereby acting as a catalyst for ground-breaking research and development undertaken by industry and academia (Mazzucato, 2013, p. 77).

1.2.   Accelerating Product Innovation and Consumer Expectations

The United Kingdom is living and competing in a rapidly changing global market. There are many examples of this change. Here are two technological examples. First, the information and data revolution is leading to exponential increase in saved and searchable data storage and thereby creating new product opportunities. Second, cost-effective human genome mapping and advances in human immune system understanding are being combined into new focused cell-based therapies that can target treatments towards individuals with specific genetics, thereby transforming effectiveness.

Equally in consumer facing sectors, for many products, the commercialisation process has shifted from seasons to 'fast fashion' with constant updates. There are moves from generic products to ones with rapid changes, in size, colour, function and style within constantly evolving consumer markets. One only has to look at the frequency of 'App' updates on 'Smart Phones' to appreciate this pace of change. Today's hot product is tomorrow's dinosaur; today's hot technology will be tomorrow's platforms waiting to be usurped. Change is fast, change is global, and consumer expectations are moving at the same pace.

The Japanese economic miracle went from 'cheap plastic items' in the mid-1960s, to initial leading edge electronic products of the 1970s (e.g. Sony Trinitron TV), to being the global product sector leaders in key sectors such as automobile design and manufacture and consumer electronics by the 1990s, to be followed by an unplanned unexpected stagnation. As shown in Box 1.2, yesterday's success and market leadership no longer guarantees future success, even in the medium term.

Box 1.2.   Smart Phone Wars

Despite a five-year head start over the iPhone, Research in Motion's (RIM) Blackberry, once the world leader in 'smartphones' and adored by the corporate mobile world, now only provides enterprise mobility management (EMM) and mobile security, having outsourced manufacturing of its handsets in 2016.

From the start a technical leader, within four years of its conception, RIM became the first technology firm, outside of Scandinavia to produce connectivity products for Mobitex wireless packet-switched data communications networks. Their next move was towards smart pagers that would exploit packet-based networks to offer wireless Internet access.

By 1998, their RIM950 Inter@ctive Pager captured the imagination as Intel CEO endorsed it saying any employee who could demonstrate a need could have one. Next with the Blackberry 5810, there was a device that could receive 'push' email from a Microsoft Exchange Server and that featured mobile web-browsing with a full QWERTY keyboard. By 2000, the stage was set for future enterprise-orientated products from the company, such as the BlackBerry 957, the first BlackBerry smartphone – a huge global sales success.

Competition would inevitably catch up, and Blackberry's fate was sealed when ARM Semiconductor Ltd (whose relationship with Apple dates back to the Newton – the world's first PDA) created a business model around licensing its microprocessor core to customers and allow them to add custom circuitry to create a final integrated circuit (Tubbs & Gillett, 2011). While RIM's secure encrypted network was attractive to corporate clients, their handsets were viewed as less engaging to consumers than the iPhone and Android alternatives. Developers simply found it easier to produce Apps on the IOS and Android platforms, which is why they continue to be ubiquitous today.

As a result, in just three years, Blackberry lost over 60 million of its users. Revenue fell from US$11 billion in 2013 to just over US$1.3 billion. In 2017, cash reserves dropped by over US$220 million, while an increase in operating costs led to a reduction in net income from losses at US$208 million to losses in excess of US$1.2 billion (CNBC, 2017).

1.2.1. *Innovation Comes in Different Forms: All Forms Matter*

Every innovation matters and every innovation can help drive competitive performance. Every viable business matters, but not every business is the same. Keeley, Walters, Pikkel, and Quinn (2013) identify 10 types of innovation ranging from the business model, to business processes, to the product itself and finally to the route to market. They stress that much progress can be made to how an existing firm works and to evolving new products in the same essential genre by improving how an existing company works. Equally there is potential for new market disrupters, 'Big Bang Disruptions' such as the Googles, Facebooks and Amazons (Downes & Nunes, 2013). In addition, as Haldane (2017) argues that we may be on the edge of a step change as artificial intelligence, robotics, the Internet of things and other innovations kick in. These changes will disrupt existing companies whilst opening space for whole new industries as yet unimagined. In global leadership terms, driving success requires a company to be in one of the top two slots globally, in a specific market segment (Welch, 2001). Blockbuster disrupters depend upon three developmental tiers: (i) basic research, (ii) development of this research into products that can be manufactured and (iii) market offers that meet profitable customer needs. Entry can be made at any tier in the structure, but the rewards from commercialised products flow from participating in the top tier. To obtain a top tier place is a common objective globally.

All types of company matter and all companies are at a variety of developmental stages. An emphasis on growing 'stars' for tomorrow must not be at the expense of failing to adapt today's workhorse companies to make them competitive in today's global markets. We need evolving processes to nudge the long tail of slow innovators to catch up with the trailblazers, whilst affirming and supporting the trailblazers to continue pushing forward (Haldane, 2017). Bringing all companies into the top-performing productivity quadrant equips them for both survival and future growth, to be at the leading, but not bleeding edge. As Andrew Carnegie once said, 'Pioneering don't pay', (Hughes, 1986) inferring that companies should adopt innovations once a clear payback is visible; an insight highlighted in Mazzucato (2013) that successful entrepreneurial innovation either requires that risks be reduced into market digestible chunks, or that the state needs to partner business to make the risk digestible.

1.2.2. A Perception of Risk: Entrepreneurs vs. Professional Managers

It is recognised that entrepreneurs and their associated MSMEs are key in the innovation and risk-taking process (OECD, 2010). What is equally important to understand is that entrepreneurial risk perception differs from that held in most mature 'managerial' businesses. Professional managers are rewarded on their ability to constantly increase earnings. This process can often occur through acquisition and subsequent cost stripping/asset sales because these offer easier risk-and-return estimation than that required in innovating a whole new product line. Product gestation and new capital investment are uncertain and therefore incur sizable risks, especially if the new product is intended to disrupt a market. It is easier and safer to buy something already developed but without the global marketing reach. Since Professional Managers' rewards comes from meeting targets and increasing the share price, they are often incentivised to see their share options increase in value, thereby giving them a short term rather than long term view. This perceived performance improvement also helps reduce the threat from Private Equity Houses and Activist Investors who may seek to replace managements that fail to deliver this growth in earnings. Examples of this in action can be seen in many companies; three such examples are Valeant (grown by acquisition followed by ruthless cost cutting especially in research and development), Heinz after its merger with Kraft under the sponsorship of 3G Capital and the 2016 failed 3G Capital bid for Unilever.

1.3. Financialisation has Interrupted Business Credit Mechanisms

We live in a financialised world. Ageing societies and financial markets responding to consequent lowering risk appetites tend to focus upon secure returns and safety for the invested principal. These returns are derived substantially from existing assets and cash flows and not from funding for new capital investment. Capital investment funding comes either from internal company financing such as in Alphabet/Google, issuing bonds (in some limited cases), equipment leasing and asset-based financing or from Capital Markets and, to a much lesser extent, Business Angels.

Banks have over the last 40 or so years significantly reduced the share of business lending and in doing this greatly increased lending to residential mortgage markets, arguably a reason for the strong relative rise in the price of residential housing assets in relation to earned incomes. This shift in lending has been reinforced by regulatory changes associated with the development of the Basel Capital Accords. This change in lending patterns is a major change with deep implications because restrictions in bank finance to smaller businesses have not automatically or adequately been matched by openings in new types of finance. In the United States, there is now a sophisticated and mature Venture Capital market, whereas in the United Kingdom and the European Union, the Venture Capital as an asset class is — notwithstanding London's role in this sector — neither as mature as that in the United States nor as ubiquitous as Private Equity, so funding flows are consequently more restricted. Real wealth increases require real productivity increases, which in turn require real capital investment and real innovation (Haldane, 2017). The juxtaposition is that savings products and derivatives effectively re-sell cash flows from previous capital investments, *less* the fees and commissions charged by each intermediary involved in the resale. These are not providing risk capital but rather looking to extract 'dividend rents' for buying the shares or bonds and having an upside of capital gains for holding the assets over time. In general, consumer financial products are marketed on their safety in returning the original capital plus their returns.

1.4.   Capitalism and the Entrepreneur

Entrepreneurs are at the centre of our innovation story. Under Capitalism, resources flow to the successful Entrepreneur, away from the unsuccessful one. Whilst it is implicit that Entrepreneurs are running their businesses for private profit, defining Capitalism by the mode of ownership alone is overly simplistic. Friedman (1962) saw the distinction as being between imposed direction of resources (feudalism, socialism, etc.) and free-market allocation via voluntary cooperation (capitalism).

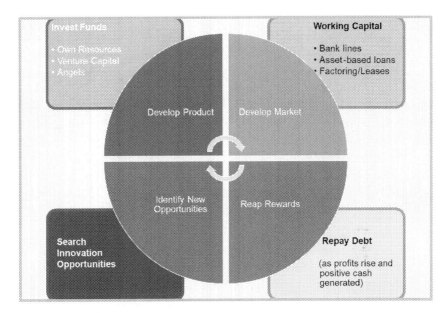

Figure 1.1.   The Innovation and Profit Generation Circle. *Source*: Authors.

We see *Mission-Based Innovation* putting the Entrepreneur at the heart of the innovation and profit generation circle (Figure 1.1).

Financialisation is different from Mission-Based Innovation (Krippner, 2005). It does not seek to promote entrepreneurial innovation and market disruption, but instead it looks for safety, to repurpose cash flows into *saver friendly* products. This is a system designed to support the economic *rentier*, where savings are not investments in entrepreneurial risk taking, but rather where savings are a delay in consumption from one period to another. A delay that either accumulates wealth for the sake of it or saves the wealth to spend at some unspecified time in the future (Keynes, 1936). Paradoxically, this financialisation *quest for safety* was at the heart of the 2008 crash, as inherently *unsafe* propositions (e.g. sub-prime mortgages) were packaged with insurance to make them look safer than they were. Financialisation in striving to remove risk from savings products misdirects resources (i) away from funding risk-taking, innovative Entrepreneurs (the potential cash flows of the future) and (ii) into funds and financing that emphasise short-term performance through reducing product and market development, asset sales and cost-reduction programmes that have short-term benefits but can be potentially damaging in the long-term.

Further impact arises from the very substantial money flows that can move from one country to another. These flows are especially substantial for the United Kingdom due to the importance of London as a financial hub. According to Borio, James, and Song Shin (2014), a change in direction in capital flows into an outbound cash drain can cause significant disruption. Such changes have occurred in the past, for example in the Asian Financial Crisis (1997) and in Iceland (2008). These are significant financial events that can be associated with a rapid decline in GDP of say more than 4 per cent in the subsequent 12 months. Box 1.3 describes the Iceland event.

Box 1.3.   Iceland's 2008 Banking Collapse

Following Iceland's accession to the European Free Trade Area in 1993, the governments undertook a process of deregulation and privatisation (especially of the main banks to create national banking champions), and a strategy to make Iceland a global financial hub. Sigurgeirsdóttir and Wade (2015) report how essentially small local banks supporting a population of just 320,000 soared to being within the 300 largest banks globally in the space of a few years in the 2000s, with their assets approaching 10 times Iceland's GDP. This process had been facilitated by 'light touch' regulation (47 staff located in non-distinct offices behind fast food shops to cover three huge banks), a strong national Credit Rating and relatively high interest rates enabling huge capital flows as investors borrowed money at lower rates elsewhere and deposited them in Iceland for higher rates. This process is known as the 'carry trade'. At the same time this wealth fed a housing and property boom, and consumption led to a growing trade deficit of over 15% from 2005 financed by inbound capital flows, raising the value of the currency and thereby further worsening the trade deficit.

The rapid growth in response to deregulation became the darling of 'Libertarian' economists. For example, Arthur Laffer (of Laffer Curve Fame) saw the fast economic growth as an example of how deregulation and tax cutting could raise growth. During a 2007 visit to Iceland, in a local newspaper article, Laffer stated, 'Iceland should be a model to the world' (Sigurgeirsdóttir & Wade, 2015). At the peak of the boom, Icelanders had moved into the top-ten per capita rich list world-wide. This was a boom which was based upon finance raised via international money markets – inbound capital flows, where bank assets that were many times in excess of national GDP always depended upon continuing foreign confidence. The 2008 Lehman's financial event broke that global confidence overnight. In Iceland, the results were catastrophic as Capital Inflows switched to becoming Capital Outflows overnight. The Krona plunged, the banks became unstable, and investors realised that Iceland could not bail out the banks to repay the debts; they were simply too large in relation to GDP.

Instead of looking for a coordinated rescue after nationalising the banks to ensure a managed insolvency, Iceland went through a slow and painful restructuring — a sort of managed insolvency. Capital controls were applied, the banks were allowed to fail, depositors were allowed to lose their deposits internationally, and the country retrenched away from finance. Unemployment went from under 2% to 9% in 2 years, and wealth and real wages were squeezed. Nine years after the crisis Iceland was able to remove the last capital controls.

The State is neither per se good nor per se bad. If the state is *effective* in investing in infrastructure, sharing technological risks, improving necessary skills (see Moudud, 1999), balancing market failures, providing necessary public goods and enabling entrepreneurship, then state spending will be making a contribution to innovation, and therefore, within reason, should be seen in a positive light. If the state is spending on transfer payments to keep resources non-productive, or taxing entrepreneurial innovators to subsidise laggards, then this spending will be unhelpful.

UK car company Rover failed for many reasons, not least that it was starved of funds to develop new competitive models to meet evolving customer needs, even though its customers were generally positive about the brand in its final years. Lucas (1988) when discussing his ideas for a growth model talks of an overemphasis in financial matters and infers financialisation acts as a growth barrier. Schumpeter (1950) returns our focus to the nub of the problem, that is not how to administer growth but how to engender it. In Schumpeter's (1934) entrepreneurial model, the financial system acts to allocate credit for expansion to the most productive projects and innovations.

1.5.   Historic Events: Our Window to the Future

Sense and foolishness can have a habit of reoccurring with solutions being rediscovered. Unfortunately, many important lessons can also be forgotten as time goes by. Smart History that looks beyond repeating dates and events into causes and solutions can offer windows into how previous generations dealt with similar types of challenge. The Ancient Civilisations understood the imperative of productive entrepreneurial finance. For example, the '*tamkarum*' (merchants) from Assyrian and Babylonian times, early in the 2nd millennium BC, played the role of the early springs of capitalism (Leemans, 1950). They funded entrepreneurs on a partnership (shared risk basis), and had such importance to the regional economies that the *tamkarum* could pass from city to city and state to state even in times of war. Whilst we do not know the role of the *tamkarum* in growing productivity, we can safely learn from them the lesson of needing risk-bearing finance for entrepreneurial activity. Entrepreneurial ideas are being embedded and are flourishing as finance is directed to the most productive investments that incorporate entrepreneurial innovations. This is a key growth engine.

1.6. The United Kingdom Today

Against a background of rapid global change in products, markets and technologies, every developed country needs to be looking to support today's successful business and to grow 'stars' for tomorrow. Such an approach requires ongoing investment into product and technology development, markets, capital equipment and skills. The United Kingdom lags behind most of its peers in capital investment levels, with current capital investment expenditures seemingly not even replacing the capital worn away by each year's production, according to the Organisation for Economic Co-operation and Development (OECD, 2015).

1.6.1. Consumers

Today's UK economy assigns significant importance to consumer spending. This spending is undertaken against challenging real wage conditions (sometimes falling, sometimes static and for the great bulk of the population subject to very modest increases if these occur). Combined with the rapid rise in house prices, there has been substantial growth in household debt as a portion of GDP since 1980, much of which is held against houses. Lending concentration (reinforced by bank regulation through the Basel Capital Accords) plus restrictive zoning and planning controls and 'Not in My Back Yard' local mentalities have arguably led to rapid house price increases and declines in home ownership amongst younger age groups.

1.6.2. Balance of Payments

There is a significant UK balance of payments deficit (between 5 per cent and 7 per cent of GDP over recent years), reflecting higher goods consumption than domestic productive capacity (there is currently a surplus on services). Capital flows that partly reflect London's importance as a global financial centre currently funds the balance of payments deficit.

Despite a significant (immediate post Brexit Referendum) fall in UK Sterling against its − trade weighted − index, there has not been a corresponding rise in exports. Export composition, exporter desire to increase profit margins, capacity restrictions and import and export elasticities may mean that modest falls in sterling will not correct the deficit. The Marshall/Lerner condition, which compares consumer sensitivity to import prices with overseas demand sensitivity to export prices to see if a devaluation will improve the trade balance, has seemingly not been fulfilled. Bahmani, Harvey, and Hegerty (2013) reviewed a number of studies and found, with one exception, that the United Kingdom is a priori unlikely to find devaluation effective. Without London's role as a hub for financial flows, such a trade deficit would most likely not be sustainable. Consequently, any loss of confidence in London as a financial centre risks very sharp adjustment as the financial activities are out of proportion with real GDP. A similar situation existed in pre-2007 Iceland, which, when the adjustment came, had insufficient financial strength to avoid a very sharp adjustment of the financial sector, its currency and the country's economy.

1.6.3. The Regions

Regionally, there is a sense of disconnection between London's economy and the economies in the regions. Regional dynamics, employment patterns, tax revenues, and house prices fall the further one moves away from London. There has been some limited devolution of activities from London, with for example some 'back office' financial services operations being located away from London. Regions also have their own industry and dynamics and in some cases have benefited from significant public spending programmes. In addition, London's own strength arises from its role as a global financial centre.

1.6.4. Manufacturing

The United Kingdom has seen a substantial decline in the size of its manufacturing sector. The manufacturing fell constantly from being around 29 per cent of output in 1979 to 18.7 per cent in 2007 (Broadberry & Leunig, 2013), and even more dramatically to 12.4 per cent, in 2007, of output at current prices. Its share of labour utilisation fell from 23.7 per cent to 9.5 per cent over the same period. Ownership has also shifted, with some key sectors, such as automotive, moving from being, in the main, nationally owned to being foreign owned. Well-paid manufacturing jobs for non-graduates disappeared and the UK experienced an increasing deficit on manufactured products.

1.6.5. Services

Significant growth in services employment has occurred across the United Kingdom, often creating lower paid and less secure (sometimes self-employed or zero-hours contract) jobs. Such works may attract tax credits and housing benefit, raising welfare spending burdens − benefits that under an alternative classification/nomenclature could be under-stood as proxy wage subsidies to employers. Wage subsidies implicitly reduce labour cost, reducing incentives to innovate and invest in new capital equipment to raise productivity and thereby enable higher real wages. Such strategies risk engendering a *low pay−low productivity* trap.

1.6.6. Generational Mismatch

The United Kingdom is an ageing society with a rising number of pensioners (making an associated strain on services and increasing pension bill). The current cohort of pensioners has benefited from rising house prices (the majority owned a house), defined benefit pensions (subsidised by current employees as they forego wage rises to divert funds to close pension fund deficits) and rising state transfer payments as the old age pension rises in real terms under the triple lock.

1.7. International Dependence

As an open, developed economy, a number of sectors in the United Kingdom following global trends have integrated internationally (especially, regionally across the EU), as some products, services and supply chains have become more complex and specialist. Equally, some sectors have become dependent upon migrant labour, some for skills reasons and some for cost reasons. Specifically, UK high-value-adding manufacturing sectors such as Automotive and Aerospace have tended to integrate into complex global supply chains, chains in which semi-manufactured products may move across national borders on multiple occasions prior to inclusion to the final manufactured item. Additionally, some sectors such as pharmaceuticals, medical devices and financial services have simplified their supply chains and customer operations through accessing common international regulatory frameworks. Manufacturing, financial services and construction businesses have accessed overseas labour markets for specific skills such as engineers, nurses and plumbers whose skills are in short supply. Other sectors such as the agricultural picking sector and the home care sector have accessed overseas labour to find staff to fill open positions.

1.8.   Today's Biggest Challenges?

What are some of today's biggest challenges? Growing new global champions, supporting existing champions, driving productivity growth into the long tail of poor performers are key challenges. Equally, closing the deficit on the balance of trade to reduce dependence on inbound capital flows, up-skilling the indigenous population to replace the need for migrant workers and weaning employers off a model of low productivity, low real wages into higher value-added sectors need to be addressed. Asset prices such as houses will eventually need to align to income levels (their supporting cash flows). Questions will need answering as to what share of resources should be given to the old.

Changes such as these can be painful. There will be winners and there will be losers.

There will be many enablers, but above all resources need to flow to the innovators of the future, to companies that will be able to command leading positions in their markets. This will require new frameworks (i) to channel capital resources into today's entrepreneurs to create tomorrow's products and (ii) to integrate research efforts and commercialise products within an understanding of commercially bearable risk. International comparison of the post-1945 'miracle states' suggests dynamic business needs to be export focused and supported by a smart and inclusive Entrepreneurial State, combined with Entrepreneur supporting banks and capital markets (Mazzucato, 2016).

Whether or not Brexit, a process that threatens to damage existing supply chains whilst threatening a key market for existing services and goods exports, will help this process is a matter for debate. What is for certain is that Brexit will mean change. Our next chapter takes us on a journey to the past to see what we can learn from previous Brexits.

Chapter 2

Brexit Paradigms

In history, a great volume is unrolled for our instruction, drawing the materials of future wisdom from the past errors and infirmities of mankind.

— Burke (1868)

The process of the United Kingdom's withdrawal from the European Union will be forever known as Brexit, which is, in itself, a rehash of the word Grexit; a term used by economist Ebrahim Rahbari to describe the possibility of Greece leaving the Eurozone, in 2012. Scheduled for 2019, as we highlighted in our last chapter, Brexit, good or bad, will bring a significant change to the status quo, that is a significant change to not only the UK's trading and political relationships — especially with the EU — but also globally (through the EU's various 'Bilateral Third Country' treaties with Third Nations). New relations and fresh treaties imply a transition that will be concomitant with the emergence of new regulatory and trading relationships.

Milton Friedman (1962), the intellectual architect of 'Economic Shock Therapy' writes:

Only a crisis — actual or perceived — produces real change. When that crisis occurs, the actions that are taken depend on the ideas that are lying around. That, I believe, is our basic function: to develop alternatives to existing policies, to keep them alive and available until the politically impossible becomes the politically inevitable.

Ultimately, the only true definition of Brexit, before Brexit is fully agreed is a tautology. '*Brexit means Brexit*' to use the words of Prime Minister May in her 11 July 2016 speech (May, 2016), which as Olin Miller opined, '*to be absolutely certain about something, one must know everything or nothing about it*' (Miller, 1950). If Brexit, in terms of detailed consequence, means everything and nothing before it is finalised, the execution risk remains unchanged and large.

Our journey continues by identifying the key issues emerging from Brexit, before focusing on how measures and environments can be structured to support the growth of Micro, Small and Medium Enterprise (MSME) firms. Our narrative is deliberately analytic. We do not seek to prove a specific point and we are expressly neutral on the wisdom or folly of undertaking Brexit. Our focus is to identify catalysing options that drive strongly rising competitiveness, improve productivity and improve per capita GNP growth within a long-term goal to achieve a neutral balance of payments. Our starting point is to reflect on the impact of three previous 'Brexits' (the end of Roman Britain, the Henrician Reformation and the Age of Elizabeth I) and explore what we can learn from each phenomenon.

2.1.   Brexit No. 1: AD 410

The British have had ambivalent relationships with Europe long before the June 2016 outcome. Arguably, the Roman Empire was the first 'European Union' with a Single Market and borderless trade, stretching from Hadrian's Wall in Britannia to the Eastern Empire and Constantinople, Near and Middle East.

Box 2.1.   Urban and Supply Chain Catastrophe Brexit (AD 410–AD 420)

Although there was a brief flirtation with an 'early Brexit' in AD 286 when Carausius tried to break away from Rome, it was all over by AD 296, ten years later (Sommerville, 2017). Further troubles in the AD 350s – led in Britain by Magentius – also proved to be a blip, and again Roman Rule stabilised. Pottery and villa remains show that the colony Britannia was still a rich trading province in the late AD 300s, and indeed there are even suggestions that it continued to prosper in the early AD 400s. One important change came with the introduction of Christianity, which saw 'The Forum' (the heart of Roman civic affairs) move from being a centre of religious and civic matters to being more of a market place. By the mid-AD 300s the elite (from archaeological finds) was based in the country rather than the towns. There is evidence that these estates continued after 410 AD and that the agricultural sector continued or prospered despite fragmenting authority. There is controversy as to how rapidly urban life fell away.

Esmonde Cleary (1989) describes how the Roman Army leaving was more of a whimper than a bang, as it was only after the AD 410 in Arles that it became clear the army would not return. Pre-AD 410, the economy was built around trading using Roman Coinage, relying on taxes to pay for the army and administration. Tax rates between 25 per cent and 33 per cent were significant (Esmonde Cleary, 1989). As ever, there was reluctance to pay the tax franchise (curiales) and the local elite pressured the peasantry and lower orders to comply, when they were reasonably frequently loath to pay themselves. The analysis of pottery artefacts suggests somewhat sophisticated supply chains, with local specialist merchandise being widely traded across the whole colony and in the rest of the empire. The later decades of the AD 300s and the first decade of the AD 400s saw continued development, but at a slow and reduced level, compared to the immediate preceding decades. It is not difficult to paint a picture of a well-off colony with a monied elite undergoing a gentle slowdown in the years immediately preceding the fall of the Roman Britain.

At roughly the same time (and it is difficult to be precise) we see the start of the collapse of towns. White (2016) tells us how the process of collapse is linked to the local elite (curiales) paying their own mercenaries for defence, rather than central tax, and that the retreat of Roman Society over a half a century happens at various paces in different parts of the country, although by AD 450 the process is complete. This narrative is supported by recent finds of Roman Coins minted well after AD 420 in Richborough, suggesting that some curiales tried to keep the Roman trading system going under own local protection. But history tells us they failed.

Ward Perkins (2013) drew this experience together in a lecture in which he ascribed the complete failure of Roman Britain (which is seen as controversial by some) to the collapse of complex supply chains that had relied upon a stable managed market (protected by the Imperial Army). This collapse, most clearly seen in pottery artefacts and changes in cropping plans — away from specialised crops for trading into subsistence crops — meant towns and associated markets were no longer needed. The rate at which each town declined is controversial, some seeing this period as lasting over centuries, others faster; and no doubt some towns' decline differed. Equally, agriculture being very local likely continued largely unchanged. For our narrative, the key issue is the overall urban decline. Also of note is how Saxon Kings such as King Offa (in the AD 700s) tended to avoid the old Roman settlements and build near them. For example in St Albans, the Abbey was built on the hill (near the old Roman centre) and the Saxon town in the valley, indicating local memory of the Roman town and Martyrdom of St Alban.

The AD 410 departure from the Roman Empire ended up over time as an economic and political dislocation (some would say catastrophe) for the civilisation of the time because complex supply chains failed (see Box 2.1). Despite archaeological finds such as Sutton Hoo, and the writings of Bede, for the common urban dweller Britannia slipped from being a rich urbanised Province of Rome into a rural peasant-based Dark Age. Towns collapsed into depopulated ruins (later revitalised in later Anglo-Saxon years), the previous monetary economy collapsed and the markets that enabled trade and impacted the ordinary person disappeared (although evidence of much more limited high-value imports at a slightly later time exists). Each town was different. For example, the decline in Verulamium[1] (St Albans) was most likely slower than some others.

Of particular note during the post-AD 410 period were both the failure of supply chains (sometimes international) and the loss of a monetary economy. In today's complex world of specialised and globalised supply chains, does a similar disruption risk to businesses dependent upon them exist?

2.2.   Brexit No. 2: Break with Rome (Again!)

The 1530–1542 Reformation (see Box 2.2) is associated with the English departure from the Roman Catholic Church and the formalisation of state organs under Thomas Cromwell. With the dissolution of the monasteries (demolishing the medieval monastic system of poor relief),

---

[1]The authors are grateful to Simon West, St Albans Archaeologist, for a helpful discussion on urban decline and agricultural continuity as Britain transitioned away from the early fifth-century Roman World.

Box 2.2. Structural Brexit (1529–1540)

Late 1536 saw rebellion in the North of England. Setting the context, by this time England had broken with Rome through a series of Acts of Parliament and associated Proclamations. The Parliamentary legislation that resulted from the Reformation Parliament, which sat from 1529, disentangled England from the Church of Rome. Clerical legal immunity and ability to respond to diktats from Rome were removed by a series of Acts of Parliament – 1529 (removing clerical privilege), 1530 (removing right of appeal to a foreign power after conviction), 1533 (stopping appeals to Rome). Payments to Rome were stopped via a number of measures targeting the 'Annates' and 'St Peter's Pence', culminating in the Act of Supremacy in 1534 and the associated Treason Act of the same year. In summary, the King was able to divorce and marry again and stopped appeal rights to the Pope in Rome. The second diverted the income that was previously sent to Rome to the Crown. This according to Elton (1975) changed the basis of English Taxation, from a situation where taxes were raised to fund war and defence, into taxes to fund general expenditure. These taxes were in addition to the 'Fifteenth and the Tenth', a form of 'Poll Tax', which had been collected since 1334. Hoyle (1994) indicates that this tax was levied at a parish level and then mainly borne by the poor.

Economically, the Reformation impact is disputed. According to Clark (2007) who created a longitudinal 'purchasing power day wage' index from the middle ages to the nineteenth century, real wages having previously risen after the 'Black Death', fell by a modest amount from the 1520s into the 1530s. This further stressed the already challenged agricultural incomes in the face of currency debasements and more acquisitive landlords.

Weber (1905) argues that these changes should be seen as the starting point in building a new entrepreneurial age, free from the monopoly and regulatory constraints of the Catholic Church. Dimot (1962) sees this as enabling a secular state that would authorise new modes of production. This assertion that Protestantism led to a work ethic and celebration of capital accumulation has been advanced to support the long-run view that economic growth and industrialisation arose from the Protestant Work Ethic liberated by the Reformation. Tawney (1926) observes that important changes to society and the economy, such as the development of banking networks, predate the Reformation. Becker et al. (2016) find Protestant states to have been more successful than Catholic states over the 400 years following the 1555 Peace of Augsberg, arguing that it is only in the 1960s this gap starts to close. Conversely, Cantoni (2015) finds no impact from Protestantism in a study of 272 cities from 1300 to 1900.

Apostolides, Broadberry, Campbell, Overton, and van Leeuwen (2008) have constructed GDP growth series for England over the years 1300 to 1700 on two bases, the first excluding the food and building industries and the second including all industries. The index is calculated on a GDP basis and on a GDP per capita basis and shows elevated growth rates in GDP from 1490 to 1650, and elevated per capita growth during the period 1490–1560. Apostolides et al. (2008) suggest this per capita growth came from an increase in working hours on agricultural land. Contrasting the fall in agricultural real wages to the small 0.6% estimated increase in GDP per capita over these decades indicates a gradual wealth redistribution away from the agricultural poor. Notwithstanding this data, Becker et al. (2016) suggest a significant impact from the Reformation changes as a result of improvements in human capital with:

- the dissolution of the monasteries and subsequent endowment of education institutions, raising the Human Capital capabilities over the next 150 years and
- the codification of a new legal framework (as the law was secularised away from the Church).

Educational change seems to have occurred in two discrete steps. The first associated with the Henrician Reformation and dissolution of monasteries saw some schools being founded to replace the now dissolved monasteries – schools that were associated with the reformed Cathedrals. The second stage in Elizabethan times saw the public charitable endowment of a number of grammar schools for the less well-off. In addition, there was a notable expansion of the Universities – Oxford and Cambridge. There were 65 BAs awarded in the two universities in 1535, rising to around 300 in the late 1590s (Heywood & Powell, 1842).

proceeds from their sale and diverted Church Taxation augmented state coffers. Some have argued this period started the backdrop to later social changes that predate the English Industrial Revolution. In the 1530s, the English Crown wished to secure freedom from Rome, political stability and additional revenue. A period of legal codification was led by Thomas Cromwell Henry VIII's leading minister, by undertaking legislative and legal codification reforms both to help raising taxation and to establish more effective public governance. The story of a 'nation state' asserting itself against Roman (Church) domination had been an underlying issue as far back as 1170 with the murder of Thomas à Becket. Cromwell introduced England to the structures and bureaucracy of a modern state, moving away from a state based on the Royal Court to one based upon ministries and active members of a newly slimmed down Privy Council. Thomas Cromwell added new social legislation to that required to formalise the break with Rome, for example by trying to restrict 'enclosure' (an issue that stirred populist dissent) and by setting a maximum on the number of sheep/cattle a person could own. In summary, this period is dominated by administrative rather than economic changes (Elton, 1953).

It is striking how Thomas Cromwell's reforms unsettle both gentry and peasants, and it is striking how fears of change, alienation from London and resentment at Land Enclosure conflate together into what becomes a serious rebellion. An echo to our own times where the 2017 general election saw a mix of issues leading to unexpected results. For many, austerity policies were a key concern, for others Brexit and for others a desire to ensure a complete Brexit happens, and for some such as in the Colne Valley constituency a local issue (protecting a hospital emergency department) linking to national concerns about austerity. Similar trends were at work in the Pilgrimage of Grace where there was unrest because previous rises in real wages had been reversed (as has also happened almost consistently since 2008). Concerns with landlords enclosing common land to their advantage (thereby disadvantaging peasants) and charging substantial fees to inherit tenancies under the label of 'improving the land' feel somewhat similar to today's lack of social housing, expensive house prices and unaffordable private sector rents. The dismantling of medieval 'Poor Relief' (Bernard, 2011) by the closure of the monasteries feels similar to today's retrenchment in welfare benefits and public services for the working poor. Justice had been centralised in London, and Parliament was regarded as having been 'packed' by interests favourable to the Crown. Today, Parliament is seen as suspect after the MP's expenses scandal. Another echo. Box 2.3

Box 2.3.   1536–1541 Insurrection and Challenge

Thomas Cromwell's reforms unsettled gentry and peasant alike, especially those more remote from London. By the start of 1536 we see an England where the nominal religion has changed, taxes that were previously paid to the Rome are now paid to the Crown and where there are modestly falling real agricultural wages, in a country that is still largely agricultural in nature.

The Pilgrimage of Grace insurrection (1536) and associated 'Pontefract Articles' reflected many underlying concerns. Bernard (2011) suggests that this insurrection reflected concerns in both gentry and peasants about the loss of local religious traditions, buildings and artefacts and the loss of the poor relief system the monasteries provided. Quelling the uprising may have taken both the fall of Cromwell and a Royal Visit to Yorkshire in 1541 to achieve. We don't exactly know and it is still a matter of controversy (i) how big the uprising was and (ii) what ended it (Sansom, 2008). Once the revolt was quashed, the Crown suppressed the rest of the monasteries for political more than economic reasons and used the economic bonus from selling monastic lands to balance an already stressed National Treasury.

Returning to the revolt, over the final months of 1536 we see the outbreak of rebellion in the North and Lincolnshire. One of the demands from the rebellion was that Parliament should meet in York – surely a reflection of local alienation from a London-based Parliament. Bush (1991) sums this up as being a reaction to heresy being imposed, and new forms of taxation, and Bush (2007) reiterates the link to Tudor tax raising and religious, constitutional and economic changes. Notwithstanding challenges from others, such as Hoyle (1994), to such economic elements, one is left with an impression that The Pilgrimage of Grace reflects a mix of factors: alienation from the political elite in London (tyranny by misusing Proclamations and Parliament), challenging economic circumstances for peasants, dissatisfaction with taxes, a fear of losing the past (in terms of the religion) and fear that local welfare for the poor was being dismantled.

There is Historical Controversy relating to the purpose, success and the meaning of the Pilgrimage of Grace. Viewed as a primarily Populist religious event looking to turn the clock backwards (Hoyle, 2001), the Pilgrimage was a failure. As he points out, the 1541

> submissions occurred with none of the 1536 requested religious changes having been undertaken. Others such as Elton and Dickens see the revolt as being gentry led and related to Royal Court politics. Above all, it seems this insurrection caused Henry considerable concern, sufficient for Henry personally to take a role in quelling it. Interestingly, there is a letter from Henry VIII personally to the Mayor of Hull thanking the City for their support (Hull, 1536). More substantively perhaps the key evidence as to concern the Pilgrimage of Grace gave the King is that after sacking and executing Thomas Cromwell in 1540, Henry VIII makes the 1541 'Progress' to York, where he enters Yorkshire through the very area where the Pilgrimage started and forces submission to him personally by the local minor gentry (Thornton, 2009).

described how all the pressures came together in the Pilgrimage of Grace insurrection.

The Reformation is upending religion that had been a feature of rural life for hundreds of years. Taxation, never a popular issue with the taxed, is viewed as having been extended by various Parliamentary Acts in 1536, so popular lore would have it that far more is being paid in order to keep the Royal Court. Maybe today's parallel is the continual tax burden and failing social services, closing local hospitals, queues and delays to see a doctor, whilst the centre still seems to be doing very well. Finally, there was some unease at the use of Crown Proclamation as a method of government. Perhaps this chimes with a feeling that many new regulations are coming from the EU and just like Crown Proclamations in the 1530s there is little if any way of influencing these. From today's perspective, it is difficult to assess the success or otherwise of such a distant revolt, although two very general statements can be made.

Short term, the revolt shows the limits of Royal Power, especially Royal Power to raise new taxes and issue Proclamations. Justice was devolved in 1537 with reestablishment of the Council of the North, the Council acts as both a court and a local arbiter on issues relating to Proclamations (Cooper & Cooper, 2015). The gap between rhetoric such as the Brexit White Paper (HM Government, 2017b) and reality in the 'Article 50 Position Papers' the United Kingdom submitted to the EU on key issues such as the European Court of Justice (HM Government, 2017d) suggests modern government too is starting to appreciate it also has boundaries. The execution of Thomas Cromwell sees, after a short delay, the start of the 1544–1551 Great Debasement (especially under Edward VI), during which coins were clipped and inflation rose as the state looked to fund its spending by effectively printing money, an illustration as to how a weak government can 'clutch at straws'. A modern parallel is to be found in 'have my cake and eat it approaches' to policy. Hard Brexit decisions and changes will not go away because we wish they would.

Secondly and longer term, the evidence suggests that in religious terms the rebellion failed as the Reformation continued and the monasteries were dissolved. At a political level though there are significant changes, although direct causality by the revolt is unproven. By the end of 1541 Cromwell has gone, Parliament has been reconvened with a different membership and a number of the direct legal and economic grievances are dealt with. Northern justice is devolved via the Council of the North and the King visits York with a significant armed group to quell further trouble. The modern parallel is not written yet, but a few signs are emerging. Regionally, both Scottish and Welsh devolved administrations have decided to work together to try to stop a perceived Brexit 'power grab' by London. Northern Counties of England have started to agitate concerning the perceived 'still-birth' of a Northern Powerhouse. Central Government has started to look for fudge to solve issues such as jurisdiction of the European Courts, and in some cases Central Government has U-turned, most spectacularly on a core manifesto pledge on how to fund elderly care, days after the pledge was made.

2.3.   Brexit No. 3: Adjustment and Stabilisation

After Queen Elizabeth I ascended the throne in 1558, she reversed her sister Mary I's policies of a return to Catholicism and links with Roman Catholic Spain. Elizabeth faced a country that had had three rulers in the previous 15 years, the economic turmoil of the Great Debasement, a divided Europe and a hostile great power in Spain. Finding stability, a religious settlement, repairing state finances and promoting well-being and economic health were all immediate challenges in addition to the need to bolster defence, especially after Elizabeth's excommunication in 1570 when Catholics were threatened with excommunication if they traded with England.

Box 2.4 gives some insight into the reverberations from this set of circumstances. Key for Elizabeth was working in partnership with

Box 2.4. Outsourced Trade Policy?

Arguably this period saw the visible decline of Antwerp as both a trading and banking centre, although its challenges had started some years before, maybe after the fiscal crisis of 1528 and the fall in mine output from South German Mines in the 1520s (Puttevils, 2010). Accelerated decline came after state loan defaults in the late 1550s (when rulers decided unilaterally to pay interest at 5% in perpetuity on outstanding sovereign debts) which led to the withdrawal of families such as the Fuggers from the Antwerp banking market (Spufford, 2010).

In 1564 English merchants found Antwerp closed (due to plague in London), so moved the crucial wool market to Emden. The next year Antwerp reopened, the trade returned, but again moved (1569) after the start of the Dutch Revolt to Hamburg. Hamburg was a member of the Hanseatic League and an important customer for English cloth (Stone, 1949). This transfer although disruptive (some wool merchants reported having been unable to sell stocks) was ultimately successful, such that English cloth exports appear to have continued at about the same level (although the product mix changed) through the rest of the sixteenth century (Stone, 1949). The London Company of the Merchant Adventurers played a key role in this transfer, having been granted the cloth export monopoly in 1564 (Bucholz & Key, 2009). Leng (2016) describes a world in which the Merchant Adventurer's organised, regulated and made the cloth market. It seems that although the State was supportive, the actual move was organised and negotiated by the Merchant Adventurers, which was an interesting outsourcing move in trade policy. In the words of John Wheeler in 1601 (from Leng, 2016), the secretary to the corporation, the aim of the company was *'engendering trust among members and with outsiders. In this reading, guilds thus helped to establish the behavioural regularities'*.

Although the data is very patchy (from Stone, 1949), it would seem that England had a sizable Balance of Payments deficit at the start of and indeed during much of this period. One significant cause seems to have been imports of luxury goods. A concerted programme of import substitution was undertaken, but this still did not stop the import of some luxuries such as wine. Faced with limited ability to open geographically near markets due to both war and religious difficulties, Elizabeth undertook two specific policies.

First, she opened trade with the Ottoman Empire (Brotton, 2016). This trade involved a variety of goods including metals for the Ottoman to melt down and form into guns. Stone (1949) tells us that notwithstanding the efforts to increase this trade, the distance and transport costs meant that any overall impact on England's then trade balance was small when compared to the cloth sales to Europe. Cloth exports are maintained, and values raised, despite England facing market dislocation.

Second, from 1585 Royal licences were issued to merchants and shippers to recover goods seized by other powers – the start of Privateering. The Court of the High Admiral was responsible for issuing these licenses and entitled to 10% of the proceeds. Fairly soon groups were able to obtain the licences without proving loss, and in some cases, they did not bother. Investors came together to finance these expeditions which could be quite costly. Andrews (1959) suggests costs ranged from say £500 for a small privateer to £3,000 for a large well-equipped vessel. Over the period 1589–1591, it is estimated that there were in excess of 235 privateer vessels in action. Some of these expeditions were part financed by the Crown and in those cases orders were given on potential targets, indicating an alignment to state. Overall privateering started to fall away once international trade took off (Hillman & Gathmann, 2011). The Queen also authorised companies by Royal Charter – for example, on 31st December 1600 – the East India Company – the company that paved the way to the conquest of India and India's inclusion in the British Empire.

commerce to drive the best result. In the case of the cloth trade, the Merchant Adventurers Company based in London played a key role. This group acted as a market maker, price fixer, transporter and standard setter for the trade, especially after it received the legal monopoly in 1564. To have maintained and grown the key English Wool Trade across 50 years of religious wars, changes in markets and main trading points represents a notable success in the face of adverse geo-political dynamics. Contrast this approach to the first 12 months of UK preparation for Brexit. During this period, Industry and Commerce have been excluded from discussions; there are stories of people who ask difficult questions being asked to leave the room and politicians have been making grand simplistic statements on extremely complex matters. One is struck by the gap between Elizabeth I's successful model and current modern practice. An opportunity to learn?

Education changed with the founding of new schools in both Henrician and Elizabethan times and by some are seen as investment in human capital later underpinning the first industrial revolution. This growing secular nature of educational institutions plus the ongoing expansion of the universities (which still focused on 'Clerical' religious courses) following the Reformation no doubt helped foster the 'English Renaissance' and later an interest in science. A long-term rather than a short-term growth impact.

Immigration concerns in the Elizabethan Age were focused at a religious 'fifth column' of papists, whose activities were regarded as treasonable requiring severe punishment. For example, the execution of Dr Lopez (a Portuguese immigrant converted Jew) as a Spanish Conspirator and papist in 1594 is seen primarily in religious rather than ethnic terms, although the anti-Semitic narrative within Shakespeare's Merchant of Venice could suggest otherwise (Campos, 2002). On the contrary, today there is a state policy of welcoming persecuted minorities. Guitteau (1942) tells us of Queen Elizabeth welcoming and offering to defend persecuted French Huguenots. The immigrants' economic contribution was valued. Muller (1989) looking at US immigration restrictions over the centuries recognises the populist issues in immigration. Notwithstanding, his view is that in both the United States and England, ever since the Huguenots' immigration, immigration, especially skilled labour immigration, has been welcome as a contribution to raising economic growth.

Contrasting this to today's public (but not industry) concerns about immigration, two immediate points highlight themselves. First, the relative skill of Elizabethan Migrants (Huguenots were renowned weavers) and, second the feeling of religious near kinship, protecting fellow travellers from persecution.

Table 2.1 summarises our learning from previous Brexits. The UK government has now published a bill to force all European Legislation into UK Law, mostly through the use of statutory instruments rather than primary legislation, allowing regulations to be recast in 'real time' in line with progress in the EU/UK Brexit negotiations. Figure 2.1 connects the main thrusts in the Bill with the lessons we have seen in Table 2.1.

Table 2.1. Brexit Challenges.

Issue	Impact	Example	Brexit Parallel
Monetary Disruption	High	AD 410 loss of Roman coinage; collapse market economy	Sterling Crisis and risks to global financial system
Supply Chain Collapse	High	AD 410 collapse of supply chains, depopulation of cities, collapse of markets; collapse market economy	Complex supply chains in key industries such as automotive and aerospace
Change in Markets	High	Merchant Adventurer's trade switch from Antwerp in second half sixteenth century, use of local trade agents to smooth trade relations and in 1580s Privateering eventually, conquest of India, short-term small impact, long-term high impact	New Free Trade Agreements Possibility for State Endorsed/Supported Local Country Agent/Export Networks
Legal Frameworks	Moderate	1530s creation of national legal framework, short-term small impact, long-term high impact	Great Repeal Bill
Overuse of Proclamation	Moderate to High	1536 Pilgrimage of Grace insurrection and 1539 Act of Proclamations	
Immigration	Moderate	Immigration was used as an aid to Economic growth – for example the Huguenot migration	Pro-Brexit Leavers see immigration as a social and job threat, whilst conversely many companies see it as an aid to economic growth

Regional Involvement	Moderate to High	1536 Pilgrimage of Grace insurrection Gentry active involvement in Reformation parliaments; eventually resolved after Civil War, Act of Union and the Jacobite suppression	Joint Ministerial Committee, co-operation between Scottish and Welsh governments on Great Repeal Bill
Access to Finance	High	Decline in Antwerp's role when the Fuggers restricted merchant financing in the late 1550s	SME Access to Risk Finance
Capital Flow Disruption	High	Iceland 2008	City of London and UK Trade Deficit
Big Bang Disruption	High	Current innovation revolution with 'Big Bang Disruption' disrupting whole industries and shortening product life cycles	Science of Innovation and Industrial Strategy
Irish Border			Not an issue in AD 410 or in 1530

Source: Authors.

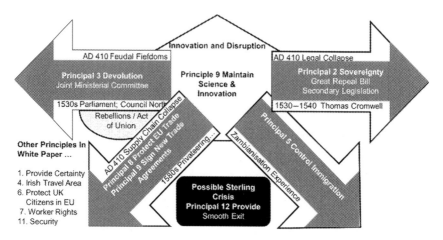

Figure 2.1.   Previous Brexits. *Source*: Authors.

2.4. Summary

Our exploration so far has identified 10 critical factors that have been fundamental to the success or failure of the domestic economy from our analysis of the outcomes and ramifications from previous Brexits. To these we have added two factors that are new to the current situation – the impact of global capital flows and the increasing speed of disruption – and then by comparing these factors to the current series of White Papers on Brexit, Industrial Strategy (H.M. Government, 2017a) and the Great Repeal Bill identified one further factor – the Irish border.

We propose that these 10 critical factors become 10 lessons that must be taken into account and addressed effectively to make this current 2019 Brexit successful.

Chapter 3

Smaller Firms: Engines of Innovation

Change the way you look at things and the things you look at change.

— Dyer (2017)

Smaller firms are an important source of Innovation. In their 2001 paper, 'An emotional business: A guide to understanding the motivations of small business decision takers', Culkin and Smith argue the way in which the UK government seeks to address the effectiveness of the small business sector is based on a flawed understanding of how small businesses actually operate. This naïve, over-simplistic understanding of the motivation of those in the small business sector continued across three different political administrations, including Labour (1997–2010), the Liberal Democrat/Conservative coalition (2010–2015) and Conservative (2015–). The many interventions that were made have been blunt instruments destined to fail, given the limited understanding of the complexity of the small business. Actions have tended to be shorter rather than longer term, with examples ranging from the demise of the UK Film Council, the end of the Business Accelerator Programme, to the £1bn + future investment in renewable energy projects that disappeared during 2016 (Green Alliance, 2016).

3.1. The 'Ambition Gap'

Divergent challenges require different solutions. Granularity in understanding needs and challenges matters. Every MSME is different, and what is good for one MSME may be counter-productive for another. Growing the next Google likely requires different skills and resources (and a few of the same ones) to opening a niche organic food store. Types of firm vary; using data from the first wave of the UK Longitudinal Small Business Survey, Saridakis, Lai, Muñoz Torres, and Mohammed (2017) (who describe small firm growth dynamics within an ownership context), report that small firms formed and run by a group of individuals are likely to grow faster than companies owned and run by families or companies owned by families and run by professional managers. It's difficult to know why this may be, but some elements stand out.

Ambitious firms matter. They play a central role in innovation with 'High-growth enterprises playing a disproportionate role in job creation'. Roper and Hart (2013) suggest that in 2008 11,800 firms with over 10 employees were responsible for creating 1.3 million of the 2.4 million jobs over the 2005–2008 review period, suggesting that maybe 4–6 per cent of fast-growing firms provide between 50 per cent and 75 per cent of all new jobs. Equally, these firms tend to focus on exports, continual innovation, exploiting their Intellectual Property and building good peer and financial networks (OECD, 2010a). For example, 56 per cent of new products in the Medical Device Sector come from MSMEs, a sector where there is also substantial acquisition activity of these MSMEs to allow bigger companies access to newer more innovative technology.

3.1.1. Mission-based Innovation Driven by 'Ambitious Firms'

Ambition is key. A group of people starting up a new venture may well have a driving ambition to create a star business – our high-growth firms. On the other hand, a family running, say, a local shop or a low-cost service business may be looking at securing sufficient income for the family, and work opportunities for the next generation. Levie (2014) identified an 'Ambition Gap' between UK and US MSMEs whereby UK firms are too often formed to house the self-employed; whereas in the United States, they are more often used to facilitate a group of individuals with a common business idea, an explanation that is perhaps extendable to explain why many family firms may appear to lack ambition.

Learning from failure matters too:

> *It's fine to celebrate success, but it is more important to heed the lessons of failure.*
>
> – Bill Gates (1995)

> *Success is a lousy teacher. It seduces smart people into thinking they can't lose.*
>
> – Gates, Myhrvold, and Rinearson (1995)

Everyone makes mistakes, everyone has successes and everyone has failures. Ask anyone about the three moments in their life when they learnt most, and these are likely to be three failures that helped them learn how to do better in the future. Whilst success is what we all strive for, we need failure to help us learn how to attain it. Support systems need to embrace failure as a springboard to success and nurture ambition as the tool to break the false glass ceilings we all tend to set for ourselves. Inevitably, the character of both the types of failure one is prepared to bear and the ambition that one holds is a reflection of an entrepreneur's passion for their product or service and their own appetite to take risk to deliver it. Arguably we could classify MSMEs by these attributes, as we can be confident the greater the risk appetite, tempered with the willingness to learn from failure and the drive to make their product or service successful, the more likely this MSME will join that segment of high-growth potential 'star businesses'.

Nevertheless, we must not forget the very real benefits that may be achieved by improving and supporting the less ambitious MSMEs as well. It is just that different mechanisms and delivery may be needed to support these.

3.2. Differing Market Landscapes

An MSME that outsources its payroll will need to understand the financial implications of changes to employee pay regimes (to be able to monitor its cost base) but does not need detailed training in the execution of the changes being handled by its outsource partner. In a complex automotive supply chain, a component or subassembly (Tier 2) supplier does not need to innovate whether the new car model will be electric or fossil fuelled; but it does need to innovate and engineer its component or subassembly to meet the demands of its customer and, ultimately the specification of the OEM automotive manufacturer. By contrast, a start-up smart phone games 'App' developer will need to innovate the whole product for the end customer to remain competitive — a skill that requires understanding where the market can be developed, rather than being able to react to a specification change from the purchaser.

3.2.1. Conventional Wisdom

The commonly used definition for SMEs comes from the European Commission (2017c) and is based upon firm size and is similar to the

Table 3.1. MSMEs by Industry (2016 Employee Count Data).

	Count		SME Total Employment		Turnover (£000s)	
Production	144,930	6.0%	1,453,682	11.2%	221,379,685	12.8%
Agriculture, forestry and fishing	147,535	6.1%	434,038	3.3%	38,977,190	2.3%
Transport and storage	92,485	3.9%	462,225	3.5%	70,259,806	4.1%
Construction	301,555	12.6%	1,077,243	8.3%	174,454,438	10.1%
Professional services	664,440	27.7%	2,190,908	16.8%	272,032,520	15.7%
Retail and wholesale	368,770	15.4%	2,103,412	16.1%	613,697,740	35.5%
Hospitality	147,455	6.1%	1,301,926	10.0%	51,150,256	3.0%
Outsourced services	254,650	10.6%	1,852,944	14.2%	172,104,937	9.9%
Health	112,380	4.7%	1,281,097	9.8%	63,965,569	3.7%
Recreation	167,785	7.0%	879,063	6.7%	52,775,486	3.0%
Total	**2,401,985**		**13,036,538**		**1,730,797,627**	

Note: Data from ONS (2017a) © Crown Copyrights. Raw dataset manipulated and edited into above table by removing Property and Financial Services counts due to high average turnover in these firms making them large firms not MSMEs.

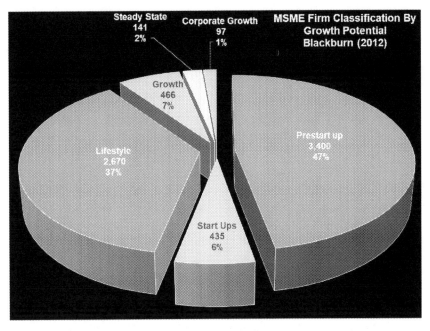

Figure 3.1.   MSME 2010 Count by Business Stage (after Blackburn, 2012). *Source*: Authors.

one in Ward and Rhodes (2014), that is companies with a turnover of under €50 million and less than 250 employees. 2016 sector data are shown in Table 3.1 (ONS, 2017a).

Figure 3.1 shows business count by business stage segment sizes for 2010 (Blackburn, 2012).

3.3.   MSME Importance to Overall Economy

Apart from the number of MSMEs and the numbers they employ, MSMEs also have other impacts, and these in turn can be used to classify them. Using 2012 data from Ward and Rhodes (2014), 41.8 per cent of medium-size companies (50–249 employees) exported and 47.7 per cent imported; and 11.8 per cent of small-size companies (1–49 employees) exported and 11.4 per cent imported. MSMEs play a central role in innovation with 'High-growth enterprises playing a disproportionate role in job creation'. For example, the 10 per cent most rapidly growing enterprises in France, Italy, the Netherlands and Greece created between 50 and 60 per cent of gross employment gains over a 5 to 10 year period, whilst in Spain this was nearly 90 per cent (OECD, 2002). Nearly 50 per cent of these high-growth firms started as MSMEs (OECD, 2010a). Equally high-growth MSMEs tend to focus on exports, continual innovation, exploiting their intellectual property and building good peer and financial networks (OECD, 2002, 2010b). For example, 56 per cent of new products come from MSMEs in the medical device sector, a sector where there is a substantial acquisition activity to allow bigger companies access to newer more innovative technology − mission-based innovation in action. Figure 3.2 confirms that the size of a sector (employment count) does not determine the sector's importance to the innovation rate. Bubble size in this chart represents sector SME employee numbers and the percentage overall sector contribution to market innovation[1] (total factor productivity, intangible capital deepening and labour composition).

The position changes if one looks at total factor productivity, as shown in Figure 3.3.

Conventional wisdom sees growth and productivity as some function of the combination of labour, capital and technology (Solow, 1956, 1957) where output and productivity result from the combination of labour and capital, with shifts in output curves related to step changes in technology. There are suggestions that this function is changing in response to changes in technology, with intangible investment rising in importance. Nesta (2012) describes intangible investment as being more significant than tangible investment − software development along with investments in improved organisation and training followed by scientific R&D and Design. Intangible investment seems to account for around 29 per cent of labour productivity growth. Manufacturing with 47 per cent of overall capital deepening has the highest intangible investment at 17 per cent of value added. Further analysis in Figure 3.4 shows the importance of E-commerce innovation in the 2000−2007 period. It is particularly striking that manufacturing which shows the most important contribution to total productivity growth spends less on

---

[1]Employment numbers for SMEs from ONS (2017c) and innovation for whole sector from Nesta (2012). We do not have segment SME innovation data. It is further complicated by Nesta sector definitions being wider than ONS definitions, for example ONS separates Retail & Wholesale from Transport & Storage and Hospitality. Goodrich has Distribution Hotels Transport. Nesta has no data for Health (not market economy). Chart indicates that further research is needed.

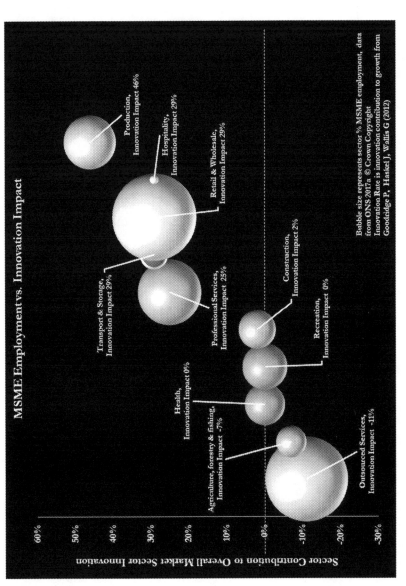

Figure 3.2. SME Employment and Innovation Impact. *Source*: Authors, using data from ONS (2017c) and Nesta (2012; data in Fig. 6, p. 55) Footnote 1 applies; data reproduced from https://creativecommons.org/ licenses/by-nc-sa/4.0/.

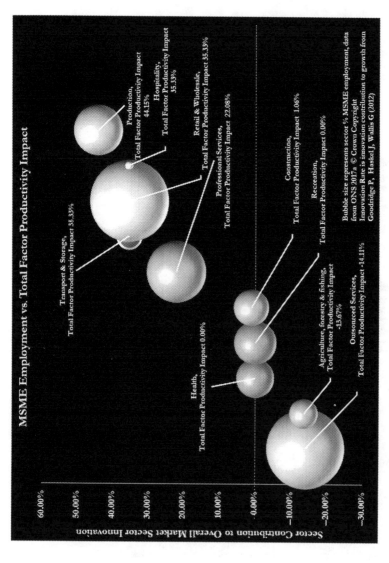

Figure 3.3.   SME Employment and Total Factor Productivity Impact.[2] *Source:* Authors, using data from ONS (2017c) and Nesta (2012; data in Table 14, p. 52); data reproduced from https://creativecommons.org/licenses/by-nc-sa/4.0/.

[2]Above footnote for Figure 3.1 applies.

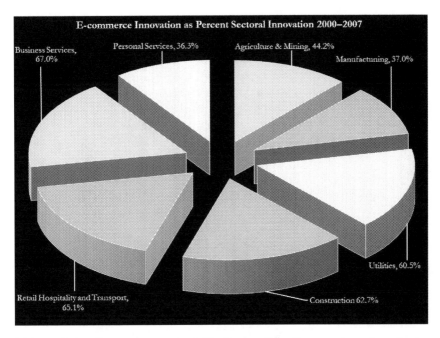

Figure 3.4. E-commerce as % Intangible Innovation by Sector 2000–2007. *Source*: Authors, using data from Nesta (2012); data reproduced from https://creativecommons.org/licenses/by-nc-sa/4.0/.

E-commerce innovation as a percentage of intangible innovation than other sectors.

It is arguable that the higher overall level of investment (about one-third higher[3]) in software, training and organisation changes compared to scientific R&D and design represents easier identifiable paybacks and the internal dominance of finance functions over marketing and product development.

Figure 3.5 shows the relationship between low pay (defined as full-time workers earning less than two-thirds of the median salary) and innovation. The larger bubbles represent higher number, so 'low paid'. Additional perspective can be garnered from Working Tax Credit Data that estimates 18 per cent of the workforce in Accommodation and

---

[3]'Scientific R&D is about 11 per cent ..., software 18 per cent, design 12 per cent and training and organisational 21 per cent' of intangibles – Goodridge, Haskel, and Wallis (2012).

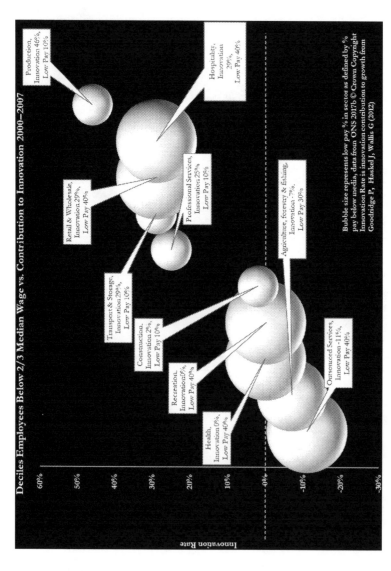

Figure 3.5. Innovation Contribution *vs.* Employees on Low Pay. *Source:* Authors, using data from ONS (2017b) and Nesta (2012)[4]; data reproduced from https://creativecommons.org/licenses/by-nc-sa/4.0/.

---
[4]Footnote from Figure 3.1 above applies.

Food Service receive Working Tax Credits, 14+ per cent in retail, 12+ per cent in social care (New Policy Institute, 2014). One unexpected feature in Figure 3.5 is the relationship between the innovation rate and pay rates in both the retail and hospitality sectors. It is dangerous to speculate, but we note (i) the continual pressure on retail gross margins because of the growth in E-commerce together with the entry of Aldi and Lidl (super discounters) to UK food retailing may be contributing to retail innovation rates *and* (ii) the data issues mentioned in the footnote to Table 3.2 may be misrepresenting the true hospitality sector innovation rate by combining this sector with the transport and storage sectors.

The question remains unanswered as to whether or not Low Pay makes it less financially worthwhile to invest when labour is relatively cheap when compared to buying new capital equipment.

Table 3.2. Sector Pre-tax Operating Profit Adjusted for Leasing and R&D.

Sector	Percentage
Renewables	32.65
Medical	23.59
Creative	17.01
IT	20.42
Microelectronics	16.14
Consumer	16.56
Tobacco	32.78
Conglomerate	12.07
Telecoms	13.31
Heavy	11.14
Health admin	13.05
Leisure	11.81
Utilities	18.52
Real Estate/Fin	22.45

Source: Damodaran (2017).

3.4. The Triangle of Opportunity

Schumpeter (1934) describes a continually innovating world, in which resources are allocated from industries that earn lower returns to industries that are earning high returns. In Marshall's (1890) world, markets reallocate resources from firms earning sub-normal profits towards firms earning super-normal profit. Schumpeter provides a key nsight by presenting this 'super-normal profit' as a reward to entrepreneurs.

Figure 3.6 presents data compiled by Damodaran (2017) on the profitability for different industries. For our purposes, we use the 'pre-tax' figure, adjusted by Damodaran (2017) for R&D and leasing expenditure by taking the 'operating charge' in the accounts and then rolling these back as if they had been capitalised, so a true operating cash flow can be inferred, which we then combine with a view on firm's financing costs. To estimate financing costs, we looked at a range of five-year commercial bond coupons being paid by companies on their debt (different from the yield the investor receives) and then informally estimated that in the current universe of issued bonds, the median for which would be approximately 7 per cent. We further assumed that equity should command a premium over bond yields and estimated a further additional equity yield over the bond yield of 4 per cent, making a total 'normal return' on equity of 11 per cent. This may be on the high side, but we are not trying to undertake a formal yield analysis, only to have a rule of thumb to segment high opportunity sectors. Our rate differs from Damodaran (2017) for the United Kingdom, which is estimated at 6.25 per cent over the ruling five-year gilt return of about 0.5 per cent, making an equity return target of 6.75 per cent.

Our target difference is based on the following: (i) we are looking at the cash payment a firm is making, not the return an investor would receive; and (ii) the Damodaran (2017) data only reports quoted companies, whereas focus of interest is the MSME.[5] We have further taken a view on what would be a 'normal rate of return' so we can segment the data and identify 'opportunity segments'. By segmenting the data, we are able to rank sectors by their profitability, and thereby highlight sectors that offer abnormally high returns over our cost of equity finance threshold.

The data in Figures 3.6–3.8 illustrate how the process can be designed. If such an approach is to be adopted we are the first to

---

[5]The authors suggest that this area would profit from a research project all on its own.

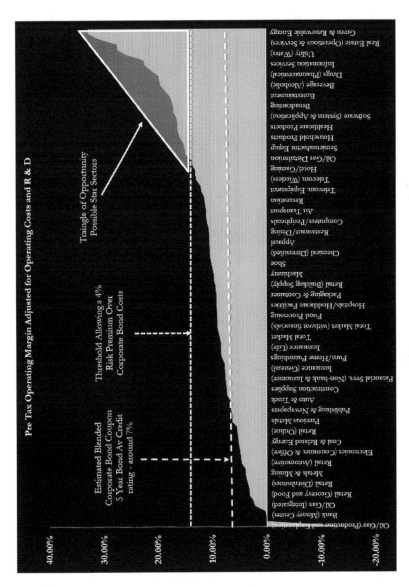

Figure 3.6.   The Triangle of Opportunity. *Source:* Authors, using Damodaran (2017) data.

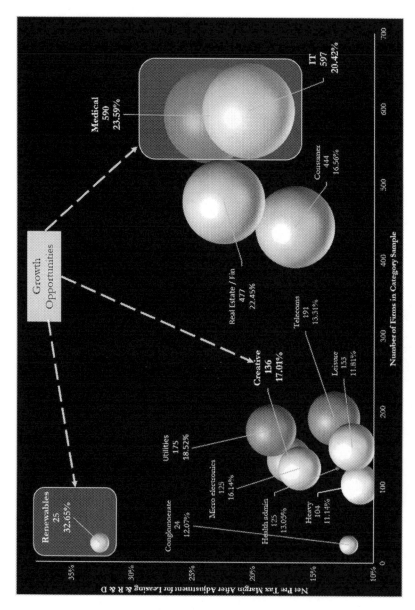

Figure 3.7.   'Opportunity Triangle' Sectors. *Source:* Authors, using Damodaran (2017) data.

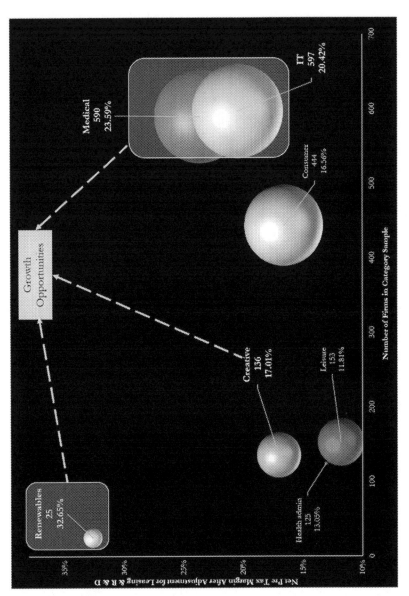

Figure 3.8.   Opportunity Triangle 'Growth' Sectors. *Source*: Authors, using Damodaran (2017) data.

acknowledge a dedicated research project would be necessary to assess for *best practice*, as opposed to the *rule of thumb* approach employed here. It goes without saying that the reader is advised against taking any operational decision based on the data in Figure 3.6. The data, nonethless seems to confirm our rule of thumb.

Separating out the sectors within the 'Triangle of Opportunity' and then consolidating these into summary sectors gives us the data in Table 3.2.

This data is then mapped into a bubble chart (Figure 3.7), the size of each bubble giving the sample size of firms included.

We then adjust this chart by removing those sectors that are earning above-average returns because of an implicit monopoly or oligopoly position (such as utilities, conglomerates, telecommunications, tobacco, etc.) or because they are essentially asset-based rent extraction industries (such as real estate or investment management). This leaves us with Figure 3.8 which suggests that sectors such as Renewables, Medical, IT, Creative, Consumer and to a lesser degree Health and Leisure have margins signaling growth opportunity.

3.5.   Zombies and New Entrants

Both Marshall (1890) and Schumpeter (1934) describe a firm-level evolution process, with new firms being born and old firms dying in the face of (i) firm-based changes in management and entrepreneurial skills and (ii) customers and the market. Often cited as a process of 'Creative Destruction', a term synonymous with Schumpeter but first used by Werner Sombart (Reinert & Reinert, 2006), this process of continual renewal serves to challenge existing companies with new innovating entrants and to clear out inefficient poorly adapted businesses. Box 3.1 gives an example of this change cycle.

An alternative to Schumpeter's 'Gales of Creative Destruction' can be the 'Zombie' company, as companies that have lived beyond their economic life, uneconomic without exceptionally low interest rates. Company Watch (2016) found 249,000 UK Zombie companies with collective debts of £115 billion.

Box 3.1.   Polaroid Corporation – 'Disrupter to Dust' in 80 Years

In the late 1930s a small technical corporation was formed in Boston, focused on innovating optical products. Setting a precedent later followed by some famous disrupting digital giants, Polaroid's leader was Edwin Land who *'As a 22-year-old Harvard dropout in*

New York, [...] sneaked into Columbia University labs to invent the
artificial polarizer, which splits light waves into separate beams'
(Boston.com, 2012). After providing optical products for the
Military in World War II, Land went on to invent his signature
product – the Polaroid Camera. Providing consumers with
opportunity to produce photographs in minutes rather than days,
and strongly patent protected (only Thomas Edison has more
patents than the 533 US Patents in Land's name), Polaroid stormed
its markets and was a US$1.4 billion corporation by 1979.

Land maintained a high level of product focus during the 43 years
he ran the company, first collaborating with and then competing
with and eventually litigating competitor Eastman Kodak. The focus
served well until markets started to change and consumer
technologies started to evolve in the early 1980s. Although Polaroid
maintained its R&D focus and indeed launched a digital camera in
1996, it failed to grab market share. The glory years were over as the
company failed to adapt to new technologies and new market trends,
leading to the company's Chapter 11 bankruptcy in 2001 and eventual
liquidation. Nowadays Polaroid instant cameras are museum pieces in
the face of ubiquitous digital cameras in smart phones.

In Box 3.2 we demonstrate that in some cases businesses don't die,
they are in fact kept on life support, but without sufficient change to
make them viable.

Box 3.2.   Alitalia Spa – A Zombie Perennial?

Founded in 1946, Italian national airline Alitalia became a problem
child for the Italian government in the early 1990s. The government
executed a restructuring plan that cut costs and reorganised the
company followed by a part privatisation, giving the employees
around 20 per cent of the company (Cuomo, 2002). By 2007, the
airline was in trouble again, and after a destabilising period of
uncertainty, it was rescued by a private Italian Consortium, who
again restructured the company, this time severely restricting the role
of its Milan hub and focusing on Rome as a base. By 2014, despite a
further 'mini-rescue' with a capital injection by the Italian Post

Office, Alitalia was again in need of a rescue, which this time came in the form of an injection from Abu Dhabi flag carrier Etihad. Despite being handed this latest lifeline, the airline was again in trouble and entered bankruptcy on 2nd May 2017.

Three underlying themes seem to run through this saga: (1) continued union and labour troubles that have hindered management turnaround plans, (2) a failure to be able to adapt the airline to meet new competitors, both from low-cost short haul carriers and higher service product long haul airlines and (3) significant and substantial losses. Bourlot (2015) alludes to total losses: *'The total amount of losses amounted to 6.1€ billion, while total costs 13.5€ billion'*. The *Wall Street Journal* reported in 2007 that Alitalia's *'share of Italian international traffic has fallen to 25% from 43% in 2001, as that market, measured by the number of airplane seats, has grown 38%'*. A case study in falling market share and accelerating cash demands, where rescue attempts have been made without finding a solution to perennial labour problems, according to industry analysts Innovata LLC in London.

Confronted with many differing ways to classify an SME, as refined across a number of researchers from Penrose (1959) to Roper and Hart (2013), we face a multi-dimensional puzzle. One firm may fit into several classifications and have needs that cut across differing categories.

Before we finally reject the commonly adhered to, 'one size fits all approach', Box 3.3 provides a short case study looking at how a 'one size fits all approach' worked out in a different way by large-scale transformation challenge − how to build an MSME sector in the former Communist States of the USSR and Eastern Europe.

Box 3.3. 'One Size Fits All': Post-1991 Sudden Shock in Russia

Following the start of the Yeltsin administration, Russia entered a controversial programme of shock treatment, deregulation and sale of state enterprise. This programme is often held up as an example of 'Shock Therapy' (named by Sachs as a term to encapsulate a series of liberalisation/deregulation policies) has been summarised by Roaf, Atoyan, Joshi, and Krogulski (2014) as 'Shock Therapy' because price, administrative and exchange controls were all removed. Stiglitz

(1999) contrasting to deregulation experience in China found that in Russia GDP fell by nearly 50 per cent and in the more gradualist China GDP nearly doubled. Sachs (2012), who played a disputed role in administering this 'Shock Therapy' and who was the originator of the term 'Shock Treatment', in a blog post distances himself from the Russian experience, despite his early involvement in the Russian programme. What went wrong? Chepurenko and Vilenski (2016) describe how the transition to a Capitalist Economy started from nothing. Whereas say Poland already had a nascent SME sector at the pint of liberalisation, Russia had none.

Consequently, initial entrepreneurship focused on 'street-based' gap filling, rather than the development of a robust-growing SME sector. 'Predatory Entrepreneurship' led to unproductive and destructive entrepreneurship. Hall and Elliott (1999) suggest success should not just be measured on economic progress but also how democratic institutions were established. Chepurenko and Vilenski (2016) highlight how Poland and Hungary already had nascent business sectors on the fall of the USSR whilst Russia did not. The 1990s 'Washington Consensus' approach we describe here demonstrates that the difficulties in adopting a 'top-down' approach used in Russia emphasises the critical role of business, regulatory and cultural capability in promoting successful growth and transition, arguably more important than, within reason, cutting taxes or deregulating.

A salutary warning to any 'Brexiteer' who sees unlimited tax cuts and regulation slashing as a panacea.

3.6.   Complexity Rather than 'One Size Fits All'

From what we have said so far, we will abandon 'one size fits all' and adopt a series of *characteristic-based* definitions as a stepping stone to formulating ideas that can be 'mixed and matched' to support each MSME category.

3.6.1.   *Group 1: High-growth Potential 'Big' (or Little!) Bang Disrupters*

> *The best time to plant a tree was 20 years ago. The second best time is now.*
>
> — Chinese Proverb (Source Unknown)

Disruptive innovations have been around for longer than history can document. Two early examples are the coming of fire and the invention of the wheel. More recently, Landes (2003) describes how the English Industrial Revolution was an age of disruption. Change resulted from the application of technology, especially first steam and later electric power being applied into redesigned production processes, transforming from artisan to mass production. New production processes transformed manufacturing with productivity rising.

Verdoorn's law (Verdoorn, 1980) asserts that as output increases and economies of scale come into play, productivity rises when the economy is in equilibrium. As, in general, increases in the output of services are not associated with the same sorts of economies of scale one finds in production, the size and dynamics of the overall production sector are an important determinant regarding productivity growth. This importance of manufacturing to overall productivity increases is re-emphasised in Figures 3.2–3.8. Firms can grow very rapidly by either opening new untapped markets or seizing market share (profitably) in existing markets.

Spotting these companies is risky and difficult. Even expert Venture Capitalists will have some successes, some question marks and some failures. Arguably, the recent disruptions from businesses such as Amazon are a modern manifestation of this continual process of change.

Box 3.4.   Technology Disrupters

Google − A Proven Success
Google started small, from academic work at Stamford University. According to Vise (2005):

> *With the help of Stanford professors and the Office of Technology Licensing, Brin and Page tried unsuccessfully to sell their PageRank system to Excite and other search engines. [...] One of Page and Brin's graduate school professors, David Cheriton, suggested that it would be a good idea for them to meet his friend Andy Bechtolsheim, a computer whiz and legendary investor in a string of successful start-ups [...]. 'This is the single best idea I have heard in years,' Bechtolsheim said. 'I want to be part of this.' Instead of discussing all the details, Brin recalled, Bechtolsheim wrote a check made out to 'Google Inc.' for $100,000, a figure he picked because it was a nice, round number.*

Uber – An Ongoing Question Mark

Uber has built a US$60 billion+ valuation based upon market promise, in an already mature market by adopting a business model to circumvent regulation (employment law, taxi licensing, etc.). Notwithstanding its valuation, Uber lost US$3.3 billion in the year to mid-2017; Uber's US market share fell 7 per cent from 84 per cent to 77 per cent in the period January to May 2017 (Hook, 2017) and in 2016 Uber lost a market battle for the Chinese market.

Kahoo – The Failure

Kahoo a taxi/ride share cost comparison application, reputed to have gained approx. US$250 million in funding commitments and claiming to have spent only US$52 million in the 6 months it traded, failed in October 2016, being unable to pay staff of creditors, with only US$5k left in the bank. During the first 12 weeks of operation in London, according to Kahoo, 300,000 users downloaded its App, which earned revenue of just under US$1 million. However, revenues were nowhere near sufficient to meet the cash burn implied by having 180 staff plus offices and apartments in various locations around the globe. The original cash call *'backers included well-known individuals such as David Kowitz, co-founder of Indus Capital Partners, the US hedge fund; Jonathan Feuer, managing partner at CVC Capital Partners, the European private equity group; and Eric Daniels, the former chief executive of Lloyds Banking Group'* (Murgia, 2016).

Today's 'Big Bang Disruption' as defined by Downes and Nunes (2013) offers no protection to existing incumbent businesses in the face of a globally disrupting new entrant and ever-shortening product life cycles. Disruption is also no guarantee of success as Box 3.4 demonstrates, echoing Landes' description of the Industrial Revolution into a digital age. Just as in the English Industrial Revolution incumbency in the textiles industry was no protection, incumbency in companies often consume substantial financial resources in their earlier stages, often finding themselves lacking in corporate governance (both Uber and Kahoo are, for example, cited for this weakness), and these firms can sometimes lack an overall business model despite an interesting product idea. Returns can take time to materialise; in the UK venture capital estimates a 3-year per annum return of 12.4 per cent, 5 years per annum at 9–11 per cent and 10 years per annum at 6.1 per cent (BVCA, 2017).

Contrasting to US experience shows a 3-year per annum return of 11.75 per cent, 5-year per annum of 14.03 per cent and a 10-year per annum US Return of 9.39 per cent (Cambridge Associates, 2016). Returns are expressed on a per annum basis, and thereby compete strongly with more conventional financial products.

Based on the authors' personal experience, the internal rate of return thresholds on business plans need to be around 30 per cent to 34 per cent, looking at the cash flows built into a 5-year business plan that ends with a final cash payment valuing a theoretical business sale. The more complicated the business is to understand, the higher the threshold needed to mitigate the risk. A high-percentage IRR approach allows for risk of the unexpected, for some failures, some firms that chug along and earn a 4 per cent to 5 per cent internal rate of return; and a few spectacular successes. The aim should be overall returns on funds deployed in line or slightly higher (say 15 per cent on 5 years) with US and UK experience cited above, thereby compensating investors for the additional risk they are taking. There is always significant risk. These companies require luck, exceptional entrepreneurs or significant additional support; or indeed all of them together to transition from idea to successful delivery. They also need to be on the lookout for the next wave of disruption as Box 3.5 explains.

Most of the issues they face will be the same, Brexit or no Brexit, although Brexit may alter the overall environment they operate in. Even acknowledged disrupters of one age can find themselves at risk if they do not continue to innovate. Box 3.5 describes how this happened in the bookselling trade.

Box 3.5.   Bookselling – Dusty Secluded Emporiums Serially Disrupted

The printed book has been around in the United Kingdom since 1476 when William Caxton a leading member of the Merchant Adventurers Company of London introduced it from Europe. Bookselling itself goes back to Greco–Roman times, with a lively bookselling trade being known in 300 BC with the accumulation of the collection at the Library of Alexandria. The printing press changed bookselling into becoming bookstores and the earliest known bookstore was the Librairie Nouvelle d'Orléans, which is known to have been in existence in 1545. Booksellers had evolved from being scribes to retailers with printed stock. The bookselling trade then continued as a specialist retail business for nearly 450 years. Consequent upon having bookstores which stocked and sold books came a separation from printers/publishers who commissioned and printed manuscripts. Publishers separated from booksellers and for many centuries the main changes were more related to public censorship and licensing than market disruptions. Bookstores and publishers worked together in an integrated supply chain. The publishers took the publication risk and the retailers took the retail risk. In consequence publisher book catalogues were considerably longer than retail title stock lists, and specialist titles had to be ordered by bookshops from the publisher. Key to bookshop economics is the ability to ensure shelf stock sales, that is stock rotated on a regular basis. A key implication is that bookshops necessarily restrict the titles they stock to those they think will sell. In practice, this restricts stocking policy to including best sellers, known authors and any specialist titles that shop may seek to hold – a very small percentage of the Universe of Books. Anderson (2004) demonstrates how by making a wider set of titles easily available, different consumer tastes can be unmasked and incremental sales gained across a wider range of titles – selling across the 'Long Tail' of titles that are normally unknown, not displayed and not sold. Opening access to the Long Tail opens a new market that Anderson estimates is nearly a third the size of that for bookshop stocked titles. *'Barnes & Noble carries 130,000 titles. Yet a quarter of Amazon's booksales already come from outside its top 130,000 titles'* (Anderson, 2004).

Book market disruption since 1980 and the gradual development of 'smart computer cataloguing' and 'product recommendation engines' have led to accessing the 'Long Tail'. Typically, a small 'mom and pop' bookstore used to hold between 10,000 and 13,000 titles (Babwin, 2006), so providing an opportunity for book 'Superstores' carrying between 130,000 and 200,000 titles to concentrate sales volume into a larger location and provide the customer with a richer experience by giving them access to a more significant percentage of the estimated 20 million titles available globally (Bowker, 2017). Peterson (2017) narrates how US book chain Borders developed from a standard bookstore into a chain of book megastores in the late 1980s and early 1990s, both through product innovation and an aggressive company acquisition plan by their then parent Kmart. Two key innovations lay behind the store's growth: first, it developed a new way of indexing and managing book inventory that allowed it to dramatically increase the number of titles it carried and subsequently to start opening book 'superstores'. Borders had opened up a new way of book retailing, capitalising on selling across the 'long tail' by holding a wider range of stock, thereby disrupting the bookselling supply chain and leading to the closure of many independent bookstores.

Roll the clock forward a further 10 to 15 years, and a second innovation arrived, this time from Amazon.com who by selling books online opened consumer access to over 2.3 million titles in the Long Tail (Anderson, 2004). Borders was unable to cope with this new disruptive innovation, remaining stuck in their previous paradigm. In their Annual Report from 2000, the company stated, *'Our online investment will be channelled to support our in-store platform, while Borders.com will continue to be utilized as a convenience retail channel'* (Borders Group, 2000). Incorrect strategy missed the opportunity and by 2011 Borders was bankrupt, in liquidation and no more. A market subject to Big Bank Disruption twice in 40 years, as technology unlocked new potential to meet and delight customer needs. A wider range available to customers, but at the cost of the old-fashioned exploration into nook's and cranny's in musty old-fashioned bookshops. No more explorations in small local bookshops, like the now closed Bury Bookshop (Bury St Edmunds Suffolk) that used to have one floor of new titles and two floors plus various higgledy-piggledy landings of second-hand books with a surfeit of unexpected finds. The nearest and second-best equivalents are specialist charity second-hand bookstores like the one in the basement of the Samaritans shop in Ipswich Suffolk – but the specialist ones are few and far between.

3.6.2. Group 2: Complex Supply Chain Players

When considering complex supply chains one could immediately think of examples from the Automotive or Aerospace supply chains, but this grouping also includes many traditional manufacturing industries such as steel and multinode central/regional distribution networks. Typically sectors with complex supply chains are fiercely competitive and dominated by large mature global players who are focused on both 'value engineering' and 'technical progress', meaning companies face a combination of tough pricing and contract terms. Some companies (such as in the defence industry) are part of complex (and often international) supply chains that are led by a major customer. High levels of interdependency between supply chain players typify these chains. Dubois, Hulthén, and Pedersen (2004) noted how supply chain issues have developed from being internal to a company to involving other linked companies. Chains can be complex with different tiers − where lower tiers are responsible for building component assemblies, which are then assembled into the final product. This sort of organisation is especially prevalent in the Automotive, Aerospace and Defence Contracting sectors. Products are complex and dependent upon embedding multiple technologies, linking different suppliers often in different countries who come together to create a single product with complex supply chains used to help manage inventory risk, ensure quality and speed product development.

Traditionally, change happened within the chain when a top-level specifying contractor or original equipment manufacturer (for example by the car company, the Defence Prime Contractor, the Aircraft Manufacturer) issued a new specification. This has evolved in response to growing technical complexity and cost pressures so that Research and Development can be shared across the chain. In some cases, changes engineered within the supply chain feed into changes in the prime product specifications − a multidirectional rather than unidirectional process across supply chain tiers.

Such a supply chain has a top tier labelled 'OEMs' which means the major big name manufacturers such as Boeing, Ford or Nissan. Below this tier are the 'Tier 1' subassembly suppliers − the Robert Bosch or Delphi's of this world. Below them are a host of SME component suppliers and raw material suppliers in Tier 3 and in Tier 4. Boeing's approach to aircraft design and development reflects this increasing supply chain interdependence, a world where development has moved from sole manufacturer command and control into a diffused set of supply chain/manufacturer relationships (as pioneered in the 787 development programme) and described in Box 3.6.

The Boeing 787 case discussed below shows how difficult it is to adapt a finely tuned structure such as a complex supply chain, and have it work in an alternative manner. In the end, Boeing had to take back control of the supply chain to resolve problems that its own

**Box 3.6.   From Prime Purchaser to Complex Tier Contractor –
Developing the Boeing 767 vs. Boeing 787**

Boeing Commercial Aerospace is in the business of building new
commercial airliners, a highly complex technical activity that is
dependent upon many different subcontractors, all of whom need to
perform to specification and deliver components on time for the final
product to come into being. In every case building a new airliner
depends upon performance across the whole supply chain, a
performance that needs to balance the needs for integration,
harmonisation, innovation and control with each other.

In the mid-1980s Boeing set about developing a new airliner, the
767. Farrell (1986) tells us how this programme was managed as an
integrated international procurement and development project across
a number of countries – the United States, Japan and Italy. The
then novel structure was conceived to reduce economic risk, but as
with all changes it raised interesting management challenges. Boeing
took 70 per cent of the programme, Japan 15 per cent and Italy the
final 15 per cent. Each partner was responsible for developing,
procuring and building its parts for the overall design. Boeing kept
control of the master design whilst subcontractors undertook
detailed design within the Boeing overall design. Boeing retained the
project and programme management roles so the project was run on
a 'top-down' basis with decision making centralised back in Boeing.
Costs were shared, risks were shared, profits were shared and
technologies protected back to Boeing and the programme; therefore,
for companies undertaking detailed design work, this was risk-sharing
subcontracting. A project structure where subcontractors down to the
lowest levels work on a command-and-control basis from the Boeing
Project/Programme Office. Innovation and change by diktat.

Thirty years later Boeing started to develop the *787 Dreamliner*.
An aircraft made from composites to reduce weight, improve fuel
efficiency and extend range. To set a new 'best practice' the goal
was that this aircraft was to be engineered and developed on a
decentralised basis, with Boeing becoming the final assembler of pre-
built modules and where the risk and project control are moved to
the module builders. Boeing was looking to redefine itself into a
financing and selling company, commissioning technology from
module suppliers. The goal appears to have been to copy Toyota's
automotive supply chain structure, that Toyota had established to
enable it to bring innovative new models to market faster than its

competitors. An opportunity to transplant 'best practice' from one industry to another. Originally scheduled for maiden flight in 2008, the 787 eventually entered service in late 2011, three years late and way over development budget. Tang, Zimmerman, and Nelson (2009) give some insight as to what caused the delays and overruns.

> *To reduce the 787's development time from six to four years and development cost from $10 to $6 billion, Boeing decided to develop and produce the Dreamliner by using an unconventional supply chain new to the aircraft manufacturing industry. The 787's supply chain was envisioned to keep manufacturing and assembly costs low, while spreading the financial risks of development to Boeing's suppliers. Unlike the 737's supply chain, which requires Boeing to play the traditional role of a key manufacturer who assembles different parts and subsystems produced by thousands of suppliers [...], the 787's supply chain is based on a tiered structure that would allow Boeing to foster partnerships with approximately 50 tier-1 strategic partners. These strategic partners serve as 'integrators' who assemble different parts and subsystems produced by tier-2 suppliers.*

A hugely complex piece of technology became a complex supply chain puzzle. The aircraft was being developed in different places and by different companies, yet everything had to seamlessly come together into a working product. Wings from Japan, centre fuselage from Italy, aft fuselage from South Carolina, cargo access doors from Sweden, flaps and wing tips from Korea, landing gear from the United Kingdom (The Boeing Corporation, 2013); the list goes on and on. All these different and in many cases interdependent assemblies needed to come together to have a working certifiable aircraft.

The programme soon started to run late and over budget. Originally estimated with a development cost of US$6bn, the final cost was US $32 billion, with the programme time nearly doubled. So how was the programme fixed? Boeing was forced to recognize that supply chains are more than financial relationships, and to work effectively, they need to be coordinated and focused on solving the same technical challenges in the same way. Contract terms alone were not sufficient to do this as they did not provide the necessary framework for suppliers to cooperate vertically within the tiers and laterally across key assemblies managed and developed by differing Tier 1 contractors.

over-ambitious organisational change had partially led to. It does beg the question as to how substantial the appetite will be in any overseas automotive or aerospace manufacturer to resolve any Brexit glitches that are not of its making, unless of course that single supplier has a unique and irreplaceable component sourced from the UK (unlikely as most supply chains hedge risk through multiple sourcing).

Similarly, complexity is a feature of the automotive supply chain, with SME companies being important in Tier 3 and Tier 4 (Automotive Council UK, 2014). This supply chain is typified by inter-firm and cross-border dependency, heightened by moves towards a just-in-time custom model build at Tier 1 OEM level. Systems schedule parts to the assembly line to build the size colour and style that reflect a customer sales order. All this is part of continual efforts to reduce inventory levels and associated needs for working capital. Notwithstanding the successful drive to increase local UK content in UK manufactured vehicles, that has risen over recent years from 36 per cent in 2011 to 44 per cent in 2017 (Automotive Council UK, 2014), there is still a desire to increase it further, with a target to raise it to 60 per cent to match Germany. With so many components sourced outside the UK, there is significant scope for Brexit-induced supply chain dislocation as components and assemblies crossing the UK/EU border could attract tariffs and time delays due to documentary and customs procedure checks. A supply manager could address the customs disruption risk by holding backup inventories, but this industry has spent the past 30 years reducing inventories to reduce working capital needs through improved supply chain management. Holding backup inventory would be a significant and costly reversal of this process. Tier 1 OEM vehicle or aircraft manufacturers can, to a large degree, specify their product development and timelines.

Knibb, Gormezano and Partners (2009) in a study of the UK East Midlands Supply Chain highlighted the limited innovation capacity due to *'management often too busy to innovate'* in many MSME Tier 2 and Tier 3 suppliers. This need for management 'time focus' on innovation is unlikely to be made any easier if the demands from revised Custom's procedures and additional Certificate of Conformity and Certificate of Origin requirements require management's urgent attention to ensure continuity of operation.

Supply chains are also evolving in other ways such that different tiers interact and work together to reduce wastage. For example, in the Aerospace Supply Chain, Tier 4 suppliers (raw material suppliers) are working with Tier 3 suppliers (machine shops and make-to-print operations) to recycle wastage from the machining process, targeting an estimated US$8 billion in material cost savings (Rhoades, 2014). Efficiency comes through integration across all levels, Tier 1 the major structure and aero system providers, Tier 2 the component and subassembly manufacturers, Tier 3 the machinists and casters and Tier 4 the material supplier. Increasingly, German automotive manufacturers are looking at collaboration across the supply chain to innovate technology in the overall product, as we see in Box 3.7.

Box 3.7.   Collaborative Innovation in the German Automotive Sector

Germany is famed for both its car industry (both volume manufacturers such as Volkswagen and high-end premium manufacturers such as Mercedes and BMW) and its successful and innovative technology SMEs (Mittlestand). Buchmann and Pyka (2012) tell us:

> *Intensified competition in the global automotive industry and particularly the catching-up of Asian firms forced German producers to significantly improve their cost structure. To escape this pressure, new strategies were developed and implemented. Innovations are identified as the key to success because they allow firms to escape a destructive price competition and to create unique selling propositions. With this an intensified innovation competition emerged as a race for innovation, shortened product life cycles as well as rising safety and quality requirements.*

In Germany the automotive sector built upon its existing supply chain relationships, is looking to develop trust and informal networking between supply chain members, sometimes facilitated by the car manufacturer, sometimes facilitated by the Tier 1 supplier and sometimes built by subcontractors themselves. These knowledge networks (which are stronger where there is geographical proximity and where there is a tradition of incorporating new learning into products) have become increasingly complex and active. Buchmann and Pyka (2012) have demonstrated the rapid increases in complexity and cross supply chain networking. The German Automotive sector has become more distributed across the whole supply chain, but more effective as it moves from a command-and-control framework, to one that utilises the knowledge of all the supply chain players.

Post-Brexit UK, there is no reason why these integration trends will reverse. UK suppliers risk being disconnected as non-tariff barriers are raised. UK-based car manufacturers risk losing competitiveness as they face restrictions on their access to EU-based supply chains.

3.6.3. Group 3: Simple Supply Chain Players

Simple supply chain subcontracting companies tend to be in 'UK only', and often in 'Region only' supply chains; across service delivery industries, UK only distribution, agriculture, large food retailers and construction. Their needs are therefore be different from business that intrinsically works across borders. These MSMEs could be working under a Prime Contractor on a government outsource programme such as the UK Government Work Programme and follow on Work and Health Programme. 'Prime Contractors' contract packages of the delivery programme from local (sometime third sector not-for-profit) suppliers to complement their own resources. Firms in these supply chains tend to have a panorama defined by UK economic performance. A 250 firm MSME construction subcontractor survey found twice as many of these firms were concerned about the UK economy as they were about Brexit, even though they felt Brexit would negatively impact their business. Their critical concern about payment lags and access to finance is indicative of their vista (Bibby, 2016).

Such contracting is both capability and price sensitive and often relates to labour intensive operations. It also normally needs standards compliance requirements as set in the Prime Contractor's contract from the originating purchaser as shown in Box 3.8.

Box 3.8.   Simple Supply Chain – The Work Programme

Commissioned by UK Central Government as a key initiative in its 'welfare to work' thinking, the Work Programme relied upon large Prime Contractors to do the detailed programme design to realise stated contract performance measures and bear the financial risk built into the programmes performance payments. Prime Contractors were urged to use:

> *specialist voluntary groups in their delivery, using their financial muscle to 'soften' the risk exposed to specialist voluntary*

> *sector subcontractors. [...] that this 'softening' had not hap-*
> *pened. [according to an early 2011 survey]. Instead, risk had*
> *been 'passed down the supply chain', with terms for subcon-*
> *tractors largely reflecting the high-risk profile of the primes*
> *contractor's own contracts, including Payment by Results. For*
> *small- and medium-sized voluntary organisations, this created*
> *enormous challenges around risk, cash flow and quality of*
> *delivery.*
>
> — Stuffins (2012)

3.6.4. Group 4: Professional Advice

UK Professional Advice, which can range from management consultancy, to architectural or engineering services through to legal and accountancy services, operates both nationally and, on more limited occasions, globally. Where traded across Europe these services may be subject (such as in France) to laws (such as the French *Law on Foreign Workers* (Law No. 2016-274)) that broadly require the issue of 'Talent Passports' for an individual to work (such as in France {Prolink, 2016}). As an example, post Brexit barriers will arise in France as non-EU Nationals who have not studied or qualified at a French University will not be automatically entitled to these. Mutual recognition of professional qualifications is another key issue, with for example in Germany certain structural engineering activities needing to be 'signed off' by a licensed structural engineer. European Commission (2017) sets out a comprehensive view of current non-tariff professional barriers for companies within Member States. Many of these barriers are associated with the need to register to undertake certain activities in specific Member States.

In addition to being non-standard and complex (Box 3.9 gives one example), the need for appropriate documentation begs the question as to how many documents will, for UK service providers, need to be translated by certified translators and then Certified and Endorsed according to The Hague Documentary Convention (an expensive and cumbersome process presently required for much documentation provided in GCC Member States). From personal experience of one of the authors, each document can cost between £200 and £300 to legalise in line with the convention, and at its fastest personally walking the document through the system can take about a week to do.

Box 3.9. SME Registration Catch 22 or Nightmare with Bureaucracy?

Sample entrepreneur comments (that align to one of the author's personal experiences in several EU countries) on registering in France from 'Start Business in France' (2017):

'Thanks for helping me navigate the bureaucracy involved in starting my auto-entrepreneur business here in France. [...]. one agency involved in the process failed to pass on my details to another agency. You got me out of this "Catch 22", and I now have my business registered and a social security number'. Entrepreneur No. 1

'The French system of setting up a business and paying taxes is complicated and easy to get lost in. I was also overdue with documents for the French authorities'. Entrepreneur No. 2

These businesses can also be dependent upon data exchanges and holding personal data on computers outside the Member State in question, thus requiring appropriate data registrations and data 'safe harbour' arrangements. Finally, some regulatory frameworks already differ – for example the DIN Building Regulations used in Germany are fundamentally different to those used in the UK.

3.6.5.   Group 5: Financial Services

Financial Services is a key sector for the United Kingdom, given London's international financial role. Both the issue of Financial Services Passporting – that is, selling financial services from a base in one Member State into another Member State – and the issue of a non-EU hub (e.g. London) acting as the Euro Derivative clearing hub have been widely highlighted and discussed. During the second half of 2017, the first evidence has started to emerge of financial services firms opening new offices in continuing Member States, but the degree to which activities and staff will move is not as yet clear. Whilst this narrative is especially focused at SMEs, and by nature of their turnover and asset bases most cross-border financial services organisations are larger than SMEs we highlight two specific issues.

First, and widely discussed, comes the issue of critical mass. Should relocating part operations into other Member States fragment regulatory capital bases, this could have knock-on effects on the UK banking cluster. Were this to lead to a repatriation of some activities to the United States as well as relocation to Europe, there could be serious knock-on multiplier effects on London-based professional/business services.

Second, and by far the most serious, is that, the UK running a trade deficit in excess of 5 per cent of GDP, UK imports and thereby consumption patterns are underpinned, to quote Carney, Bank of England Governor, by '*the kindness of strangers*' (Carney, 2017) in their capital deposits and investments in UK businesses and real estate. A significant reversal of these capital flows could engender a 'Sudden Stop' (Eichengreen & Gupta, 2016) event. Such an event has the capability to initiate a significant macro-economic adjustment (more about this later).

Some reports suggest that major financial institutions are considering splitting their capital bases post-Brexit (Lewis & Noonan, 2017). Such a restructuring could affect the location of funds under management by UK-based Asset Management. A recent study (The FCA, 2017a) estimates that there are £6.9 trillion of assets under UK management of which £2.7 trillion are owned by overseas clients. This makes the UK Asset Management industry the second largest in the world. Of the £6.9 trillion under management, it is estimated that £1.7 trillion is in UK-managed funds domiciled either in the United Kingdom or overseas. It is unknown how much of this is in sterling assets that are susceptible to being sold in the event of a loss of confidence in the United Kingdom. Abstracting published data investment holdings (The Investment Association, 2016), one can estimate maybe up to £2.3 trillion of the £6.9 trillion is held in UK equities and UK debt, assets that are very likely to be Sterling denominated.

3.6.6. Group 6: Local Retail and Artisan Products

Local retail, artisan products and local services have to compete within a local context. This was as true for the artisans at the gate of the Roman Forum in Verulamium in AD 409 as it is on today's high street. In stable times, the major pressures are keeping up with local competition and maintaining positive cash flow. In the Men's Clothing Industry (especially, suits) some companies have adapted to market changes and some have not. Business evolution has seen a progression from individual tailors, to 'off-the-peg' manufacturers who became retailers, to including the suit in an overall 'fashion concept'. Post-Middle Ages, tailors had an elite status, for example Allen (2006) tells us in respect of Edinburgh tailoring in 1635:

> *Two of the tailors were also placed on that main artery for economic activity and one was located on the Cowgate,*

*between Horse Wynd and Niddry's Wynd. The elite status
[...] is again highlighted by the fact that their known businesses seem to have been placed only on main streets.*

An elite trade that maintained its position until after the First World
War and that entered into steep decline after the Second World War. This
decline seems to have been related to cheaper ready-to-wear fashion being
available for the masses, although tailoring still maintained a superior sense
of style (Ugolini, 2000). As ready-to-wear products and supplies developed,
branding identities became more important. They started to unlock
elements of consumer personality (Lee & Rhee, 2008), so allowing ready-
to-wear products to attain a premier fashion position. This branding revolution was combined with retail brand upheaval. Table 3.3 sets the context
by giving sample data from census records for the past 150+ years.

Men's high-street fashion has gone through many changes during the
last 120 years. For example, a retailer such as Next (2017) evolved from
being a tailor founded around its manufacturing plant in Leeds into
today's unisex fashion. As we demonstrate in Box 3.10, Jacobean society put a premium on fashion whereby 'Luxurious clothes and accesso-
ries were essential items for the wealthy and powerful members of
Jacobean society' (V & A, 2017).

Table 3.3. Number of Tailors Operating in the United Kingdom.

1851	1861	1871	1911	1921[a]	1951	2001
152,672	136,390	149,864	140,919	204,705	109,963	22,651

Sources: 1851–1871 (Bloy, 2017); 1911–1951 (Vision of Britain, 2017); Census Data For 2001 (2017).
[a]1921 has no Scottish data so may understate the numbers.

Box 3.10.   Tailors, Ready-to-Wear and Nuanced Branding

This importance of tailored style has continued through the centuries
into modern day fashion retailing and brand identities. Style and
garment design have joined in seeming perpetual competitive
symbiosis for at least five centuries. In the 1630s this was reflected by
the premier city locations tailors occupied (Allen, 2006); in the
Victorian age this was reflected by the tradition of buying suits for
special occasions. Jobling (2005) describes the advance of quality
'off-the-peg' tailors through the development of Austin Reed.

Progressing from readymade shirts in the pre-1914 period into semi-finished suits, Austin Reed sold the convenience of 'off-the-peg' as having the quality and style of a 'bespoke' suit. Whilst the likes of Hepworth & Son and 50 Shilling Tailors competed for 'Class C' customers, Austin Reed started to make an off-the-peg market for 'Class A and B' customers. Off-the-peg was gaining a 'flagship' brand to help drive consumer change. This change being driven through the aggressive use of advertising, and changing the product proposition in the whole industry, not just the segment addressed by Austin Reed.

Class perception was a key driver in product positioning. Ugolini (2000) tells us how the chain stores such as 50 Shilling Tailor and Montague Burton presented clothes at an affordable price that then lifted the perceived social class of the buyer, as a key customer selling proposition. In some ways 'advertising puff':

> *Despite these claims, the notion of a new inter-class homogeneity in interwar clothing should be treated with a degree of caution, as the experiences of a certain David Henry Campbell can help to show. On the night between 25 and the 26 of February 1932, the 21-year-old Campbell broke into the tailoring shop of Castell & Son, in one of Oxford's premier shopping streets, and stole clothing to the value of £1.10s. The stolen items included a jacket, trousers and a bathing suit. There is little doubt that Campbell's subsequent discovery and arrest were aided by the unemployed bricklayer's decision to wear the stolen clothes while residing at Stratton St Mary Public Institution (The Oxford Times, 15 April 1933). By wearing garments intended for University undergraduates, rather than those suitable for a young man living on the margins of society, Campbell had made himself conspicuous, and had attracted the unwelcome attention of the law.*
>
> – Ugolini (2000)

This change rippled out to provincial cities and market towns. For example, Grimwades in Ipswich, a family-run men's outfitting store, became an anchor for the local community and town centre, even having the street it was located on named Grimwade Street. The Grimwade store became synonymous with being the 'local Austin Reed' – the store with the quality and the style for the man of class.

A business founded in 1845 and described in later years as *'one of Ipswich's oldest and best-loved institutions'* (*The Ipswich Star*, 2007) before it closed in 1996. Grimwades had evolved from being a bespoke tailor into a combination of 'off-the-peg' and 'made-to-measure'. The Grimwade family also played an important role in town life, providing mayors, footballers and philanthropic works. A small local business.

In the early 1980s, Hepworths was a traditional, although a bit sleepy, manufacturer/retailer of somewhat-dated men's suits that had survived the Austin Reed and Fifty Shilling Tailor disruptions, by changing and evolving into a local icon, only to fall at the wayside with next great wave of change when national consumer branding and media lifestyle generation were to replace social class as the drivers in the product proposition. In a competitive and evolving market, it faced challenges that required it to change strategy and direction. Top management was changed with the bringing in of a new chairman (Terence Conran), chief executive and chief financial officer. Initial changes were made by acquiring parallel business Kendall & Sons — buying market in the woman's wear sector. This acquisition was then transformed into Next, at first for women, and then a couple of years later as Next for Men. Prior to undergoing a period of strategic change, this company J Hepworth & Son was described as *'[...] a tailor in the Montague Burton mould, with an uninspiring business in off-the-peg suits and a less well-known sideline in made-to-measure outfits for the self-respecting teddy boy'* (*The Times*, 1985).

Next became a 'style'-driven retailer; the factory closed. The revamped business subsequently became reliant upon a variety of suppliers instead of upon its own factory. Further expansion came via the acquisition of Grattan Mail Order in 1986, the subsequent launch of 'Next Directory' in 1988 and finally solidified into a single product channel over both a retail store and mail order strategy in 1993. This strategy was then extended into a combined online, mail order and retail strategy in 2009.

The AD 410 experience we discussed in Chapter 2 shows that when faced with massive disruption, businesses have a tendency to regress. In AD 410 this regression was extreme, moving from urban centres to village as centres of population. Even in villages business has to innovate. For example, in the village of Angmering in West Sussex, there is evidence of a postal service from about 1793 (Rogers-Davis, 2013). The first village post master was noted in 1851 and was 27-year-old Allen Johnson, the son of a local grocer. By 1861 the role of post master had moved to his mother, and by 1871, Allen Johnson had been demoted to postal messenger. The business had moved into Mr Elliot's combined Grocer and Draper and from here on in, as in many villages, the post office and sub-post master were combined with other businesses, at first the local drapers and then later the local grocers. Innovation started with the son of an existing SME holder (Allen Johnson) becoming postmaster and then evolved until the new product could be combined with something else to make it economically viable.

One constant of business is the need to continually change to meet customer needs and aspirations. Some changes involve 'range extensions' by including new products in the range, some by improving existing products and some by expanding sales and distribution channels. Companies may innovate through finding new customers by buying other businesses, grabbing their customers and gaining new sales points.

For example, the UK garden centre market is worth around £5 billion, excluding landscaping and amenity sectors (The HTA, 2017). In the United States, this market is worth around $14bn with some 20,000 firms, mostly employing 20 people or less. Box 3.11 describes how a local UK player branched out.

Box 3.11.   Notcutts Nurseries: Change through Expanding Distribution (as well as Range Expansion)

Notcutts Nurseries was started in 1749 by Thomas Wood (on former monastery land seized by Henry VIII in Woodbridge Suffolk) and run by the Woods family until 1897. *'The last of the Woods, John, always wore a top hat and carried a small stool. He used to select a customer's tree or shrub personally and would sit on the stool whilst personally lifting it'* (Westerndarp, 1968). During these years, business was with large country estates and town houses, an elite market for fruit and forest trees.

> *John Wood's catalogue of Fruit Trees and Roses, published in October 1895, lists no fewer than 95 apples, 35 pears, 25 plums, 16 cherries, 20 trained peaches, 7 nectarines and 123 varieties of roses. He produced his last full catalogue in the autumn of 1896 and died without succession in 1897.*
> — Notcutts (2017)

The purchase of the business by Roger Notcutt in 1897 introduced a new entrepreneurial drive. He was the second son of an established Ipswich legal family that already had an interest in the Natural Sciences (his elder brother read Natural Science at Cambridge). Roger had already developed his own flower business based on award-winning Chrysanthemums, and his nursery was outgrowing its premises, so Roger's purchase of Woods solved three problems, the succession at Woods, the lack of space at his own nursery and provided new product lines to expand the Woods business. The Notcutts family had an interest in Natural Science, with a tradition of academic studies at Cambridge and in some cases species development at Royal Botanical Gardens. Post 1945 the family started to bring in professional management to work with the family. Two major events were to challenge and transform the business, first the harsh and long winter of 1963 led to a delay in being able to fulfil orders by mail order, and so customers started to discover that they could buy plants at the nursery itself. A trend that was accelerated by the second event in 1971 — a national postal strike. Together with shifts in demand away from large local authority purchasers into individual customers, today's modern Garden Centre was born. Notcutts both developed its own business and from the early 1980s started to acquire other garden centres across the country and now has 18 such units. This was a case of expanding distribution outlets in the face of a challenge. Still a private company with family involvement, the family moved to sell the business to the management during the 2000s.

Such trends towards retail concentration are well established. We note Brexit may especially impact some sectors such as agriculture and horticulture if the previous EU export markets become inaccessible. (Historically, the EU has protected Agriculture and the Common Agriculture in its third-state trade deals).

3.6.7. Group 7: Labour-intensive Service MSMEs

Another substantial group of MSMEs are labour-intensive small-scale local businesses such as family-owned shops, local social care and health, hairdressers, leisure and tourism, sandwich bars, cafes, restaurants, local cleaning firms, agricultural labouring, etc. These firms are typified by their

Box 3.12. Southern Cross Healthcare

Adult social care is a growing market driven both by an ageing population and by an increase in conditions that require some sort of care provision, such as dementia. The market changed significantly following the passing of the 1990 NHS and Community Care Act becoming dominated by Private Care providers. The sector attracted significant new capital and grew rapidly in the years leading up to 2008, based upon favourable demographics (ageing population) and the revised state care spending in line with a policy favouring private sector care over public sector provision. Capital entered the market to support new builds and mergers and acquisitions to create significant size care groups.

One of the best known of these groups was Southern Cross, a private care home provider that grew rapidly during the 2000s as Private Equity House Blackstone invested capital. From 2001 when it had 70 care homes (making it a 'top-ten' player), Southern Cross grew (mainly by acquisition) to 750 care homes with 37,000+ residents in 2011, meaning that in 2011 it had over 10 per cent of the market (Scourfield, 2012). Blackstone continued a pre-existing sale-and-leaseback policy (Blackstone, 2011). Sale-and-leaseback looks to unlock asset values by separating the property assets into a separate company and establishing long-term leases on the properties with the operating company (in this case Southern Cross). The remaining operating company was floated in 2007. Despite rent being such a significant expense, the official pricing documents for the Southern Cross Health Care IPO (Southern Cross, 2006) show the Southern Cross operating margin in terms of EBITDAR (Earnings before Interest, Tax, Depreciation, Amortization and Rent), an approach that continued into the Southern Cross annual reports (Southern Cross, 2008). For Southern Cross, the average 2008 rent per bed was £4,672, rising at around 4.5 per cent per annum (Southern Cross, 2008).

With locked-in rising rents, the Southern Cross business model depended upon rising fees and continued high occupancy to stand still. The Great Recession and consolidation in public budgets led to squeezed fees, lack of available cash led to an increasingly poorly viewed care business with few (higher fee paying) private clients, and it went bankrupt in 2011.

low level of technology, not currently prone to rapid technology-driven productivity improvement and, in general, tend to be labour intensive. Being labour intensive means that wages, employer taxes and labour regulation have significant importance to their costs, and in many cases, occupy rental premises with rent being a significant cost, as shown in Box 3.12.

Typically, if one excludes property costs, these businesses have fairly low fixed capital requirements (unless they own the property they are in) but may face working capital needs to fund stock and in some cases delays in customer payments.

These businesses are also subject to extensive regulation, ranging from employment and health and safety law, to food safety, chemical safety, local planning ordinances and licensing, signage rules, etc. They often operate in fiercely competitive situations, and are differentiated mainly by customer perception about the product or product range they offer. Such businesses are often the cornerstones of local communities, but do not offer immediately attractive propositions to bring in additional capital. In consequence, financing is limited to bank overdrafts (if available and sometimes secured against personal assets), invoice factoring, trade credit, leasing and rentals. Attempts to change or increase scale in these businesses have had questionable success and raise important financing questions.

3.6.8.   *Group 8: Knowledge-driven Innovators*

Typically, these are companies involved in Creative Media, Software Development not covered elsewhere and Medical Industries, including medical devices and pharmaceuticals. They rely on workforce innovation, and skill capacities are often dependent upon large commissioning organisations, although they can have additional or independent routes to market from the commissioning body. Their value is in their copyright, patents and brand perception, that is value created by an innovative and creative workforce often organised into teams. At an MSME level, although the output may be marketed globally, these companies are local in character with a tendency to be focused into clusters.

Box 3.13.   Event Cinema

Digital cinema has dramatically changed the cinema landscape. The cinema itself is undergoing a radical transformation, and technology continually changes every facet of the business. Once a showcase for Hollywood studio content, the cinema now offers a range of entertainment from ballet to sport, comedy to live music, opera to theatre, museums to art gallery exhibitions, and much of it is broadcast live by satellite and directly via Internet streaming. While experiments had begun as early as 2002, Melissa Cogavin, CEO of The Event Cinema Association (ECA) reckons that,

> *'the last 10 years has witnessed this initial offering of the arts expanding, so that today the industry is worth $750m worldwide. Even conventional cinema took about 10 years before talkies took over, and another 20 years before "The Golden Age of Hollywood" peaked in the 1940s [...]'.*

Worldwide estimations put the likely value of the Event Cinema industry at $1bn by 2019. Providers such as the Royal Opera House have designed value creation opportunities during the intervals (e.g. interviews with choreographers, cast members, backstage tours), prohibited at the live event itself.

Research conducted by the Arts Council in 2016 showed that far from 'cannibalising' the traditional arts, the effect of Event Cinema on ticket sales for the theatre, ballet and opera has actually been minimal, and that the medium of live broadcasts in cinemas has done much to promote the arts amongst audiences who would not otherwise attend such events for reasons such as awareness, budget and accessibility. David Hancock, who runs the Film and Cinema team at IHS Markit and is the President of the European Digital Cinema Forum, believes the ECA can become a major force for this increasingly important sector in the marketplace by supporting the industry by supplying vital box office data and for distributors and exhibitors as well as raising awareness of the sector and lobbying national and supra-national bodies.

> *Hancock believes that 'at present, very little data exists freely and this access will provide investors with the infor-mation they need to invest in this sector with greater confi-dence and promote its growth'.*

As for the future, the United Kingdom remains the most buoyant and developed market; however, the ECA reflects the appetite for Event Cinema content worldwide. As David Hancock points out,

> *China has seen unprecedented building of cinemas through-out the country, with 2 multiplexes a day opening for some*

years now. The focus of this new sector has been on building audiences for films, and Event Cinema has passed the country by. However, as this content is not subject to the same quota system on foreign content as for feature films, the opportunity is beginning to be explored.

As a solution to this, some Chinese exhibition companies are envisaging a time within the next decade where 50 per cent of all cinema content is Event Cinema, which is apparently not subject to the same censorship restrictions (see Figure B3.13).

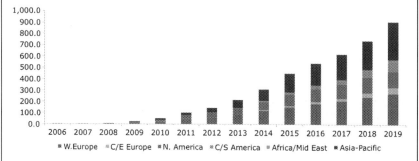

Figure B3.13.   Global Event Cinema Revenues, by Region ($mn).
Source: IHS Markit.

Event Cinema emerged as a happy accident, a by-product of the digitisation of cinemas; nobody saw this opportunity coming. As Cogavin is quick to point out,

Event Cinema is a steady and profitable revenue stream for exhibitors in the UK, and the content itself is a magnificent promotional tool for UK Plc as we pointlessly navigate the treacherous waters of Brexit over the coming years. The government has recognised the value that this revenue stream provides and the ECA has been in preliminary dialogue with the DCMS and Arts Council about research to register the impact of Event Cinema overseas, but the essence of those meetings had been that there is no "magic money tree" to do much to promote the business of Event Cinema overseas as a successful British export.

Cogavin asserts that 'Event Cinema is the most innovative cinema content the world has seen in decades has no

> *roadmap to success, and everyone involved is learning from their mistakes and growing from their triumphs. The industry at large is all too aware that we have had a fortunate start, but we need to keep innovating and anticipating the "next big thing" in cinemas to remain as culturally relevant and commercially vital as we have become in 2017.*

Bio Technology research companies are often associated with academic or large research institutions, and so can in some cases be 'clustered' near other similar companies, although in today's high-speed broadband world they can also be part of much wider virtual global clusters of scientists and researchers with similar interest. Equally, the building of Salford Media City has spurred media innovation. The BBC anchors the project (which is still ongoing) and now employs over 7,000 people across a range of business (Media City, 2017). The rapid rate of change in the Creative Industries is emphasised by our description of the development of Event Cinema in Box 3.13 above that gives an example of one of these innovating sectors.

3.7.   Diverse Groups Requiring Differing Brexit Outcomes

The contrast between a village shop and a new technology Medical Device MSME is obvious. Their interfaces with the customer, business, regulatory, trade and financial worlds are different. Brexit will change these interfaces by altering the environment the companies work in. We will return to this theme later in our journey, but for now in Table 3.4 is a summary of some of the main potential impacts.

3.8.   Summary: Brexit Implications

This chapter has emphasised the complex and diverse MSME landscape that exists today. To recap, as Table 3.4 summarises, each MSME is different and some very different. Perhaps for many, Pre-Brexit, the EU is not their biggest worry as they cope with rising costs, especially minimum wage changes, pension auto-enrolment, rent, business rates, etc., changing regulations, relatively expensive banking and poor access

Table 3.4. Potential EU Impacts.

Dimension	EU Component	National Component
Customer	Goods – free movement with no tariffs or additional documents	VAT Return and Intrastat
	Common product standards	Approved standards bodies
	Data safe harbour	Sector watchdogs
	Late payment protection	(e.g. supermarkets)
Business	Mutual recognition for services	
	Passporting (sell from one EU country to another using a branch)	
	EU-wide competition law	UK competition law
	EU-wide public contracting	UK public contract rules
	Free movement	
Regulatory	'New Approach'[a] directives	Approved notified bodies
	Health and safety	Local transcription/enhancement
		Pension auto-enrolment
		Apprenticeship levy
		The Provision and Use of Work Equipment Regulations 1998
		Building regulations
	Food safety directives	Local transcription/enhancement
		Electrical wiring regulations
		Minimum wage regulations

Table 3.4. (*Continued*)

Dimension	EU Component	National Component
	Employment rights	Local transcription/ enhancement
Trade	EU free movement	
	Bilateral trade agreements	
Finance	Bank capital (from Basel Regs)	Bank capital rules
	Regional, social grants	
	EIB loans especially infrastructure	
	EIB Venture Capital Fund Support	
	CAP payments	Administration

[a]'New Approach' directives look to reduce regulatory burdens by using a self-certification regime that is audited by qualified privately owned 'notified bodies'. One example is Medical Devices. List available at European Commission (2017d).

to finance, all in a fiercely competitive and often concentrating market-place. These issues are set out in Table 3.5.

The first and most obvious conclusion is that each and every MSME will face some form of change as the UK executes Brexit. For some the impact will be far higher than for others, but every business owner will need to adapt their organisation in some respect to the new situation. A key challenge in this adaptation will be to ensure minimal (ideally no) disruption to the innovation mechanism. On the contrary, the innovation mechanism will need to accelerate to compensate for the loss of competitiveness some firms will face. In 410 AD, the innovation engine was unable to handle the scale of changes thrown at it.

During the Great Debasement of 1544 to 1551 and indeed up until the Elizabethan stabilisation, business was stretched, but in some ways protected by the interrelationships of many commercial actors and most especially by the connections and reach of the London Company of the Merchant Adventurers. The Elizabethan stabilisation helps us to appreciate a few key points. State and commerce needed to work hand in hand to effect the changes and avoid the risk. The Merchant

Table 3.5. MSME Sectors *vs.* EU Impact.

No	Description	Attributes	Current EU Impact	Current Non-Brexit Threats
1	High-Growth Disrupters	Fast-growing, often cash-consuming attacking global markets	European Investment Bank support for venture capital funds EU R&D programmes Open borders give access to full European Market 'New Approach' directives less onerous than some US regulations such as FDA approvals for new medical devices EU standards conformity auto-homologates products into many markets Free movement helps acquire technical resources	Missing the market (too late) Insufficient capital/access to finance Inadequate management in face of growth rate Wrong product
2.	Complex Supply Chain Players	MSMEs integrated into mainly Pan European supply chains	Open borders give access to full European Market No EU customs declarations, Certificates of Origin or Certificates of Conformity Minimal port delays supporting 'just-in-time' manufacturing Common regulatory standards with single local audit No tariffs No need to prove value added originated within the EU.	Global consolidation Product innovation Cost base including currency movements and transit costs Pension auto-enrolment Business rates revaluation Access to finance

3.	Simple Supply Chain Players	MSMEs integrated into UK-only supply chains	Labour regulations Health and safety regulations Availability of cheap migrant staff	Pension auto-enrolment Business rates revaluation Minimum wage changes Customer payment delays Access to finance Food retailers (some) Labour regulations Health and safety/food inspections
4.	Professional Advice	Consultants, lawyers, accountants, architects, surveyors, etc.	Mutual recognition aids market access Free movement aids market access	Business rate revaluation Customer payment delays Access to finance Changes in regulations
5.	Financial Services[a]	Boutique financial advisers	Mutual recognition aids market access Free movement aids market access	Robo-adviser/tracker products Increasing regulation/MIFID Business rate revaluation Miss-selling compensation
6.	Local Retail and Artisan Products	Owner run small business with a 'local only' dimension,	Labour regulations Health and safety regulations	Retail concentration Rent increases Pension auto-enrolment

Table 3.5. (*Continued*)

No	Description	Attributes	Current EU Impact	Current Non-Brexit Threats
		including local shops and restaurants	Food standard regulations (some) Availability of cheap migrant staff	Minimum wage changes Business rate revaluation Access to finance Health and safety/food inspections
7.	Labour Intensive	Service businesses such as social care/ care homes, cleaning, etc.	Labour regulations Health and safety regulations Availability of cheap migrant staff	Pension auto-enrolment Minimum wage changes Rent increases Business rate revaluation Access to finance Health and safety/food inspections
8.	Knowledge Based	Creative media including Internet product developers	Free movement aids market access Free movement helps acquire technical resources	Pension auto-enrolment Minimum wage changes Rent increases Business rate revaluation Access to finance

[a]The reader will be surprised by the failure to mention 'Passporting' and 'Euro-based activity'. It is our understanding activities are mainly located in much larger non-SME firms.

Adventurers looked at both maintaining their market share and improving their product. They did not try to compete by removing regulation or cutting wages or prices. Instead they used their control of regulation and their network of relationships to maintain and grow their competitive position.

Whilst not unique to our time, especially important to a successful transition, will be a rebalancing between asset holders and income generators. Subsidies are not a long-term option, given that long-term subsidies distort markets and thereby retard long-term competitiveness. Customer driven innovation that drives an economic rebalancing into value adding activities will be the key.

Implicit subsidy is already an unhelpful challenge. Weaning business off the implicit wage support provided by Universal Credit and its prior benefits to industries where 'low paid' wage rates are insufficient for the earner to maintain a basic standard of living is a key issue. Wages and therefore the related jobs are not economic if workers can only work in them with the addition of state hand-outs, and if removing these state hand-outs means that the bottom of the workforce cannot afford a roof over its head. Although labelled individual welfare by many, if wages are uneconomic or rents are unrealistically high, these welfare payments in effect become a hidden subsidy to either the business that is paying uneconomic low wages or to the rentier charging uneconomic rents that are not affordable at current income levels or indeed both.[6] Removing subsidies is always painful and needs to be carefully signalled and transitioned to minimise social costs and/or business disruption. Low pay where workers cannot afford a roof over their head is not economically sustainable in the long term[7] and will have to adjust, most likely by a major fall in housing costs relative to income. Such a house price fall would represent a significant transfer away from asset holders (home

---

[6]A rough calculation suggests when adjusting the benefits bill to focus on welfare for earners (say single, in a couple or in a two-child working household – allowing welfare to be for the out-of-work, disabled and large families) suggest this subsidy is currently worth around £25 billion per annum.

[7]Labour-intensive cost advantage resides low wage/low housing costs/low social protection environments such as Vietnam or Bangladesh. Higher wage/social protection environments derive from higher value adding, a drive to competing by low wages alone would require adjusting the United Kingdom to a Bangladesh-type economic/social framework. Even then it would not work unless housing costs are appropriately downward adapted. Marxist theory which suggests wages will always tend to a subsistence level as a core level of unemployment is maintained to 'discipline labour' is not applicable.

owners) into wage owning non-home owners and will be difficult to handle economically, politically and socially.

Consequently, many of what are regarded as 'safe savings' such as copper bottom lease commercial property or 'buy to let' may become unsafe should circumstances change dramatically. The Southern Cross example shows how institutional and contractual arrangements appropriate to one set of circumstances became uneconomic when circumstances changed. An oft-repeated story. For example, vacant retail units on high streets are dynamic proof of how market changes impact previously long-standing commercial arrangements. Many former BHS stores still stand empty and other former stores have become charity shops, as a testament to out-of-town retailing. Now, in turn, out-of-town retailing is being disrupted by online retailing.

With Brexit, we can expect many such changes in many sectors, as previously established business dynamics become uneconomic. Since businesses will face change with perhaps staffing issues in the face of migration restrictions, changes in customer demand, and / or possible non-tariff and tariff barriers, some businesses may face profitability, sales volume and cash flow challenges. This may result in there being more zombie companies/insolvencies.

Perhaps the state may choose to support these companies through subsidising low wages and unaffordable housing costs for the working population more than it already does, through rises in Universal Benefit rates. Or perhaps there will be a sharp macro-economic adjustment that will bring low-paid wages in line with living costs, either through substantial wage increases or through significant drops in residential property prices in the face of a generalised economic downturn.

Chapter 4

Shocks Revisited

Man has a limited biological capacity for change. When this capacity is overwhelmed, the capacity is in future shock.
— Toffler (1970)

Once a shock materialises it immediately turns into a historical event, thereby changing the available possibilities - not least - by removing that action (the shock) as an option. When a stone is dropped into a pond you cannot 'un-drop' the stone; instead you have to watch the ripples and adjust your actions accordingly, to deal with the ramifications. But imagine the stone is not merely a pebble. Unintentionally, it is now an enormous boulder that triggers a Tsunami capable of overwhelming local coastlines. In this case, one's focus necessarily moves from dropping the stone to protecting the affected coastlines.

The *ripples* of our stone in the pond are transmitted as *financial signals* that then generate real economic impacts. In the same way that the Tsunami is a force of change, financial signals can announce forthcoming changes. Money is not a neutral add-on; rather, it is the transmission medium that drives change as its financial signals via price, cost and resulting profit changes determine the products and services to be sold, and thereby deciding which firms prosper and which firms die.

Yet complex models often start from the paradigm that money is neutral and thereby bypass or perhaps do not know how to simulate money's role in delivering a dynamic general equilibrium. Is it a surprise that so many models find it challenging to predict discontinuities? Keen (2015) observed:

> *I know that sounds like an outrageous statement .... Now that is to my way of thinking, a bit like saying well you can be on the Serengeti Plains and you can perfectly ignore the approaching hill herd of Wildebeest ....*

4.1.   Recap from Historical Brexits

In Chapter 2 we looked at earlier times when England left Europe, and we ended that chapter with Table 4.1, setting out historical issues and Brexit parallels and linking this to the groups we highlighted in Chapter 3.

4.2.   Our 'Stones' and 'Ripples'

Our Brexit shock starts with the Referendum result, which saw an immediate financial markets reaction in the fall of Sterling, as shown in Figure 4.1. This fall continued after the Mrs May 2016 Conservative Party Conference speech outlining her view of a 'hard Brexit'.[1]

This fall in Sterling was the first 'ripple' to the 'Brexit Stone' being dropped in the pool. Now the question was what subsequent ripples this 'stone' would create, how big these would be and if they would decay into mere murmurs or slowly build into a tumultuous Tsunami? The early movements were quite small as business started to look for reassurances, but somewhat later, inflation began to rise and personal living standards came under pressure, by the second half of 2017. (It is normal for significant exchange rate changes to take many months to feed through into price changes.) In another analogy, one could look at these as small 'foreshocks' that may or may not augur (as in the natural world) an altogether larger seismic event. Box 4.1 describes one such initial ripple.

The shocks then started to build in frequency, but still as minor unfelt tremors. Requests for reassurance morphed into initial precautionary steps after the March 2017 Article 50 Notification to Leave. Preliminary actions were set in motion, especially in Brexit vulnerable business such as Banks, as we see in our example in Box 4.2.

The decision point for large firms to make potential structural changes to accommodate Brexit is likely to come as they establish within their 2018 fiscal year budgets plans to execute contingency measures if negotiations suggest a loss of market access. The more detailed

---

[1]Evaluating sterlings movement is often done against the US$. In Early 2018 the £ / US$ rate has appreciated as the US$ has fallen against many currencies. The sterling trade weighted index has not shown the same appreciation and we remain of the opinion that the overall traded weighted measure of sterling best reflects changes in the sterling exchange rate

Table 4.1. Lessons from Previous Brexits.

Anticipated Impact Rank	Issue	Historical Impact	Example	Brexit Parallel	Big Bang Disruption	Complex Supply Chain	Simple Supply Chain	Professional Advice	Financial Services	Local Retail and Artisan	Labour Intensive Service	Knowledge-Driven Innovators	Total Impact Score	Impact Percentage
1	Monetary/Capital Flow Disruption	High	AD 410 loss of Roman coinage; collapse market economy	Sterling Crisis. Sudden Stop balance of payments event/risks to global financial system/Iceland Event. Significant loss in confidence in Sterling accompanied by a reversal of capital flows, moving funds from sterling-denominated equities and bonds; strongly rising UK Bank Rate to defend currency; calls against interest rate and currency hedges; drop in consumer confidence, residential mortgage debt arrears, sterling-driven rise in inflation coupled with falls in real wages. 'Sudden Stop' event impacts: funding for new and existing company's stopping development of Big Bang Disrupting companies, challenges complex supply chain contract profitability and cash flows, interrupts simple supply chain contractor, local retail and artisan business cash flows, hits leisure spending reducing need for labour-intensive services, reduces consulting work, stops construction of new projects, disrupts financial services and knowledge-driven innovators.	10	10	10	8	10	8	8	8	72	90%
2	Access to Finance	High	Decline in Antwerp's role when the Fuggers restricted merchant financing in the late 1550s	MSME Access to Risk Finance. Exit arrangements mean a change in European and hence the global role of the City of London. Immediate regulatory causes are removal of Euro clearing rights and an end to 'passporting' with no stable 'equivalence' regime; financial institutions relocating operations into EU to maintain market access being forced to set up fully capitalised operations, driving strategic review on ancillary operation repatriation to the United States by US institutions vs. consolidation in an EU city. Potential for funding challenges for new and existing company's negatively impacting development of Big Bang Disrupting companies, with challenges to supply chains, hedges, and cash flows, also negatively impacting local retail and artisan business and knowledge-driven innovator's access to finance. Likely reduced leisure spending reducing the need for labour-intensive services; reductions in consulting work, disrupts construction of new financial centre office. Potential for disruption and structural change in non-UK customer-driven financial services.	10	10	8	8	8	5	5	8	62	78%

Table 4.1. (*Continued*)

Anticipated Impact Rank	Issue	Historical Impact	Example	Brexit Parallel	Big Bang Disruption	Complex Supply Chain	Simple Supply Chain	Professional Advice	Financial Services	Local Retail and Artisan	Labour Intensive Service	Knowledge-Driven Innovators	Total Impact Score	Impact Percentage
3	Legal Frameworks	High	1530s creation of national legal framework, short-term small impact, long-term high impact	International Access Treaties/Great Repeal Bill	7	10	7	10	10	4	4	8	60	75%
			Examples of Brexit legal framework risks: (i) UK fails to re-negotiate key elements of 759 international treaties that need completion before Brexit Day; with consequent risks to air transport, aircraft licensing, nuclear material transport, etc. (ii) Failure to establish key regulatory agencies and agree equivalence protocols invalidates product approvals in pharmaceuticals and medical devices stopping shipment, customs system not developed, long queues at ports due to physical inspections and checking origins. (iii) Many UK service providers and many knowledge-based innovators prevented from selling in EU if the UK cannot handle EU personal data due to failure to negotiate and establish a data safe harbour agreement											
4	Supply Chain Collapse	High	AD 410 collapse of supply chains, depopulation of cities, collapse of markets; collapse market economy	Complex supply chains in key industries such as automotive and aerospace	4	10	6	7	4	8	6	4	49	61%
			Failure to resolve legal frameworks and/or failure to implement the legal changes into working and efficient operational chaos as firms try to ship goods and services across borders without working systems. Additional tariffs add to costs, making existing contracts unprofitable and pricing suppliers out of contracts. Data safe harbour restrictions restrict data transfer, thereby inhibiting services. Lack of regulatory approval or agreed equivalence hold goods from release. Certificate of Origin systems not adapted to complex cross-border movements and Origin rules.											

No.	Risk	Likelihood		Description									Total	%
5	Big Bang Disruption	High	**Current innovation revolution with 'Big Bang Disruption' disrupting whole industries and shortening product life cycles**	Markets disrupted by new innovations, often with only one or two surviving champions (for example Amazon and Ali Baba). Disrupters who fail to command leading position are survival challenged (e.g. search engines AltaVista and Excite). Companies with established business model challenged (e.g. Borders books vs. Amazon). Previous disrupters may themselves be disrupted by new disrupters.	10	7	7	7	8	1	4	5	49	61%
6	Change in Markets	High	**Merchant Adventurer's trade switch from Antwerp in second half sixteenth century, use of local trade agents to smooth trade relations and in 1580s Privateering eventually, conquest of India, short-term small impact, long-term high impact**	New Free Trade Agreements/ Possibility for State Endorsed/ Supported Local Country Agent/ Export Networks. Post-1945 has seen several significant changes in markets, first the German and Japanese economic miracles of the 1960s, the 1970s oil price shock, then the rise of South East Asian economies Taiwan and Korea and more recently the rise of China. In all but the oil price shock emerging economies mentioned moved rapidly from basic manufacturing to embodying knowledge in products and securing this with patenting and copyright and therefore threatening existing businesses. Typically, emerging market service economies are less developed and more protected by non-trade barriers, thereby requiring service companies to adapt to be able to compete.	6	8	5	9	9	3	3	4	47	59%
7	Immigration Controls	Moderate	**Indigenisation programmes such as Zambianisations, reductions in productivity dependent on positions changed and skills of local replacements. Zambian study suggested 20% productivity fall**	Immigration control central to changes. Immigration restrictions will bring differing impacts to different sectors. Sectors that rely on high-skilled immigrants may find EU citizens less willing to work in the United Kingdom (for both financial and ambience reasons). Higher salaries may help overcome this, leading to top skill wage inflation and associated cost pressures. For sectors dependent upon cheap unskilled labour, the impact will be disruptive (replacing existing staff) and costly as wage rates rise to attract more locally based staff. An alternative to wage rises would be mass unemployment, driving down wage costs so the cost of the adjustment is paid by unskilled workers.	2	4	2	3	4	4	8	8	35	44%
8	Overuse of Proclamation	Moderate to High	**1536 Pilgrimage of Grace insurrection and 1539 Act of Proclamations**	Hung Parliament, legal challenges. All sectors will be at risk from poorly worded secondary legislation that has not been adequately 'sanity checked' by Parliamentary debate and sectors may face poorly scrutinised secondary legislation issued to satisfy media campaigns or political hobby horses, giving high opportunity for unintended consequences. Desire to buy off voter and interest groups may raise downward price pressures on outsourcing contracts to reduce government spending but distance governments from being seen as responsible for cuts.	4	5	7	3	0	3	1	1	24	30%

Table 4.1. (*Continued*)

Anticipated Impact Rank	Issue	Historical Impact	Example	Brexit Parallel	Anticipated Impact Score									
					Big Bang Disruption	Complex Supply Chain	Simple Supply Chain	Professional Advice	Financial Services	Local Retail and Artisan	Labour Intensive Service	Knowledge-Driven Innovators	Total Impact Score	Impact Percentage
9	Regional Involvement	Moderate to High	1536 Pilgrimage of Grace insurrection, Gentry active involvement in Reformation Parliaments. Eventually resolved after Civil War, Act of Union and the Jacobite suppression	Joint Ministerial Committee	2	5	6	5	3	0	0	1	22	28%
			With so many decisions to make and implement so quickly, decisions will be challenged to match operational needs. These challenges will be exacerbated, should devolved governments not be fully involved as both (i) important local knowledge may be missed and (ii) devolved governments will have no ownership or incentive to adapt their own legislative programmes to complement changes coming from London. Opportunities for confusion and delays especially in letting medium-to-low priority outsource contracts may multiply. Contract definition may not be as rigorous as required due to administrative overstretch.											
10	Irish Border	Low		Not an issue in AD 410 or in 1530	0	6	0	0	0	0	0	0	6	8%
			At its worst, a hard Irish border may be similar in impact to risk 4 (described above) 'supply chain collapse' with an added civil disturbance risk. Assuming that a soft border is implemented, the difficulties will be adapting to its administrative requirements.											

Source: Authors.

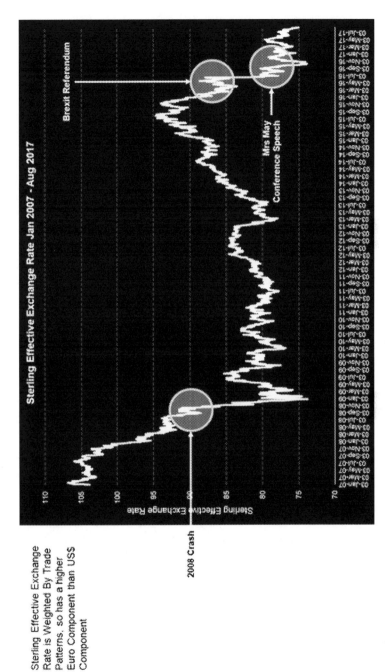

Figure 4.1. Sterling Effective Purchasing Power. *Source:* Bank of England (2017) revocable data license.

Box 4.1.   First Ripples – An Automotive Example

Dependent upon complex global and especially EU supply chains, Nissan, a key operator in the automotive sector, sought and received unspecified early assurances from the prime ministers so as to maintain its existing model launch schedule for its North East UK Manufacturing Facility.

Colin Lawther, Senior Vice President for Nissan Motor Manufacturing in Europe (House of Commons International Trade Committee, 2017), in January 2017, made clear that these assurances were related to shorter term infrastructure, training and local business capability whilst highlighting future Brexit-related issues. He highlighted (i) the need to avoid tariffs; (ii) the importance of smooth movement through borders, emphasising that only about half a day's stock of the 5 million parts the plant uses each day are held at the plant; (iii) the need to raise the level of UK parts' content; (iv) the challenges of Big Bang technological disruption such as Electric Vehicles; (v) that production decisions are long-term and made on a model life basis. Some estimates of incremental tariff costs were discussed, should the United Kingdom not have a non-tariff agreement with the EU. These were estimated at around £500 million additional cost versus a UK profit of around £150 million.

Overall, the automotive sector has significantly reduced capital investment from £2.5bn in 2015 to £1.66bn in 2016 and an estimated £644 million in 2017 based upon first half 2017 investment rates (Campbell, 2017).

---

these plans become, the more the costs will become visible, and the more the 'gaps' in transition thinking will be understood, and consequently the more vocal business can be expected to become. Detzer (2005) quoting the nineteenth-century military strategist Field Marshall Helmuth Graf von Moltke the elder reminds us that, *'No battle plan ever survives contact with the enemy'*.

Executing the required changes to adapt to the post Brexit world will be different for every industry and indeed for every firm. These changes will be driven by (i) the lead times required to execute changes; (ii) existing investments and how these can be run down; (iii) anticipated financial pressures if the changes are not made; (iv) absolute dates set by

---

Box 4.2. Waves in the Financial Sector (Banking and Insurance)

Quarter 2, 2017 has seen a series of location announcements by major financial institutions whereby they are opening new operations in countries such as Ireland, Luxembourg and Germany. France is also campaigning to attract these institutions. Insurance giants AIG, RSA and Hiscox are opening Luxembourg operations; Lloyds and QBE are setting up functions in Brussels (Ralph, 2017). Japanese banks and Daiwa have announced intentions to establish in Frankfurt (Turvill, 2017). Barclays has chosen to move its European Headquarters to Dublin (Bloomberg, 2017a). These relocation decisions allow the institutions to go through the regulatory approvals and then make the decision about what functions to fully transfer as Brexit negotiations and results from these unfold.

Recent estimates in a study by the Boston Consulting Group and Clifford Chance (BCG, 2017) suggest the restructuring will cost upwards of €15 billion and require an additional €40 billion in regulatory capital of which €20 billion will be additional equity capital.

---

changes in compliance and regulatory regimes and (v) available management capability, finance and resources. For large businesses, these factors will determine whether the ripples become a major seismic event, such as a Tsunami and, if they do then the speed and force with which any such wave arrives.

The impact upon each industry will differ.

Financial services will need to take early actions to maintain continuity, given the lead times to gain Banking Licences and regulatory approvals if there is an end to financial passporting with no matching equivalence regime. By contrast, automotive manufacturers will be able to continue to sell products but initially face substantial cost hikes to mitigate port delay risks to production, and could face additional documentation and checks together with possible tariffs. 'Relocation' is more likely by introducing new models in non-UK plants over a period of years. As Nissan says, no plant is safe in the long term (House of Commons International Trade Committee, 2017). Either Cliff Edge or 'Creeping Death' will imply change for MSMEs in complex supply chains, changes that will continue to ripple through multiplier effects. If a factory closes and say 1000 skilled jobs are lost, this significantly

Box 4.3.   A Village Multiplier in Action – Grimethorpe

Grimethorpe in East Yorkshire, England was home to one of the most productive coal mines in the United Kingdom until the last coal was mined in 1992 and the colliery was closed in 1993. The pit was the anchor of the local community, employing 7,000 at the point of closure, which was significantly more than the entire population of the village. Longitudinal average earnings data by voting ward is not available for this period, so we are forced to look at anecdotal data. Quoting local MP Eric Ilsley, 'Grimethorpe colliery was one of the most profitable collieries in the country until it was closed. Now that it is no longer there, the village has no visible employment' (Hansard, 2000). Most likely this contains some element of hyperbole, although by 1994 Grimethorpe was recognised by the EU as one of the most deprived villages in England. The South Yorkshire mine closures had a significant impact on regional GDP per capita, which fell from around 83% of the EU norm in 1991 (Eurostat, 1991) to below 75% by the later 1990s, leading to South Yorkshire receiving EU Objective 1 status. Grimethorpe per capita income had fallen to below 66% (Hansard, 2000).

The village (with a world-famous brass band) was the inspiration for the movie 'Brassed Off' (1996). Ten years later, Herbert (2006) writes,

> *the much-loved chip shop In Cod We Trust, which featured in the film, is bricked up. Even the local Kwik Save supermarket is to close following the company's sell-out to Somerfield. The grim facts of commercial life here are that just 37 per cent of Grimethorpe's adult population is economically active, the average household income is £8,000 compared with a national average of £20,000, nearly 46 per cent of locals are on housing benefit and 33 per cent are unemployed.*

This, however, represents a significant recovery from 1994 when unemployment was over 50 per cent, young people were leaving and house prices fell to the point where a house could be purchased for £200. The recovery was due to public regeneration funds (under Objective 1) building a new road to improve access and a positive policy to encourage demolition and rebuilding of old housing stock together with building an industrial estate to raise employment (McVeigh, 2015).

Table 4.2. Disruption Events.

Shock	Category	Risk	Risk No	Historic Impact	Impact Today
A	Financial System	Monetary/capital flow disruption	1	High	90%
		Access to finance	2	High	78%
B	Legal/Regulatory	Legal frameworks	3	High	75%
		Overuse of proclamation	8	Moderate to high	30%
C	Operational Disruption	Supply chain collapse	4	High	61%
		Change in markets	6	High	59%
		Immigration controls	7	Moderate	44%
D	Market Disruption/ Innovation	Big bang disruption	5	High	61%
E	Regional Execution	Regional involvement	9	Moderate to high	28%
		Irish border	10		8%

Source: Authors.

impacts the local community. This process is called the 'multiplier effect' and is described by Keynes (1936). Part of the assessment of the 'multiplier effect' comes from how we define 'local'. The seepage from spending to other localities is greater if 'local' is defined say as a town. Box 4.3 gives an example of this in the village of Grimethorpe.

The Grimethorpe case demonstrates how *in extremis* this downward (but it can also be ascending) multiplier impacted a local community when there was a major structural change, in this case losing but not replacing the anchor employer. On a wider level, the same 'multiplier' relationship exists in the UK economy. Table 4.2 pulls together our narrative so far by suggesting how risks we have identified could materialise into 'shocks' which we will then explore in more detail.

4.3.   Shock A: Financial System Disruption ('Sudden Stop Events')

It's not speed that kills but the sudden stop.
            – Banker Aphorism (Eichengreen & Gupta, 2016)

Providing overseas parties are prepared to deposit funds in the United Kingdom to cover a Balance of Payment Current Account deficit, expenditure is not trade balance constrained. When this does not happen, this can lead to a 'Balance of Payments Sudden Stop Event' (Eichengreen & Gupta, 2016) such as during the 1998 Asian Financial Crisis or the 2008 Iceland crisis. During a visit to Kuala Lumpur, Malaysia in 2007, the modernity of the essentially new Central Business District near the Petronas Towers complex was striking, as was the rapid transit system from the airport into the city and at first sight the monorail. On closer inspection we find that only the first stage of the monorail has been built, there are also some deserted partly completed buildings visible in the Central City zone. Anecdotally, word on the street was that these part-finished monuments are a testament to the severity of the 1997 Asian Financial Crisis. Not only was there a Sudden Stop, but also according to an estimate by Barro (2001) the Asian Crisis reduced GDP growth from 3 per cent to 2 per cent over the following 5 years. This example is one of many over the ages. Table 4.3 provides some examples of various financial Sudden Stops.

Some will remember a time when newspaper headlines and economy watching were dominated by news relating to the 'Balance of Payments', loans from the IMF, currency controls and fixed exchange rates being devalued. Suddenly after 1980 this narrative disappeared. Why? The 1980 change coincided for the United Kingdom with a one-off windfall to the trade balance from the growth of North Sea Oil (now in decline) and then the inbound financial flows associated with London's growing role as a global financial centre.

The UK's Current Trade Balance Deficit, sometimes over 5 per cent of GDP, is a key UK economic weakness. Significant falls in sterling in 2008 and 2016 have not successfully closed this gap. Export composition, capacity restrictions and import and export elasticities may mean that modest falls in sterling will not correct the deficit.

Kristin Forbes, a former member of the UK's Monetary Policy Committee, demonstrated that impact of a Sterling upward revaluations is to widen the trade deficit, in a speech entitled, 'The economic impact of sterling's recent moves: more than a midsummer night's dream'. In her model,

Table 4.3. Sample Sudden Stop Events.

Event	Timing	Narrative
AD410 Brexit	Starts in AD410	The change in GDP in undocumented, although archaeological, evidence suggests urban collapse whilst agricultural GDP (then the most important GDP component) being maintained[a]
Great Depression	1929−1933 Worldwide impact	GDP decline 30−40% in real prices (Marcuss & Kane, 2007)
Asian Financial Crisis	1998	GDP decline 3−16% (Barro, 2001)
Iceland	2008	GDP approx. 10% over 2 years (Krueger, 2016)

Source: Authors.

[a]"Significant economic changes did occur but these affected the most visible parts of the economy catastrophically. The biggest slice of Romano−British GDP, the largely invisible agricultural economy, remained resilient and may even have prospered once the burdens of the Roman Empire had been lifted. This allowed diversification and a move to a less-efficient pastoral economy, which manifested itself in the way landscapes were managed and perhaps increased calorific intake [...] rural economy actually rested upon relatively small blocks of land, [...] connected in some cases by ownership tenurial obligations and kinship [...] Together [with] [...] other forms of social practice, as well as economic linkages, defined so-called "small words"' (Gerrard, 2013).

imports rise faster than exports fall (Forbes, 2014). The Marshall/Lerner condition (comparing sensitivity to import prices with overseas demand sensitivity to export prices) requires that export markets respond positively to a devaluation and that domestic consumers reign back import consumption as import prices rise, has seemingly not been fulfilled, a finding validated by review (Bahmani et al., 2013). They find that for the UK a priori devaluation is ineffective in reducing the trade deficit. Summers (1995) writes, *'close attention should be paid to any current account deficit in excess of 5 per cent of GDP, particularly if it is financed in a way that could lead to rapid reversals'*. 'Sudden Stop' risks are heightened by high UK levels of personal indebtedness as percentage of GDP (Eichengreen & Gupta, 2016) and inflated house prices vs. income (highlighted in Sufi & Mian, 2014).

Funding the trade deficit relies on inbound capital flows to either (i) purchase existing UK assets such as the foreign investors buying UK companies (selling the family silver) or (ii) arrive as portfolio or short-term balance investment (mortgaging current and future family silver and in the event of a lack of confidence event subject to reversal). Should these flows stop, let alone reverse, the United Kingdom could face very difficult and economic waters. Some look to a reduction in UK payments to the EU to cushion any adjustment. Currently, net UK contributions to the EU are about £8bn per annum or 0.4% of GDP (The IFS, 2016). Payments from the UK to the EU will continue through any transition and will be followed by significant although as yet unquantified 'divorce' payments over many future years.

Any 'divorce' contributions will most likely be combined with some form of 'market access fee' that may be required by the EU for continued market access in specific areas. Assuming such sums are set as monetary amounts rather than as a percentage of GDP, were any Brexit shock to reduce GDP, these fixed payments would become a rising burden as a percentage of GDP.

4.4.   Shock B: Legal and Regulatory Risk

Business and trade are executed within trade and regulatory frameworks, some of which are national and some of which cross borders. The European Union's *'acquis communitaire'* requires Member States to align their national legislation to European Union norms in areas where the European Union is given competence under its treaties. Some of the legislation, for example implementing workers' rights, are domestic in nature whilst others are in turn international in character, such as the Capital Requirements Directives that require Member States to implement the Basel Banking Capital Accords, and others are 'European' in origin such as matters that implement the Single Market and the Customs Union. Member States also pool sovereign rights on to some Treaty Negotiation and thereby access to some international treaties via their membership of the European Union. Significant complexity exists in the interaction between various treaties, European Union Directives, transcribed UK Law, EU Regulators, UK Regulators and implementing regulations and associated approvals.

In particular the EU has negotiated a series of treaties with other countries supranational blocs on various bases. In some cases, these are bilateral, meaning that UK access to the Treaty provisions is via its membership of the EU. When the UK leaves the European Union, it will lose access to these treaties as it will no longer be an EU member. These bilateral treaties can, and in many cases, have clauses that bind both Treaty Parties to cancelling any previous bilateral treaties between individual Member States and the other contracting State.

By implication, the UK upon leaving the EU leaves any EU bi-lateral Treaties with 3rd Countries and it is not in the 'gift' of the EU to unilaterally grant the UK access to these treaties once the EU is no longer a Member State. Both signatories plus the UK would presumably be required to agree to an addendum that gives the UK access to any existing treaties. One imagines that in some cases this could be subject to ratification processes in some countries, with such a ratification process dependent upon whether such a Treaty was to be called a 'New Treaty', an exchange of 'Diplomatic Notes' or a revision to an existing Treaty. Grandfathering the existing Treaty across by whatever legal mechanism at its simplest assumes no third country will want something in return from the UK for signing the change to the Treaty, and that all third countries are happy that the UK has both the infrastructure and institutions to comply with the Treaty once it is disconnected from the European Union. One example of the complexities in this process relates to air safety which is described in Box 4.4.

Box 4.4. 3rd Country Treaties, Airplanes, Gunboats and All That

The UK Civil Aviation Authority works under the umbrella of the European Aviation and Safety Agency whose operation is confirmed and continued under European Union 'Regulation 216-2008' and that has a 'Treaty' role, with it being the named party for the safety relationship with the United States (9.11.2011 Official Journal L291/3). The 2011 Treaty mandated the repeal of the previous 1995 US–UK bilateral agreement. Without valid aircraft certifications (which currently require the above framework to be valid), even though will be the same aircraft flying with the same crew to the self-same standards on Brexit Day as the day before, the regulatory approval will have been voided. Muttukumaru (2017) state:

> *Strict position is that, absent an EU/UK agreement, certificates of safety issued by the UK CAA would cease to be valid in the Single Market on Brexit day. Without valid safety certificates, an air operator certificate could*

> *not be issued to a UK-based air carrier which seeks access to the Aviation Single Market. Equally if there is no agreement at the EU/UK level, the UK could refuse to rec- ognise EU carriers' safety certificates. But that would be wholly implausible*

A solution is required, but with no assignment provision in the EU/US Treaty there may be a requirement for a new Treaty, which requires a two-third Senate vote approval.

Equally, mutual recognition on air safety issues requires the FAA accept the CAA (the UK regulator) has the competencies to do the job, which it clearly does not at the current time, as the EU Regulator has to perform some functions that the CAA is not performing. FAA head Michael Huerta is quoted in an interview with Skift as saying:

> *With very limited exceptions the United Kingdom's aviation products are currently certified by the European safety agency or EASA and service providers such as maintenance repair and overhaul facilities are certified using EU regula- tion and EASA procedure [...]. If the UK does not maintain an associated or working arrangement with EASA upon leaving the EU, the UK will quickly need to re-establish competencies in specific areas especially around certification of new aviation products*
>
> *– FAA (2017)*

The CAA (UK regulator) has made clear that they 'want to remain full members of EASA [...] should not be planning for a new independent aviation safety system in the UK [...] [and have] [...] decided not to do that work as it would be misleading to suggest that's a viable option' (CAA, 2017). Norway and Iceland are members of EASA, but they also have their own 2011 treaty ('Air Transport Agreement') with the EU and the United States to facilitate this working. The United Kingdom will need a similar agreement.

Medical devices are approved for sale into EU markets based on the Medical Device Directive. Unlike the US Food and Drug Administration, this directive relies on a 'self-certification' and audit approach to oversee product safety. Approved products carry a 'CE' mark which links back to a manufacturer who has a registered address within the European Union. The manufacturer's products, manufacturing, R&D and other operations are independently audited against ISO standards by an independent notified body such as TUV or BSI. These notified bodies are themselves certified and approved to be added to a centralised EU list maintained by the EU Commission showing the approved Member State. Product packaging must include the CE Mark plus the authorised EU representative responsible for complaints and product surveillance.

Will existing UK-based notified bodies be grandfathered across into the new post-Brexit world or will this change and will product need to be recertified to the new arrangement if it is to be sold in the EU? Will there be enough time for any changes to be operationally executed before Brexit Day, or will the only feasible business option be to relocate the regulatory elements of the business into a continuing EU Member State before Brexit happens (DEXU, 2017b)? Specialist micro sectors will also risk being impacted as we see in Box 4.5.

Two other areas already given considerable media profile are (i) the 1995 agreement which regulates movements of nuclear material between the United States and the EU. This started as an extension to a 1949 agreement but broadened to include new and complex 'non-proliferation

---

Box 4.5. UK Butterfly Exports to the EU

Small companies and micro exporters to the EU will be impacted by Brexit. Stratford Butterfly Farm (*The Stratford Herald*, 2017) is an important supplier of Butterfly Pupae across the world. It sources the Pupae and then looks to deliver them to farms world-wide before the hatch. Its business is time critical as should the butterfly hatch whilst it is in transit it is likely to break its wings and so be fatally damaged.

Specimens can come from all over the world and are subject to the 2009 EU health checks on live imported animals. These checks require appropriately qualified veterinarians, thereby limiting the airports that can be used. Currently, these checks are handled in the United Kingdom and the appropriate UK veterinarian certificate accepted across the EU. The owner Mr Lamb fears that these certificates will not be accepted in the EU after Brexit, meaning health controls need to happen in the EU, so adding time to the transport process and risking wiping out 50 per cent of his £1.2 million per annum export business.

issues', and waited some time before US Senate ratification. All civil nuclear material shipments were halted for 3 months as without a treaty the product could not be moved. (ii) The European Open Skies Treaty giving unrestricted EU landing rights (this is different from the Air Safety Treaty).

With an estimated 759+ treaties (McLean, 2017) requiring replacement, it would be unsurprising if some of these treaty negotiations are incomplete by Brexit Day. Some of these concern mutual recognition between regulators such as the 1998 *Agreement on Mutual Recognition between the European Community and the United States of America* (EUUSA, 1998) that specifies mutual rights for regulators such as the FDA in certain sectors (such as Pharmaceuticals, Medical Devices, Electrical Safety, Telecommunications and more), thereby simplifying cross-border operation. For example, the treaty allows the FDA to recognise the integrity of an inspection (and thereby avoid a second inspection in the United States) of an EU manufacturing location by an EU-approved body under the Annex focused on Pharmaceutical Products for confirming adherence to Good Manufacturing Practice (GMP). This recognition is based upon a mutually agreed equivalence and upon authorised inspecting bodies. For this there must be mutual recognition of regulators, agreements on equivalence regimes and agreements on inspecting bodies. Such a detailed process risks being complex and time consuming. Faced with such risks some businesses may opt for a 'third-way' contingency plan that allows them to switch operations to continuing EU locations if the United Kingdom cannot deliver the necessary legal, new internationally recognised regulators and treaty frameworks.

4.5.   Shock C: Brexit Day Operational Imperatives

Legislative and regulatory framework changes risk operational disruption. Some sample operational challenges that must be successfully handled for Brexit Day are as follows:

(i) Third-country treaties must be in place to replace critical EU bilateral treaties. Some areas include air safety, open skies, peaceful movement of nuclear materials, and mutual recognition arrangements for regulators.

(ii) New regulators will require new (even if grandfathered) registrations or revised registrations.

(iii) Operating procedures and business processes will need to adapt to the new environment; computer systems require updating to match revised business processes and operating environment.

(iv) Corporate restructurings, asset hive downs and business relocations will need to be executed to match new legal and regulatory environments.

(v) New suppliers will need to be engaged to replace suppliers who can no longer supply or to provide additional services required (such as customs entry processing at ports of entry).

(vi) Staff must be trained into the new environment; databases may need to be split to conform to revised data safe harbour requirements.

(vii) Dependent upon negotiation manufacturer-held inventory may need re-labelling to be saleable in EU markets.

(viii) Certificates of Origin and Certificates of Conformity will most likely be required for EU shipments.

(ix) Some EU migrant staff may need replacing if they decide the United Kingdom is no longer attractive and new staff sourced, trained and recruited.

(x) Commercial terms and conditions may need revision.

(xi) Transport arrangements may need revision if UK freight drivers are no longer licensed to haul freight within the EU.

(xii) New 'boiler plate' contract formats and existing contracts may need revising, especially for EU sales.

We comment on a small sample of potential consequent risks. For example, if the new treaties are not in place, power supplies from nuclear plants and nuclear medicine could be disrupted; aircraft may not be able to fly and some industries face regulatory turmoil as their inspections and recognition arrangements may be invalidated. The United Kingdom will again need to use Certificates of Origin and Conformity. In concept, this is a simple change, but one with possible administrative complexities. For businesses in complex Pan EU supply chains, these certificates will need to be produced according to World Trade Organisation rules in the context of any potential EU–UK Free Trade Agreement. For example, in the automotive sector, relief, cars will need over 60 per cent of the value-added to be 'local' to benefit from a zero tariff in the event that a UK – EU Free Trade Agreement is similar to existing EU third country Free Trade Agreements. Currently, the UK 'local' percentage content is about 37 per cent of the content, although this would look larger if a Free Trade Deal allowed EU-sourced components to be rolled into the local content percentage

(Holmes, 2016). Such a set up may require specific and verifiable tracking systems to be put in place. Blanket 'Origin' approvals are available through 'Binding Origin Information' decisions (which can be applied for). With these 'decisions' there is a requirement that the imported products are identical to the Binding Origin Approval.

Further disruptive complexity may arise from any requirements for 'officially translated and certified document requirements' (not mandatory but a barrier that can arise) and the need for technical certificates of conformity. Production, confirmation and certification for complex industries can be a non-trivial process unless computer systems are adapted to automate the process.

Bank and lender restructuring to meet the new operating environment may heighten 'access to finance issues', splitting bank regulatory capital, thereby reducing lending capacity. Banks globally are regulated in line with the Basel Capital Accords. Summarising and simplifying a complex area, there are several key elements to the regulatory framework. First is the need to maintain adequate shareholder capital and loss absorbing debt (i.e. debt that converts to capital upon bank losses exceeding a specific threshold) to cover potential loan losses. Second, to estimate potential loan losses the 'risk-weighted assets' value is calculated. Each loan is categorised with a list and a percentage of its value is calculated as being the 'risk' to the lender. The risk can range from 0 per cent for high-rated sovereign debt of modest amounts for secured residential mortgages with loan-to-value ratios under 75 per cent through to much higher weightings for business loans. The risk weightings vary between lenders; some lenders used weights calculated on previous loan experience, and others used 'standard' published risk weights from the regulatory authorities.

Risk offsets are possible against the assessed risk if the loan is fully guaranteed by an organisation with a lower risk (e.g. a sovereign state with a good rating) or by cash offset. Lenders need to maintain sufficient regulator capital as a percentage of risk-weighted assets plus meet a target leverage ratio. Regulators have the option to add additional capital requirements as they see fit. A recent study suggests restructuring costs could be €15 billion requiring €20 billion more equity and a further €20 billion of Tier 2 risk capital (AFME, 2017). The volume of Customs Entries is estimated to rise fivefold and there is a risk that the Customs Administration may struggle to cope, causing port delays, thereby disrupting air and sea transport (Harra, 2017). For the United Kingdom, this risk is heightened as Customs expect to launch a new IT system (called Customs Declaration Service) around the same as Brexit.

This system was designed based upon pre-Brexit volumes. According to the Treasury Select Committee *'If there are even modest delays, there is potential for major disruption to trade and economic activity'* (Tyrie, 2017).

4.6. Shock D: Continued Market Innovation

Brexit will not execute against a 'steady state' in terms of ongoing market and technological innovation. For example, both automotive and technology companies are putting significant resources into developing both autonomous cars and electric/hybrid cars. Several major technology companies such as Waymo, Apple, Tesla and Uber have been pushing development of a self-driving car. Waymo, the self-driving car unit of Google parent Alphabet, which describes itself as 'a self-driving tech company with a mission to make it safe and easy for people and things to move around', relies upon light-based technology LIDAR as the eyes of the car (Waymo, 2017). The sensing from these eyes then needs to be processed by some form of artificial intelligence to be able to instruct the car to anticipate and handle challenging situations. This deep learning and predictive intelligence is the focus of some artificial intelligence innovators in Silicon Valley. This type of learning needs access to vast amounts of sensor data that can then be interpreted and resolved into the artificial intelligence self-drive component and used to avoid hazards. For example, in September 2016 a Google Self-Drive test car had a serious accident when the driver of the other vehicle 'jumped' a red light. Despite light jumping being illegal, self-drive vehicles still need to be able to predict it, but not over predict it to the point that they are 'too hesitant' to go on a green light! Developing this understanding requires processing the huge amounts (giga bytes) of data self-driving cars can generate over just a few miles of driving. Wireless transmission is not currently feasible for this volume of data, so restricting development work to manual downloads from the cars. Maybe a faster transmission technology could help? The University of Edinburgh has developed a new network topology based on light known as LIFI that has (in cooperation with other UK universities) been able to reach laboratory transfer speeds of 224 Gb/sec (Gomez et al., 2015). Such a technology could *ceteris paribus* handle the data volumes from self-driving cars, giving opportunities to transform the man/machine learning interface.

With self-driving cars expected to arrive on the market between 2018 and 2022, and manufacturers such as Volvo announcing moves towards all electric vehicle ranges, much change can be anticipated in the automotive sector (McGee, 2017). The United Kingdom continues to lead in certain enabling technologies such as LIFI; we also know that the scientific research base is recognised in the EU commission and that the Brexit negotiating position seeks to maintain EU access to UK technology, through maintaining post-Brexit joint EU−UK academic research programmes. Will UK-based commercial firms have the management focus or resources in a Brexit adaptation phase to seize these opportunities, and will global firms wish to build centres of regional excellence in a country divorced from its wider regional market?

4.7. Shock E: Regional Execution

Historically, feelings of regional remoteness from London have caused political tension. The 1536 Pilgrimage of Grace was in some sense characterised by remoteness from London, not least by the demand for local judicial procedures via the 'Council of the North'. Present day tensions have been handled through the 1998 Devolution Settlement that granted certain powers to Scotland (as amended in 2012) and differing ones to Wales, the 1999 Good Friday Agreement that set a framework for Northern Ireland and the more recent and more informal appointments of executive mayors in some urban areas. Brexit execution is complicated by Scotland and Northern Ireland voting to remain in the EU and Wales voting to leave in the 2016 Brexit Referendum. With an unwritten constitution, the United Kingdom has to some extent evolved Constitutional Law by means of 'Conventions'. These can be defined as 'malleable' understandings that evolve with events over the passage of time. For example, the operation of the 'Salisbury Convention' whereby the House of Lords will not challenge legislation presented to it that enacts a manifesto commitment from a winning General Election manifesto was interpreted more flexibly during the 2010−2015 Coalition Government.

The fundamentals of the 1998 Devolution Settlement still hold: some matters are reserved for the Westminster 'UK' Parliament and some matters are within the local competence of each devolved administration. To cover the reality that sometimes the Westminster Parliament may need to legislate on matters that have been devolved, rather than having a formal constitutional procedure, a convention − the Sewel

Convention — was put in place. In essence, this provides for devolved administrations to pass motions of 'legislative consent' in the event Westminster needs to legislate on a devolved matter. Nowadays the procedure is, in the main, uncontroversial — with maybe 10 or so such motions a year. A reasonably frequent occurrence with more than 150 such motions in Scotland since 1998, and indeed 2016 legislation gives legal basis to the 'Convention' by formally accepting its role in Scottish matters. The Convention does not give Scotland a veto over a UK matter such as the Brexit Referendum result as a whole. In January 2017, the UK Supreme Court refused to rule on this issue deeming it a matter of 'High Politics'. There can be tensions where a matter is both devolved but also partially reserved for Westminster. Inevitably a number of these will arise with Brexit.

Farming and agriculture is a devolved matter under the Scotland Act 1998 and has been incorporated within a Scottish Government Ministry for Rural Affairs. Currently (pre-Brexit) a key work component is to administer payments under the Common Agricultural Policy. Brexit will remove the United Kingdom from this scheme. Given that over 50 per cent of farm incomes derive from CAP payments, these payments have a significant impact upon farming and rural landscapes; and, as a consequence, rural incomes from tourism. The 'Great Repeal Bill' White Paper has suggested that the United Kingdom replaces the CAP with a UK wide scheme, thereby arguing (notwithstanding the 1998 Devolution Act) agriculture will be a Westminster and not a Scotland issue.

> *In areas where the devolved administrations and legislatures have competence, such as agriculture, environment and some transport issues, the devolved administrations and legislatures are responsible for implementing the common policy frameworks set by the EU. At EU level, the UK Government represents the whole of the UK's interests in the process for setting those common frameworks and these also then provide common UK frameworks, including safeguarding the harmonious functioning of the UK's own single market. When the UK leaves the EU, the powers which the EU currently exercises in relation to the common frameworks will return to the UK, allowing these rules to be set here in the UK by democratically-elected representatives.*
>
> — H.M. Government (2017c)

The Common Agricultural Policy (CAP) subsidy is complex. CAP funds from Europe are delivered under two pillars, the first of which contains the 90 per cent of funds allocated to 'Direct Farm Payments' and the second of which represents funds that can be used for Rural Development. Member States can move up to 20 per cent funds from Pillar 1 to Pillar 2 (The Scottish Parliament, 2017). Under the current devolved government settlement, this decision is made independently in Scotland from England. Consequently, the transfer percentages are different, with England transferring 12 per cent and Scotland transferring 9.5 per cent in 2014. Current Westminster input to Scottish Agricultural Policy is from (i) its influence at the EU as a Member State and (ii) from Treasury control of local UK co-funding amounts.

Furthermore, agriculture is one of the more controversial areas in trade deals, and international policy is a reserved power for Westminster. Agricultural price support is restricted under World Trade Organisation Rules with an exception where there have been historic schemes. Each exemption must be negotiated separately and is not automatic. Currently, Scotland has two schemes (one from beef and one for upland sheep) that are eligible for restriction by being exempted under the EU block exemption (The Scottish Parliament, 2017). Current regulatory frameworks are complex and confusing and may well benefit from simplification, although foundation elements such as the EU sanitary, phytosanitary (SPS) and veterinary standards help obtaining the Export Health Certificates necessary for international trade.

Rural development policy in Scotland has just over £1.6bn allocated to it over a 5-year period of which about 50 per cent comes from the EU via either the rural development pillar or transfers into the pillar from direct farm payments. Direct farm support payments are worth about £390 million per annum. The UK government has guaranteed these until 2020, but has hinted they may no longer be paid after that date. Without direct farm payments, only dairy farming would be viable in Scotland (The Scottish Parliament, 2017). Scotland with 8 per cent of UK's population currently receives 17 per cent of the UK Agriculture Budget. England with 84 per cent of the population receives 65 per cent of the spending. Whether post-Brexit Agriculture is a matter 'reserved' for Westminster rather than being devolved is currently a matter of contention and debate. Two serious risks seem possible. First, the process of legislative consent, or further attempts at court action to require such consent, could be time consuming (thereby delaying the preparation timetable for Brexit Day); second, any tug of war between the

Westminster and the devolved administrations would raise uncertainty and alienation from Westminster in the regions.

For the hill farmer in need of state support or the rural MSME looking to invest to support tourism, such uncertainly is likely to be less than helpful.

4.8. Summary

In this chapter, we have seen how Brexit carries many diverse risks, from a 'Sudden Stop' event (similar to Brexit AD 410) through to risking regional alienation that could become similar to the alienation behind the 1536 Pilgrimage of Grace.

Anecdotal hearsay has it that during the 1940s, a man jumped out of a plane to practice a parachute jump, his parachute failed to open and he died. What on earth could be good about that story? For the person who died nothing, but for others the shock of the event led to the packing and carrying of a reserve parachute for every jump, thereby making sure the same event could not happen twice. The same could be said for the 2017 Grenfell Tower fire disaster. There is nothing good about this for the people who were in the tower at the time or for the firefighters who tried to handle it. But one hopes that the lessons from this tragedy will be learnt and implemented into regulations so it can never happen again. In both the above cases, the learning process required regulations to stop it happening again. Some call these 'red tape', whilst others would call these essential protections.

Did anyone in the policy-making elite in AD 408 plan or desire that towns and cities be depopulated and the Roman system of exchange stop? Did anyone in the elite in Iceland want the 2008 banking crash? Putting one's head into the hot desert sun will make neither midday sun nor it's heat go away. Just as when I visit the desert, whether I am hot or not is dependent upon forces I cannot control; the ripples of change Brexit will cause cannot be controlled. How likely is a policy maker whose head is buried in technical details likely to anticipate UK 'Sudden Stop' risks or a major loss of jobs and exports through structural change?

Is there a way to transform risks to become opportunities? Could a Sudden Stop event and significant structural changes be utilised to: (i) update the UK's economy to leapfrog other leading nations by investing in new technologies and markets as old ones fall away; (ii) realign asset prices, especially housing to income; (iii) realign inter-generational policies with more emphasis on equipping, investing in and enabling younger generations. There is a belief that leaving the EU will remove a layer of bureaucracy and red tape, and by so doing, unleash a new 'entrepreneurial age'.

There may well be many things that don't make much sense and that can be rationalised. But underneath these may be and indeed is likely to be some fundamental need that will not go away. With the CAP, doing away with direct farm payments does not do away with the issue of Upland Sheep farming in Scotland or the Lake District needing support to continue. In 1536 the closure of the minor monasteries closed down the then 'outsourced' method of poor relief. A factor in the Pilgrimage of Grace uprising and an issue – welfare for the poor – that remains as controversial today as in the 1530s. Monasteries made a very local and very unscientific decision between who was needy and who was feckless. The way of delivering the decision may have changed but the issue remains the same. Implicitly things are never as simple as the 'Tabloid Red Top' newspaper headlines – headlines are by definition highlights that may not exactly correspond to reality. Removing one piece of so-called red tape may expose the reason why it was there in the first place, or it may not! But people usually do things for a good reason, so rather than describing 'bonfires of red tape', the smart questions to ask are: (i) 'why is the red tape regulation here?' (ii) 'Is there an easier way of doing it?' and (iii) 'Am I letting the minutiae of legal certainty overrule the common sense of dealing with the issue?'

In the next chapters we will look at how the risks and challenges that we can sense from our narrative so far can be mitigated and turned to opportunity. We will look to learn from the experience of other countries that have been through similar transformations and from these lessons of history to tease out a menu of support measures to deal with the most serious risks, challenges and seize the best opportunities.

Common sense under another name? And ... perhaps an echo from a prior age as our slightly modified quote from Keynes suggests:

> *'Very few of us realize with conviction the intensely unusual, unstable, complicated, unreliable, temporary nature of the economic organization by which Western Europe has lived for the last half century. We assume some of the most peculiar and temporary of our late advantages as natural, permanent, and to be depended on, and we lay our plans accordingly. On this sandy and false foundation, we scheme*

*for social improvement and dress our political platforms,
pursue our animosities and particular ambitions, and feel
ourselves with enough margin in hand to foster, not assuage,
civil conflict in the European family. Moved by insane delu-
sion and reckless self-regard, [Brexit?] overturned the foundations on which we all lived and built. But the spokesmen
of the [EU?] peoples have run the risk of completing the
ruin, which [Brexit?] began, by a [Settlement] which, if it
is carried into effect, must impair yet further, when it might
have restored, the delicate, complicated organization, [...]
through which alone the European peoples can employ themselves and live [...]*

*In England the outward aspect of life does not yet teach us
to feel or realize in the least that an age is over [...]
Evidently we did not exploit to the utmost the possibilities
of our economic life. We look, therefore, not only to
[continuance of] the comforts [...] but to an immense
broadening and intensification of them. All classes alike thus
build their plans, the rich to spend more and save less, the
poor to spend more and work less [...].*

*The greater part of the population, it is true, worked and
lived at a low standard of comfort, yet were, to all appear-
ances, reasonably contented with this lot. But escape was
possible, for any man of capacity or character at all exceeding the average, into the middle and upper classes, for whom
life offered, at a low cost and with the least trouble, conve-
niences, comforts, and amenities beyond the compass of the
richest and most powerful monarchs of other ages. The
inhabitant of London could order by telephone, sipping his
morning tea in bed, the various products of the whole earth,
in such quantity as he might see fit, and reasonably expect
their early delivery upon his doorstep; he could at the same
moment and by the same means adventure his wealth in the
natural resources and new enterprises of any quarter of the
world, and share, without exertion or even trouble, in their
prospective fruits and advantages; or he could decide to couple the security of his fortunes with the good faith of the
townspeople of any substantial municipality in any continent
that fancy or information might recommend.*

> *He could secure forthwith, if he wished it, cheap and comfortable means of transit to any country or climate without passport or other formality, could despatch his servant to the neighbouring office of a bank for such supply of the precious metals as might seem convenient, and could then proceed abroad to foreign quarters, without knowledge of their religion, language, or customs, bearing coined wealth upon his person, and would consider himself greatly aggrieved and much surprised at the least interference. But, most important of all, he regarded this state of affairs as normal, certain, and permanent, except in the direction of further improvement, and any deviation from it as aberrant, scandalous, and avoidable. The projects and politics of militarism and imperialism, of racial and cultural rivalries, of monopolies, restrictions, and exclusion, which were to play the serpent to this paradise, were little more than the amusements of his daily newspaper [...].*

Writing after discussing the provisions of the 1919 Treaty of Versailles, most especially the scale of German Reparations and the scale of Allied debts (e.g. public sector debt) that was unlikely to be repaid from reparations:

> *All these influences combine not merely to prevent Europe from supplying immediately a sufficient stream of exports to pay for the goods she needs to import, but they impair her credit for securing the working capital required to re-start the circle of exchange and also, by swinging the forces of economic law yet further from equilibrium rather than towards it.*
>
> – Keynes (1920)

Chapter 5

Brexit: The Conventional Wisdom

[...] the madman was once a regular comic figure; that was how Hamlet got his opportunity before Shakespeare touched him. The originality of Shakespeare's version lay in his taking the lunatic sympathetically and seriously, and thereby making an advance towards [...] consciousness of the fact that lunacy may be inspiration in disguise.

— *Major Barbara* (G B Shaw, 1907)

The pro-Brexit slogans 'Take Back Control' and 'Reclaim Our Sovereignty' contain elements of hope for a more predictable and personally safer world with echoes from a darker age. Yearning for greater certainty and safety is conflated with a sense of nostalgia and a use of resources to match national priorities (£350 million extra per week for the NHS). Combined with a longing in some to relive a lost 'golden age', this engenders a sense of independence. There are also echoes from a darker European age that championed nationalism, economic autarchy, an age that burnt books and rubbished non-conforming experts. An age with leaders (on both left and right) who thought that whilst '*Capital is the property of individuals; its use also affects the welfare of the state; [...]. economic boundaries should coincide with political boundaries*'[1] (Fairweather, 1932). Both strands express the championing of the 'Nation State', proud in its identity and proud of its historic birth right. A State ripe for (in the words of media commentators) Empire 2.0. A United Kingdom strong in its borders and emboldened in its international relations. An age that recognises British Bulldog superiority.

---

[1]The 1932 news article quote comes from clarifies how globalization vs nationalism was seen from the perspective of an American liberal living in a different age. The context of this quote is the article author describing Hitler's economic philosophy.

5.1.   The Optimistic Case

Once the United Kingdom is free of the EU, the removal of bureaucratic barriers will free the British 'Prometheus'.

(i) Nations of the world will be lining up to be granted access to the UK market to sell their foreign delicacies, their Camembert, BMWs and Peugeots; their TVs and smart phones; their fancy foreign holiday destinations, etc. It's happening already with US President Trump suggesting the United States will offer a *'very, very good'* (Bloomberg, 2017b) trade deal to the United Kingdom.[2] Lord Digby Jones (former head of CBI and Brexit supporter) in response to news of potential US and Australian trade deals 'tweeted' *'So that's trade deals with both the US & Oz [...] in the bag'*[3] (Allen Green, 2017).

(ii) Bundles of 'red tape' will disappear, taxes will be cut and the innovative capabilities of the market unleashed.

Citing Cobden and earlier arguments between 'mercantilism' and 'free trade' Minford et al. (2017) frame the Brexit debate as a 'modern' debate on the repeal of the Corn Laws:

> *The prize from the UK adopting global free trade today is an additional long-term GDP gain of 4% and a fall of 8% in consumer prices, compared to remaining in the Single Market. These gains are achieved even if other countries do not reduce their tariffs against the UK. This does not include additional benefits gained from decreased regulation, eliminating annual EU budget contributions, etc.*
>
> — Minford et al. (2017)

Their gains come from import prices into the UK being reduced by the unilateral removal of tariffs so improving consumer real incomes and reducing industrial input costs. They do not see 'regional gravity' in trade patterns; for them it is as easy and as cheap to export to China

---

[2]UK International Trade Secretary visit to US July 2017.
[3]Twitter Lord Digby Jones 'tweet' 12.24 am, 11 July 2017 (Allen Green, 2017).

as it is Germany. They do not see a further slide in sterling but rather manufacturers being 'supported' by the UK Government able to maintain the same prices for European Sale and a gradual rise in sterling's value. In Box 5.1 we see that the immediate impact of mid-nineteenth-century tariff liberalisation was positive for the United Kingdom, and according to Bairoch negative elsewhere.

Box 5.1. Corn Law Repeal Revisited?

Minford et al. (2017) believe that Brexit will drive similar benefits as those perceived to have flowed from the 1849 repeal of the Corn Laws — a much older debate of Free Trade vs. Mercantilism, one to which many have contributed over the years. They assert that unilaterally removing tariffs gives the highest benefits as consumers and industry benefit from cheaper food and goods from non-EU sources because removing tariffs reduces the price of imports. For example, the price to the importer of food imported from Brazil or the United States could reduce as the tariff is removed, but tariff removal says nothing about whether this benefit is pocketed by the importer, the supermarket or the consumer or indeed if the exporting nation raises its prices to improve its own earnings. Equally this price benefit only occurs if the sterling exchange rate is steady or rising. Minford et al. (2017) explicitly assume sterling will not fall further and that it will rise to its pre-Brexit Referendum value within 10 years. Their study does mention the importance of 'non-tariff' barriers and they suggest these could in some cases be equivalent to a tariff of 18 per cent to 20 per cent — that is higher than most money tariffs. Copy the 1846 repeal of the Corn Laws and the benefits will flow.

So what happened in the mid-nineteenth century? First there is the context of Empire and Britain's then military might. O'Brian and Pigman (1992) see Britain as the global rule setter during the second half of the nineteenth century. They find evidence of this in the Far East with for example the opening of Chinese Markets via (the still resented) Nanking Treaty (1842). Contrarily in Europe there is little British Intervention.

The 1860 Cobden Chevalier Treaty between France and the United Kingdom reduced tariffs and duties and introduced 'Most Favoured Nation Status' (MFN) where all MFN treaty status nations gain the same rights even if only one country negotiates a change. Following the 1860s saw a spate of 56 bilateral trade treaties signed between 13 European nations (mostly not with the United Kingdom). Lampe (2011) finds these agreements were mainly to increase trade with near neighbours (distance matters) to improve or protect an existing export industry, generally made with larger states first and were possibly to 'free ride' 'MFN' clauses. Bairoch (1976) alludes to the post-1860 Cobden Chevalier Treaty between France and the United Kingdom, creating a unique European low tariff area that gave the United Kingdom a significant advantage due to its more advanced industrial base. Reviewing Bairoch's findings, Glazier (1980) finds:

> *Under free trade the gap in development levels between Britain and the Continent became more pronounced, income differentials widened between 1860 and 1880, and investment and innovation on the Continent declined. With the reintroduction of protective tariffs between 1890 and 1913 on the Continent, however [...] per capita incomes in the less developed (continental) countries rose, while growth in Britain lagged.*

Accominotti and Flandreau (2008) commented, '*A striking aspect of the conventional wisdom on the nineteenth-century experience is its complete lack of empirical foundations; there is simply no empirical data on trade for that period*' and created a revised dataset from which they suggest that trade liberalisation in Europe started before 1860 and that the 1860 Cobden Chevalier Treaty and subsequent agreements were deepening a process that had already happened. Tena-Junguito, Lampe, and Fernandes (2012) build a data set that looks at the level of manufacturing tariff protection country by country. They comment, '*average tariffs fell during the 1850s, although little of it happened in North-western Europe. Subsequently, Cobden-Chevalier affected a substantial share of world trade and reinforced previous unilateral liberalization trends*'. Data from The Maddison-Project (Bolt & Zanden, 2014) are re-combined in Table B5.1.

Table B5.1. Selected Europe Trade Data for Nineteenth Century (Authors' Table).

Decade	GDP Per Capita (From Madisson 2013)				Tariff Burden vs. United Kingdom (from Tena Jungui to 2012)			(From Madisson 2013)	
	UK	Ned	Fr	Ger	Ned	Fr	Ger	UK	Continent
1840s	10.0%	2.4%	10.1%		8.0%	11063.0%	1451.0%	5.7%	2.9%
1850s	19.7%	−3.0%	11.1%	9.6%	6.0%	11068.0%	1395.0%	5.4%	5.4%
1860s	7.1%	11.6%	6.0%	13.5%	4.0%	214.0%	625.0%	3.8%	5.4%
1870s	5.1%	0.5%	4.1%	10.3%	6.0%	495.0%	83.0%	2.6%	3.2%

Yet within a few years there were to be calls for 'Fair Trade' culminating in a full campaign to restore tariffs. What had changed? Box 5.2 takes up the story.

Box 5.2. Industrial Change and Tariffs

Kaldor (1977) explains:

> *whilst Free Trade suited Britain perfectly while it served to enhance **the share of UK manufactures in the world market** [...] the reverse was the case when other countries – Germany, France, the United States, Japan [...] began to foster their manufacturing industries behind the shelter of protective tariffs. Our continued adherence to Free Trade meant that a lot of **new** industries [...] could not be properly established here' (emphasis as in Kaldor's original notes).*

The theory of Comparative Advantage (Ricardo, 1817) postulates an overall gain where countries specialise in the products they are most efficient in. Hume (1742) tells us Comparative Advantage is not absolute and shifts over time – we have seen this in recent manufacturing shifts to low labour cost Asian countries.

For industries being challenged in export markets, and especially after the 'Long Depression' that started in 1873, there was a rising call for protection that can be summed up by Joseph Chamberlain, speaking in Glasgow in 1903:

> *[T]he protected countries which you have been told, and which I myself at one time believed, were going rapidly to wreck and ruin, have progressed in a much greater proportion than ours. That is not all; not merely the amount of your trade remained stagnant, but the character of your trade has changed. When Mr. Cobden preached his doctrine, he believed [...] that while foreign countries would supply us with our food-stuffs and raw materials, we should remain the mart of the world, and should send them in exchange our manufactures. But that is exactly what we have not done. On the contrary, in the period to which I have referred, we are sending less and less of our manufactures to them, and they are sending more and more of their manufactures to us.*
>
> – Chamberlain (1914)

The story had moved on. Countries other than the United Kingdom are starting to follow the United States in raising tariffs, and industrialisation is raising output in countries such as Germany and the United States. Britain becomes the financial hub of the world. Operating under the Gold Standard, it invests surpluses overseas in countries with lower cost bases and protected by tariffs. Britain's export growth becomes dominated by export to its colonies as other markets become more challenging. New innovation industries such as chemicals and electricity find easier ground in other countries. The scene has moved from the 1860's when Bairoch (1976) found the United Kingdom benefiting most from Free Trade to Chamberlain perceiving the UK was losing from Free Trade and campaigning for Tariff Protection in 1903.

5.2. The Mainstream Case

Based upon models that economists have developed over the past 50 years, (these models take a 'stylised view' of the economy) in that they formalise supposed economic relationships into a series of equations, and then calculate anticipated results based upon the input data. The 2008 crash demonstrated that these models are fairly good at predicting continuing status quo but not so effective in dealing with discontinuities or 'black swan' events.

The two forecast cases shown in Table 5.1 are a small sample of the many pre-referendum studies, all of which, with the exception of the 'Economists for Brexit' study pointed to Brexit economic losses. The immediate post-Brexit impact was a sharp fall in Sterling (fairly well predicted) but very little other impact as consumers kept spending, and inflation impacts took time to feed through the system (Table 5.1).

Initial GDP growth and inflation figures seemed to undermine mainstream forecasts, although as time rolled on, inflation rose in response to the Sterling fall, real wages were squeezed and there started (although inconclusive at time of writing) to be signs of ebbing growth in consumer borrowing, down shifting in base consumer purchases such as food, as trade shifts towards food discounters. These are early indicators, but more time is required to establish a trend. Box 5.3 explores some reasons why mainstream forecast expectations have been incorrect.

Table 5.1. Mainstream Case Examples.

Forecast Body	Short Term Compared to Pre-Brexit Forecasts (GDP Still Rises)	Long Term (2030) Compared to Pre-Brexit Forecasts (GDP Still Rises)
NIESR	• Sterling 20% fall on result • Inflation 2% to 4% more than would have been • Fall in confidence and investment • GDP 1% lower in 2017 • Unlikely to drive recession	• GDP fall 2.7% to 7.8% • Consumption Fall 4% to 9.2% • Real Wage Fall 4.6% to 7% • Foreign Direct Investment Fall 24% • Share of exports fall 50% to 72%
Treasury (Short-term Shock Scenario) (Long-term Central Case Bilateral Agreement)	• GDP 3.6% lower than would have been by end of year 2 • Sterling fall 12% • Inflation 2.3% higher than would have been • Unemployment 0.5 million higher than would have been	• GDP 6.2% lower than would have been by end of year 15 • Reduction in EU trade −14% to −19% • Foreign Direct Investment Falls 15% to 20% • Productivity Fall 3% to 6%

Sources: NIESR (2016), H.M. Treasury (2016a, 2016b).

Box 5.3.   The 'Missing' Hurricane, Black Swans and Conspiracy Theory

I think people in this country have had enough of experts.
                                                      − Gove (2016)

In 1987 the weather presenter, Michael Fish, famously assured the public there would be no hurricane in the south of England and there was. In 2016 economists promised an immediate economic challenge if the United Kingdom voted for Brexit. Nothing happened − the hurricane that never was. Was it incompetence? Was there a dark conspiracy to falsify the forecast so the people would vote against Brexit? Or was it something else?

Economics, sometimes known as the 'Dismal Science' (Carlyle, 1849), and in recent years has (using mathematics) tried to create a predictive model upon four pillars: (i) General Equilibrium Theory (Arrow, Debreau, Malinvaud Hahn, etc.); (ii) Econometrics using data to substantiate model; (iii) 'Rational Expectations' to assume away uncertain futures (Lucas); and (iv) evolving Dynamic Stochastic General Equilibrium forecast models. Tovar (2008) describes models that have improved over the years but that still have some way to go to mirror real life. Genberg and Martinez (2014), from the IMF independent evaluation office (which evaluates IMF Forecasting performance), find that whilst IMF models in general match the performance of other non-IMF models, all models including the IMF model fail to predict step changes such as recessions (in this case being consistently over-optimistic). Malinvaud (1981) (writing at another moment when macroeconomic modelling had a bad name for not predicting events) writes:

> *[…] success or failures of macro-econometric models is identified with the success or failure of […] policies adopted by their governments […]. Macro-economic policies are not all-powerful; notably they do not permit our societies to avoid the adaptations required by the new conditions of the world economy. […] proposed theoretical models bring hypotheses into play which are very unrealistic because of their simplicity and which reveal themselves as increasingly unrealistic as they are better explained […].*

By their very nature, these models rely on mathematical functions validated upon past data which is then extended into the future. A great tool for forecasting within the status quo, but just like their failure to see the 2008 financial crisis, these models are not equipped, designed or built to deal with step discontinuities like Brexit. In this context, it is a credit to the mainstream forecasters that they foresaw the immediate fall in Sterling, even if their models did not map out what immediately happened with consumer demand. Black Swans, discontinuities, step changes need models and constructs relevant to them. Try to use the wrong tool and don't be surprised if there is a sub-optimal result.

5.3. Tinkerbell and the Art of Wishful Thinking

The moment you doubt whether you can fly, you cease for ever to be able to do it [...]. Whenever a child says, 'I don't believe in fairies', there's a little fairy somewhere that falls right down dead.

– Barrie (1911)
Term 'Tinkerbell Policy' first coined by
Abrams (2014) and restated by Elledge (2017)

Tinkerbell policy is the policy made on the belief that one only has to believe it will work, and success will happen. Economic development comes from combining ideas and entrepreneurship with capital and labour to deliver innovative products. The economic and political landscape is littered with 'idea baskets' that can offer false dawns, as they easily correspond to political philosophies, but prove to be less than well supported in economic delivery. Here are some policies that may count on the 'Tinkerbell Effect'.

5.3.1. The Laffer Curve

On the right of the political spectrum, the Laffer Curve is an example of how important context and environment can be for a potential policy measures effectiveness. Box 5.4 discusses this.

The proposals we will later suggest do not mention cutting the corporation tax rate or slashing labour regulation, two oft-quoted 'Growth' measures. Balanced and consistent labour regulation and non-punitive

Box 5.4.   Growth on a Napkin? The Laffer Curve

The Laffer curve is believed to have started its life after being sketched on a napkin during a 1974 meeting Dr Laffer and others had with Ford Administration members Cheney and Rumsfeld. Laffer himself claims the theory has deeper origins. The theory says that growth rises when taxes, especially personal taxes, are cut. It has been extended over the years by some more extreme US-based think tanks to suggest that personal tax rates need to be set below an optimum level to drive growth.

Easy to comprehend, easy to action, but in real life this delivers poor and unsubstantiated results (Goolsbee, 1999). Despite Goolsbee's findings, intuitively one would expect that a cut in top tax rates from say 99 per cent to 50 per cent would have some impact, not least by removing an entrepreneur's incentive to emigrate in the face of very high personal tax rates. There is anecdotal evidence that French President Holland's raising of the top personal tax rate did make French entrepreneurs look to start up elsewhere in the European Union — a decision open to them as a result of the EU's freedom of movement principle. Without freedom of movement substantial prior wealth would likely have been required to obtain residence in the UK (most likely through an *entrepreneurs investment residency*) thereby acting as a movement barrier and probably reducing this migration effect. Laffer Curve credibility in *non-tax cutting think tank circles* was not helped by Arthur Laffer's unfortunate newspaper comment (Laffer, 2007) that Iceland was an example for all the world to follow shortly before its banking system and economy crashed in 2008. Notwithstanding, Laffer and the Laffer curve have been central to the *cut tax and grow narrative*.

Interestingly and anecdotally in AD 410 tax sent from the colony Britannia to Rome was cut dramatically as the inhabitants refused to pay for an absent army, but this does not seem to have stimulated economic growth.

taxation are important growth-enabling conditions; but as Box 5.4 discussing the Laffer Curve demonstrates, cuts in tax do not automatically generate growth. Equally our data on low wages and productivity suggest that focusing on reducing labour cost is a way to become globally uncompetitive, as higher wages provide an incentive to invest in labour saving equipment and processes, and in any event the United Kingdom will never find it acceptable to pay people on Bangladesh or Vietnamese pay scales. Cost competitiveness matters. In this context and as a consequence of rises in productivity there needs to be a laser focus on *unit labour cost* reduction. This improvement is most likely achieved through investment, skills uplift, better working methods and making the most innovative and best of class products in the sector. People don't buy a Rolls Royce because it's cheap; they buy them because they are 'best of class'.

Government has an important role to balance different and competing societal interests, and to level the regulatory playing field between businesses.

Are businesses that side step regulations to grow at the expense of existing businesses (online ride share and food delivery businesses come to mind) that reduce their relative costs through self-employment and avoiding licensing schemes true sector disruptors and productivity drivers, or do they mainly win through sidestepping regulations? Does reducing the tax on a multinational's transfer pricing profits add the same value as reducing the tax of a company that invests in new plant, equipment and intangibles to launch new products, grow export markets, grow employment and grow GDP? How important are tax rates or labour regulations to an MSME facing bankruptcy as the bank withdraws its working capital credit line?

Box 5.5. Etymology! Savings, Investment, Frittered Debt and Economic Rents

Definitions and words used in these definitions matter. Much economic debate tends to be confused by multiple uses of the same word. For example 'investment' can be the placing of savings or can be buying new machinery to increase production, or spending on research and development to create new products and patents. We examine some potential sources of confusion below.

Ricardo (1815) describes an agricultural model for corn with three components: labour, capital and rent. Wages and capital are assumed to be at set levels; therefore, any increase in the price over that needed to reward labour and capital constitutes a 'rent'. He implicitly defines rent as being a payment in excess of the profit rate required to attract capital into the industry. Extending this, any payment to shareholders that is not required to solicit funds for new Capital Investment can be defined as *Economic Rent*.

Non-Corporate *Savings* are made to shift spending from one-time period to a later one; the instrument the savings are held in (stocks, bonds, bank savings accounts whatever) is determined by a savers trade-off between risk, access to cash and potential rewards. The savings provider manages the asset mix to deliver the risk / reward balance savers seek, and regulators monitor providers to make sure that in most cases 'savings' are safe. Consequently, most savings are invested into some form of existing assets and associated cash flows, not into new Venture or Angel Seed Capital and not into new share issues to fund Capital Investment. Savings rewards are a call on asset cash flows that are not directly related to Capital Investment. This implies that rather than acting as a spur to economic development they act as an 'Economic Rent' extracting value from existing businesses rather than investing in new products, innovations, skills and capital expenditure to raise future growth, productivity and future profit levels. Share Buy Backs are a device to raise the level of 'rent' extracted and not the performance of the base assets. Better managements can extract more from their assets, raise the rent they pay and so raise the share price (and if rewarded by stock options raise their own rewards).

Capital Investment drives future returns, provided it is invested in the right things — products, research and infrastructure that will drive future income. Wicksell (1898) spots a key relationship — the natural rate of interest must be at the level that matches the return upon the least profitable new project. Profit in Wicksells model is the return on capital investment, and relating this to Schumpeter (1934) needs to equate the return to the entrepreneur. We discuss this again later on.

Frittered Debt is debt used to fund current consumption — it must be repaid from future income. It is consumed and gone. Frittered Debt can be incurred by both private individuals and the state. In an open economy it is Frittered Debt that can cause long-term Balance of Payment's problems, as it builds up overseas debts that can only be repaid by progressively squeezing other expenditures.

Churchill in 1940 did not talk about how to fund replacing equipment lost in the Fall of France, he focused on preventing a feared invasion. Recovering from near death requires focus and strong an appropriate action. Even in a benign economic environment, firms face near death every year as global competitors innovate new products that threaten a firm's market position. Firms need to constantly invest and innovate in new products and technologies that their customers want if they are to remain competitive. Brexit will add an additional pressure as companies need to adapt to Brexit changes as well as normal competitive demands.

5.3.2. Government Debt, 'Austerity' and Crowding Out

Again, on the right, some have suggested that having a set maximum percentage of government debt to GDP is crucial to growth (Reinhart & Rogoff, 2009) and supposedly supported this assertion with statistical data, only to find the proposition challenged by different analysis of this self-same statistical data (i.e. Nersisyan & Wray, 2010; Parent, 2012).

This debate links to assertions that the public sector 'Crowds Out' investment in the private sector. 'In short, if the combined ratios of private consumption and non-market spending rise, and current account balance of payments equilibrium must be maintained, the ratio of market sector investment must inevitably become lower. Hence in these conditions "crowding-out" of market sector investment is inescapable' (Bacon & Eltis, 1979, p. 411). Whilst this statement holds true when a country is on the 'Gold Standard' it does not correspond with the modern reality of endogenous credit creation in the banking system, as described by the Bank of England (2014). Banks can create unlimited credit subject to liquidity and risk-weighted asset ratios. UK Government bonds are fully discountable for cash at the Central Bank and carry a zero-risk weighting, thereby having minimal impact on Bank credit creation potential for the private sector. The modern limitation is hinted at by Bacon and Eltis (1979), namely that the overall limitation on credit creation relates to overseas confidence in the currency. In this context both private and public credit volumes matter. To be effective the credit being raised must be invested in future productive capacity that will increase wealth, or otherwise the credit raised is 'frittered' on consumption (Box 5.5).

5.3.3. Inequality

'Left-wing/Marxist income distribution economics' highlights the economic impact of wealth distribution showing growing inequality, supposedly supported by statistical data, but equally questioned by differing analysis of this self-same statistical data (Piketty, 2017; Wolfers, 2014). Richer consumers spend less of their income, so there is insufficient demand to support economic activity. We do not explore these 'distributional' arguments. A key Brexit objective is to raise international demand for UK products through expanded exports from the UK. We view the 'distribution argument' as to how economic benefits are divided between earners and capital holders as to be unrelated to our narrative.

Chapter 6

Our Assumptions

Three econometricians went to the fair and came across a coconut shy. The first econometrician threw but missed, by a meter to the left. The second econometrician threw but also missed, by a meter to the right. The third econometrician didn't throw but shouted in triumph, 'We got it! We got it!'

— Authors

Conventional economic models are based on mathematics ignoring Marshall's (1890) warning

[I had] a growing feeling in the later years of my work at the subject that a good mathematical theorem dealing with economic hypotheses was very unlikely to be good economics: and I went more and more on the rules — (1) Use mathematics as a shorthand language, rather than an engine of inquiry. (2) Keep to them till you have done. (3) Translate into English. (4) Then illustrate by examples that are important in real life. (5) Burn the mathematics. (6) If you can't succeed in (4), burn (3). This last I did often

— Brue (1993)

Brexit implies changes to foreign trade patterns and restrictions on free movement. A recurring and indeed current theme is a desire to reduce tax and to avoid paying for anything (for Brexiteer's especially if this is related to the European Union) that may not have a direct perceived benefit. We will never know, but it is easy to imagine a similar narrative occurring amongst the taxpayers of Britannia during the period AD 401 to AD 409. Britannia was a rich, independent-minded colony, so why did it need to make such a huge contribution to Roman defence costs? Especially when the army was defending the towns, when anyone with a sense of style had long left for the comfort of their rural villas that they knew they could protect themselves. What could not have been imagined in that discussion was the soon to be felt impact on supply chains, trade and urban locations, as with a lack of new Roman Coin the monetary economy started to dry up Britannia stopped paying taxes to the Empire, and how quickly things can change.

From our visit to the nineteenth century in Box 5.1, we can see 'free trade' is helpful to all parties when all the participants are at about the same level of industrial and technological evolution. Equally, protection can help when nursing infant industries to make them globally competitive. For example, Nunn and Trefler (2010) demonstrate through a study of 63 countries in a 28-year period up to the millennium that tariffs can make a significant contribution to developing high-skill innovative industries, even when accounting for tariff inefficiencies induced from some tariffs being set based upon 'special pleading' from specific interest groups.

We also found that geographical proximity ('gravity' to use the technical term) has been historically important in trade patterns and trade liberalisation. If proximity is important for general trade, it is even more important for manufacturing supply chains. A detailed study looking at value adding in complex cross-country supply chains by Timmer, Dietzenbacher, Los, Stehrer, and Vries (2015) shows the key and rising importance of regional proximity in the Automotive Supply chain. For example, for cars built in Germany, domestic German content fell from 78.9 per cent in 1998 to 66 per cent in 2008, whilst other EU and East Europe content that was 13.2 per cent in 1998, rose to 18.6 per cent in 2008.

6.1. Assumptions

> *A physicist, an engineer and an economist are stranded on a deserted island. They carry with them some canned food but have no ordinary means of opening the cans. The physicist suggests gathering some wood and starting a fire and then holding the cans over the heat, counting on the expanding contents to burst open the cans. The engineer thinks it would be better to try smashing the cans open with some of the rocks lying around. The economist begins, 'Assume we had a can opener […]'.*
>
> – Adapted from Keen (2017)

1. Brexit happens on Brexit Day, Friday 29 March 2019.
2. Domestic legislation and government systems are ready for March 2019 (this is a heroic assumption that may not be met, but where it is

not met we assume that either an 'as is' transition is in place or manual but expensive workarounds will be in place in all mission critical – such as customs declarations – areas).

3. Treaty cover is available for the most important areas such as air safety, peaceful nuclear movements[1] (although this could be 6 months late as it may require ratification in foreign legislatures) but there are gaps in important secondary areas.

4. No treaty cover is available in areas such as data safe harbours, key body mutual recognition, etc., but the cliff edge is softened on these through a maximum 2-year transition agreement on these specific issues. The transition allows free flow between the United Kingdom and EU but not with third countries, as the United Kingdom having left the EU will no longer be able to access the benefits available under EU third-country treaties.

5. The UK regulators that control product standards do not benefit from automatic mutual recognition and firms need to re-apply the regulatory base to sell products into Europe, but there is a 2-year transition agreement to cover this.

6. Euro-denominated transactions must from Brexit Day be processed by a regulated entity within the remaining EU, and parties processing retail transactions for EU-located parties must be located in remaining EU states. Banks and other financial sector institutions relocate portions of their operations to other EU states before Brexit Day. Capital and portfolio flows out of the United Kingdom occur as this adjustment occurs.

7. Existing EU workers are allowed continued residency; work permits for new non/low-skilled EU workers are not attractive due to their cost, minimum salaries and bureaucratic difficulties. The agricultural worker picker regime is re-established with Ukraine and other CIS states.

8. Companies start to adapt supply chains through restructuring purchases and investments and the lack of a clear transition deal 15 months before exit date. (Company financial annual budget planning cycle's force plans for 2018 execution to be budget approved in Q4 2017.)

9. A transition agreement is restricted to the time needed to establish a 'mutual recognition treaty' to give UK standards bodies validity

---

[1]The need to establish a new treaty is set out in 'Nuclear Materials and Safeguards Issues Position Paper' (DEXU, 2017c).

in testing to EU Standards and to establish a data protection data safe harbour arrangement. Negotiations run to the wire, and transition arrangements are agreed too late for business to rely on.
10. No EU Free Trade Agreement is available Day 1 with a default back to WTO most especially for 'services' at the end of any transition period.

6.2.   Assumptions Basis

We know from the Article 50 notification letter that the intention is to leave the Customs Union and Single Market. Consequent upon this we know cross-border movements into the EU will require full

---

Box 6.1.   Could We Face a Major Shock?

Brexit risks being a major macro-economic and structural shock to the UK economy. A possible worst case would see a shock on the scale of say the loss of the First World War, Versailles Treaty and 1921 Ruhr Occupation in Weimar Germany, Iceland in 2008 or the Greek Euro Crisis. These events suggest potential risk for a 24–36-month fall in GDP of between 10 per cent (Iceland) and 25 per cent + (Greece). By way of contrast, official data on US recessions saw a 43 per cent 'contraction' in the period 1929–1933 (NBER, 2012). A 'Sudden Stop' event.

From a structural view-point we anticipate multitudinous changes affecting multiple industries. The degree of change will be directly related to each industries' dependence on international trade (longer term most especially exports and imports from the European Union, especially when these trade flows occur within complex pan European Supply Chains) and upon the degree of internationally accredited regulation (industries dependent upon complex internationally recognised standards will face the greatest impact when mutual standards and regulatory control regimes are accessed globally via treaties held by the EU and not by bilateral treaties). We note the Repeal Bill (Parliament, 2017a, 2017b) does not deal with the need for UK access to working Third Country Bi-Lateral Treaties, an issue also not mentioned in associated briefings, although referred to by individual treaty in Article 50 briefing notes.

---

customs declarations for each movement (a C88 plus Certificates of Origin and Conformity plus any other Common Community Tariff required documentation). We know that transport will be disrupted, as UK haulage firms and drivers will not have licences to drive in the EU, as required by EU directive 1072/2009. Transport access will revert to access via the 'TIR Convention' which allows for sealed containers (so each end inspection rather than inspection in each country of transport and deferred duty payment (subject to financial guarantee) plus under preamble clause 3 to bi-lateral treaties with Member States).

We do not know whether all UK-manufactured Pharmaceuticals and Medical Devices held outside the United Kingdom on Brexit Day will lose their EU registrations as UK regulatory and notified bodies require treaty cover to establish competence and mutual recognition. That treaty has not been negotiated yet. We do not know, for example, if UK-registered airplanes will lose their FAA safety certification as a result of the United Kingdom losing access to the EU/USA Air Safety Treaty (2011) that specifically cancelled the 1995 UK Bi-Lateral Treaty.

The issues around the Financial Sector regarding possible loss of Financial Services Passporting and Euro Clearing have been well aired. Box 6.1 gives a downside view on the potential shock.

In summary, more uncertainty than precision, but with something so complex and with so many items to be handled, inevitably with significant opportunity to wreak disruption. This is the background to our next chapter.

Chapter 7

Coping with a Brexit Shock

> **Shock**: *noun; Meanings:* **1**. Waking up and finding today is just the same as yesterday; **2**. Waking up and finding the world has completely changed; *Interpretation:* meaning 1 usually applies until there is a step change when meaning 2 applies. Neither was an anticipated outcome.
>
> – Authors

Whilst no experience is ever exactly the same, building on the previous chapter, we assume that firms will need to start to execute contingency plans to mitigate against risks to their business operations, at some point before Brexit day. Structural change will accelerate from this point on. Equally, at some point Sterling may undertake further adjustments as markets take a long-term view on the UK's revised situation. It is questionable if the Sterling fall so far fully reflects the future trade-deficit risks. Such an adjustment is likely to be in the context of our Chapter 4 discussion on Sudden Stops.

It seems likely that drastically changing the arrangements that govern 44 per cent of foreign trade, and most especially establishing procedural non-tariff barriers will negatively impact the trade balance in a country already running a dangerously (Summers, 1995) high trade deficit of over 5 per cent of GDP.[1] Equally, it seems likely that there be a significant structural adjustment and, restructuring in Financial Services, in response to as yet unspecified changes in how the UK interfaces with the EU regulatory regime. Complex supply chains, especially those in the Automotive and Aerospace, and possibly Pharmaceutical sectors also look like they will be significantly impacted.

Given that firms must plan, fund and undertake projects to cope with regulatory changes, which in some cases (e.g. trading Euro denominated derivatives) threaten to exclude them from markets, there will be a point in time when the state-to-state negotiations become less relevant and

---

[1]This links to Sudden Stop risks already discussed in Chapter 4.

contingency plans must be executed, as it becomes too risky to leave things any longer. In practical terms with Brexit this anecdotally is most likely to be during the first three quarters of 2018. Restructuring in financial markets may involve raising substantial additional capital (Afme, 2017) and relocation of some asset holdings. The sums could be substantial (billions) and result in a capital outflow that magnifies the funding gap in the Balance of Payments (e.g. a negative trade balance plus negative financial flows). This reinforces the risks of a further fall in Sterling.

This 'double whammy' of Trade Deficit and Capital Flow risks generating pressure to raise UK interest rates to both defend the currency and stop inflationary wage expectations setting in. A rise in interest rates, will likely ripple through into drop in consumer spending with associated falls in employment. There is significant risk that a combination of higher interest rates, squeezed real wages and a fall in employment could lead to a material housing market adjustment. The housing market has an important role in economic stability in countries such as the UK. Because of the housing market's key linkages to other economic parameters such as Consumption, significant changes in the housing market have significant impact throughout the economy. In this context it has been called the 'elephant in the room' (Muellbauer, 2012). A material negative adjustment in the housing market will have negative impacts on overall economic demand and may help depress growth rates. In the UK major downward changes in sterling coupled with significant interest rate rises and knock on effects in the housing market are likely to be important transmission corridors for any Sudden Shock event.

Even without a Sudden Stop event, significant structural adjustment in response to changes in European Supply Chains as they restructure to re-optimise in a post Brexit environment can be expected. It is likely that this adjustment will raise unemployment levels in some industries and professions. Structural adjustment, especially if this is combined with falls in demand (associated with EU based firms moving supply sources from the UK to other EU countries to maintain supply chain efficiency as they face tariff and especially non-tariff barriers) will most likely impact on overall economic confidence. This confidence impact will most likely lead to banks and other lenders drawing in their horns and looking to minimise risk to all sectors including the MSME sector. This change in lending profile, is likely as in 2008, to negatively impact MSME's. Common sense affirms the dictum that '*Financial Policy must not be so imposed to thwart the energies of enterprise*' (Macmillan Report, 1930). Poor policy of any type risks damaging enterprise.

MSMEs will in response to a shock likely face (i) further restricted lending flows, (ii) an increase in financing costs compounding (iii) supply chain changes, with (iv) in some cases, orders falling and large companies deferring payment. This challenge risks raising death rates for some types of firm and also for others creating fertile conditions for a 'zombification moment'. Box 7.1 helps us understand that 'zombification' can be an opportunity if it becomes a spur to innovation.

Box 7.1. The 'Zombification Moment'

Just as in a car crash when there is that moment of stunned unreality and silence, which to the participant seems like an eternity but is in fact only a micro second of shock before one adjusts to one's new circumstances; a business facing a 'sharp economic shock' goes through a 'slow motion' silence moment as entrepreneurs and managers comprehend the shock that their world has suddenly changed.

Marketing agency WDMP had an annual turnover of around £10 million as it entered the 2008 financial shock. The shock struck. Large clients cancelled contracts and within months, annual turnover had fallen to a rate of £4 million. The business reacted by moving their product up the value chain to offer high valued-added 'advice' at the expense of cutting back on 'volume operational work'. Whist there was less turnover, and costs were cut (staff were reduced from 65 to 17 and monthly expenses fell from approximately £300k per month to less than £70k per month); value added rose and together with funding taken from reserves, survival was assured. Moving from survival to growth found banks who would not grant credit lines, with growth requiring additional finance, customers provided support through advance payments. By 2012, turnover was rising again, up to £5 million (Bartrum, 2013). This is an example of a company undertaking radical restructuring to avoid 'sudden death' or 'zombification'.

Some SMEs fail to adjust, but become 'zombies' as they are kept on 'life support' for public policy reasons or to avoid bank loan losses. Imai (2016) in a study of over 4,000 Japanese SMEs during 1999–2008 found 4–13 per cent were 'zombies' who were not benefiting from being kept on banking and government guarantee 'life support'. These companies were stuck where they could innovate out of being a Zombie, yet life support seem a better option to their lenders and the state. Zombie company's distort resource allocation away from innovative business into supporting lifeless business.

On the other hand, rapid and strong action can innovate the company back into growth. Makin Metal Powders UK is in the main a 'Tier 4' automotive supplier, selling base copper and copper alloy powders. The company had a turnover of £30 million with a forecast £0.5 million profit as it ran into the 2008 crisis, but within months, turnover had dropped 40 per cent as customers cut orders. By changing their business, cutting raw material and 'consignment stocks', focusing product lines into higher margin products, developing products to anticipate customer needs, keeping a laser eye on yields and waste and squeezing working capital by invoice factoring, the business was back in growth by 2012. (Bartrum, 2013)

7.1.   Action Points

We will now discuss each potential action in turn.

> *A bank is a place where they lend you an umbrella in fair weather and ask for it back when it begins to rain.*[2]
> — Attributed to Robert Frost (1949)

It has long been recognised that smaller businesses can face challenges in accessing the funding they need to grow. A 2012 report estimated a 5-year UK MSME funding gap of between £84 billion and £191 billion (BEIS, 2012). Funding availability changes over the economic cycle, so the figures in this estimate may overstate today's gap. Quantifying any funding gap is in any event likely to be imprecise. For example paragraphs 379 to 396 of an early 1930s' House of Commons Report into the relationship of the then 'Big 5' joint stock banks and industry (Macmillan, 1930) carries many echoes to the 2016 British Business Bank report (British Business Bank, 2016): a tale of a great financial centre with relatively (when compared to say Germany) weak MSME domestic business credit provision. As we demonstrate in Box

---

[2]A similar adage appeared in a London accounting magazine in 1905, and earlier unconfirmed attribution has been given to Mark Twain.

7.2, access to financial challenges is not new, and post-2008 experience is not unique. Since 1921 there have been a number of attempts to improve UK business lending flows, although not all of these have been targeted at MSMEs.

Box 7.2.   Recent (Post-1914) UK Lending Support Measures

During the 'interwar' years, the United Kingdom experimented with a number of schemes. For example, the 1921 'Trade Facilities Act' which allowed industry to *'to guarantee, in respect of interest or principal or both, loans calculated to promote employment in the United Kingdom'* (House of Commons, 1922). This scheme focused on helping large legacy industries, with support provided to sunset sectors such as ship building rather than to newer sunrise sectors. The same may be said of the 'Securities Management Trust' which was created to hold government stakes in companies. In 1929 these initiatives were extended to form the Bankers Industrial Development Company to support industrial restructuring engendered during the previous 1917 'British Trade Corporation' export initiative. Additionally, in 1929 a Bank of England initiative supported the Hire Purchase market through a stake in the leading Hire Purchase Financier of the time, United Dominions Trust. It is understood Bank Governor Montague Norman wanted Hire Purchase to be extended into MSME companies to help their funding; however, the relatively small size of the loans and short loan terms resulted in little MSME take up.

Cerretano (2009) suggests these changes reflected a dissatisfaction with the UK financial system especially when contrasted to the *'alleged superiority of German Universal Banking'*. British banking maintained the *'time-honoured principle of English banking, of not participating in the management of industry, which had developed through generations of self-financing'* (Lucas, 1933). It was felt banks were ill equipped to provide the capital and management pressure to drive investment, rationalisation and competitiveness. Sir W Guy Granet (head of the BIDC) said *'I do not see how you can secure a really effective connection that find the money and the management [...] It is not your function to supervise management, and when I am told that the German banks have done it I wonder if it is effective'* Macmillan (1930). The BIDC was wound up in 1945 and replaced by the Industrial and Commercial Finance Corporation (ICFC) aimed at MSMEs and the Finance Corporation for Industry aimed at large companies. In 1973 these two companies were merged into 'Finance for Industry' which was rebranded to 'Investors for Industry' in 1983 and privatised in 1994 as '3i'.

In the early years the MSME-focused ICFC jointly funded by the Commercial Banks and the Bank of England provided long-term fixed-rate finance to SMEs. Over the years it funded many companies. Amongst its success stories was Oxford Instruments. In the 1950s it was squeezed by commercial banks that saw it as both a cost and as a competitor, eventually leading it to establish a regional organisation to embed local knowledge. This framework allowed a 'hands-off' approach to management when things were going as per plan (along with some gentle advice) and more direct intervention if things went off the rails. As mentioned above, the two organisations merged in 1973 into Finance For Industry which was then able to access capital markets to raise its own capital. The 1974 recession saw a focus on earning shorter term returns through restructuring larger businesses.

The institution's old MSME work increasingly focused on high-technology ventures. By the late 1980s, 3i Ventures was a pariah to the more conservative 'Private Equity' focused group and it faded away especially in the lead up to privatisation in 1994. Merlin-Jones (2010) writes *'As soon as shareholders began to take a stake in the Corporation, they were given an incentive to exert pressure to raise immediate returns, which jeopardised the original principles of MSME funding'*.

Three other pre-2010 initiatives complete the picture: (1) the 1966 Industrial Reorganisation Corporation, funded by the state, was created to consolidate industries and was wound up in 1971; (2) the series of 'Small Firm Guarantee Schemes' which looked to give commercial banks security when they could not find it and (3) the allocation of Venture Capital Funds to Venture Houses by the European Investment Bank to help 'pump prime' the venture capital market.

From the failure noted by the Macmillan Committee in the 1920s through to the present, SME funding has been caught in a tug of war between bank and capital market actors claiming they have it covered. Limited state intervention has most recently focused on guarantees and limited venture capital investment and philosophical disputes between 'laissez faire' and 'interventionism'.

Repeated attempts have been made by the UK government to improve access to finance. The latest was to amalgamate a number of existing schemes to create a British Business Bank in 2014 (Parliament, 2014). Looking forward the British Business Bank with a suitable extension of its resources and mandate could both help mitigate the Brexit loss of current European Investment Bank venture capital and infrastructure funding and help free funding flows to MSMEs. Funding and further enhance lending and risk capital flows to MSME's.

> *The industry of the society can augment only in proportion*
> *as its capital augments.*[3]
> — Adam Smith (1776, Section IV, Chapter 2, para 13).

7.1.1. Proposition 1: Create New 'Family Silver' (to Sell at a Profit)

Economic growth requires capital expenditure in R&D, design, machines, software, etc. be combined with entrepreneurship and labour to produce new products sold to customers for a profit. The market signals which are the most attractive products and services to produce through the profit mechanism — the surplus of price over cost. Costs are fixed by how the product is created; prices are set by what the customer will pay and so represent Adam Smith's 'Invisible Hand' directing where resources are to be used. Figure 7.1 stylises Smith's Invisible Hand in its purest perfect competition setting.

Figure 7.2 relaxes one assumption and allows us to see the growth in some sectors and contraction in others as resources are reallocated, but still within a closed world where the overall economy is static, prices are stable and no new money is created. 'Rentiers' are interested in complementing successful entrepreneurs in investing in growing their businesses to compensate for the loss of income they will experience from the shrinking business. Overall resources are neither created nor destroyed in this set of assumptions, just reallocated to different markets.

---

[3]Smith goes on to say *'and its capital can augment only in proportion to what can be gradually saved out of its revenue'*. This statement holds true if the country is operating under the Gold Standard, but is not correct in a modern financialised economy where money is created by Banks in response to demand for loans (Bank of England, 2014) and credit/money creation is not restricted to a Gold Base or pseudo gold base (for example the Corset in the 1970s).

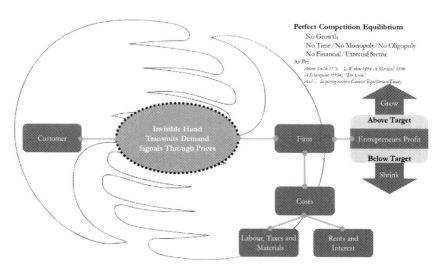

Figure 7.1.   Basic Invisible Hand Model. *Authors Note*: Graphic partially includes artwork derived from Vecteezy (2017).

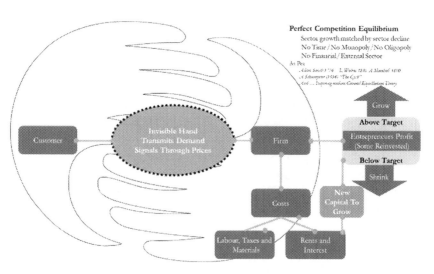

Figure 7.2.   Basic Invisible Hand Model with Resources Reinvested in Growing Sectors. *Authors Note*: Graphic partially includes artwork derived from Vecteezy (2017).

The equilibrium[4] condition in Figure 7.2 is as follows:

$$\text{Rate of Interest} = \frac{\text{Entrepreneurs Profit}}{\% \text{ on Capital}} = \text{Rent} \% \text{ on Land} = \frac{\text{Risk Adjusted} \%}{\text{Dividends on Capital}}$$

This equation is in effect another way of stating equilibrium in a simple economy at Wicksell's (1898) 'natural rate of interest'. Our next step is to add a financial sector. Drawing again on Wicksell (1898) together with Schumpeter (1934), Keynes (1936) and Minsky (1986) we add a very simple financial sector. Shortly after this, we will add a growth-and-credit model that will include Hahn's (1920) thinking in addition to those we have just named. Figure 7.3 adds this very simple financial sector in which the 'rentier' can allocate their funds to either support the company in its capital investment needs, or they can invest in second-hand real estate, second-hand equities or bonds or derivatives.

Adding a financial sector looks simple, but it fundamentally changes the model rules, as rentiers can now earn a return from two different sources: (1) dividends and rents and (2) capital gains on their assets. Take, for

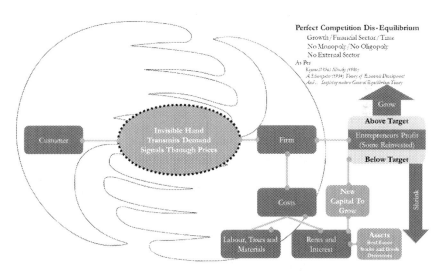

Figure 7.3. Basic Invisible Hand Model with Financial Sector. *Authors Note*: Graphic partially includes artwork derived from Vecteezy (2017).

---

[4]We could express these mathematically, but as we focus on innovation rather than economics we will express these relationships in text and leave formalising the full model until another day.

example, real estate — the rentier owns the asset or part of the asset, but they can now 'gamble' on the price going up if they think it is an attractive property in an attractive location. Keynes's (1936) speculative casino has been introduced to the model, and becomes pervasive because, implicitly by allowing asset markets into the model, we now introduce time into our model. The rentier has no idea how customers' tastes may change, so firms look fairly unsafe; therefore, maybe real estate or second-hand bonds look safer as they are promises to pay from a firm's currently known cash flow. We now have a cash leakage from the model where cash can go into second-hand assets and fail to fund the capital investment needs of firms.

We now move to include monetary growth to facilitate overall growth. For this we draw on Hahn (1920) and Schumpeter (1934) in seeing banks as 'credit allocators' rather than 'savings allocators'. This credit model matches current money creation in the UK and is explained in far more detail in Bank of England (2014). To summarise, money is an *endogenous* variable created by commercial banks in response to loan demand and *not* (with a single exception) an *exogenous* variable created by the Central Bank. The sole exception to this is Quantitative Easing, where the Central Bank creates money to buy bonds from the bond markets. The constraint on creating money lies in the relationship between the Commercial Bank risk assets and their regulatory capital. In our financing model this can either come from savings (mainly by the firm itself as it reinvests its profits) *and/or* increases in the money supply through additional credit extended to the firm.

Unfortunately, distortions arising from the Basel Capital Accords, political imperatives to support home owners and Quantitative Easing that has inflated bond and stock prices have meant funds that could have been used by MSMEs to fund capital investment have been misdirected by Banking System and political distortions into inflating asset prices relative to wages and salaries. As Smith (1776) makes clear, the Invisible Hand is much better than people at deciding which ventures should be invested in. Market distortions distort the work of the invisible hand.

Take, for example, UK Residential housing prices (a key asset price). These have risen as multiples of average wages for many years, as Muellbauer and Murphy (1997) state,

> *Theory suggests that financial liberalisation of mortgage markets in the 1980s should have led to notable shifts in house price behaviour. The evidence supports the predictions of theory, suggesting shifts took place in wealth effects, as in the consumption function, and that real interest rates and income expectations became more important.*

It is highly likely that the market will, at some point, force adjustment by reducing asset (for example house) prices until they align with cash flows supporting them.

This happened in 2008 in the United States, Spain and Ireland. It did not happen in the United Kingdom largely because of government intervention to protect the UK housing market, Government measures to stimulate demand (that led to ballooning public sector borrowing, Quantitative Easing and the very rapid drop in interest rates) during the final quarter of 2008. This combined with ultra-low interest rates, state pressure for lender forbearance, activist monetary policy to support residential mortgage lending and an active Help to Buy subsidy scheme averted a UK house price crash.

Asset prices that are out of line with incomes can lead to financial instability (Sufi & Mian, 2014). Affordability challenges for younger people with no inherited wealth from 'the bank of mum and dad' plus the rise of 'Buy to Let' has transferred wealth and financial opportunity from the younger to older generations and from the less well-off to the more well-off. It has also deprived many MSME firms of the vital credit they need to operate and grow, including some MSMEs that help in commercialising new innovations.

Bearing this in mind, we propose a mechanism to deliver financing to remedy overall MSME funding difficulties and improve lending and risk capital flows to MSMEs, and address Basel Capital Accord MSME distortions. Our scheme offers the opportunity to innovate how the UK government supports capital investment spending by both state and private sectors. Our suggestions greatly increase British Business Bank resources and create a structure to provide existing banking and financial sector actors with financial returns in return for contributing their credit expertise and maintaining MSME lending flows.[5]

At the heart of our proposal is a mechanism to reduce the risk capital penalty that Banks currently incur for MSME lending, through a nuanced (and long-term profitable to both state and lender) use of the 'credit mitigation' feature in the Basel Capital Accords. Figure 7.4 shows this suggested structure to improve finance flows into MSMEs. This structure seeds/replenishes an 'arm's length' state-owned fund to support capital expenditure through a dedicated state bond issue fully purchased and held by the Bank of England. The proceeds of the bond issue are flowed into the state-owned fund, but because the matching

---

[5]This proposal conforms to the Basel Capital Accords via Credit Risk Mitigation as set out in The FCA (2017b).

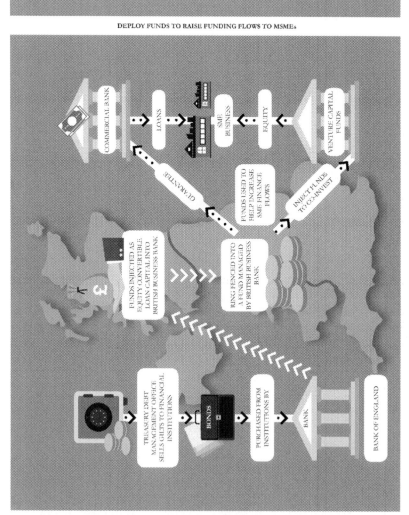

Figure 7.4.   Proposed MSME Funding Support Flow.

debt (as in Quantitative Easing) is held by the Bank of England, the creation of this fund does not distort existing capital allocations. The fund merely plugs a gap that is not currently covered.

Profits from income and successful investments being sold to the private sector are repaid the fund and are used by HM Treasury to redeem and cancel the bonds. In the long term the fund is targeted to make a profit to be paid to the Treasury after fully redeeming relevant bonds and contributing to appropriate reserves. Failed or failing investments will be exited as necessary and certainly by a defined date (a 'sunset' clause). This structure is similar to the one used in Germany and described in Box 7.3.

Unlike previous UK[6] attempts to address this issue, this solution (i) ensures the state is commercially financially compensated for its share of the risk (ii) structures the guarantees to make MSME commercial bank lending more profitable for commercial lenders and generate a higher relative rate of return on capital (a key bank measure internationally), (iii) incorporate private market discipline. Our structure[7] temporarily raises the state debt to GDP ratio but in the long term it reduces as the debt is repaid with profits and growth raises tax revenues.

7.1.2.   *Proposition 2: Link Public Procurement to MSME Innovation — Example: Use 'Block Chain' to Establish Event-triggered Payment System for MSMEs*

MSMEs face payment challenges on collecting outstanding debt from (often larger) customers. Sometimes, MSMEs resort to expensive invoice discounting to ensure their cash flow. Traditionally, sharp financial shocks see larger companies extend payment times to smaller suppliers and squeeze their own customers for early payment. Block chain technology allows payment to become event driven within the terms of the commercial contract (Box 7.4). Successful trials for

---

[6]Bossone, Cattaneo, Gallino, Grazzini, and Sylos Labini (2015) suggest something along the same lines for Italy.

[7]Such a structure is consistent with EU State Aid rules due to the block exemption for SME assistance under Commission Regulation (EU) N°651/2014 of 17 June 2014 (EuroLex, 2014) as updated and amended by Commission Regulation Commission Regulation (EU) 2017/1084 of 14 June 2017 (EuroLex, 2017). The increase in the GDP to state debt ratio may violate the Growth and Stability Pact in the Maastricht Treaty (non-binding) so incur and EU Commission comment, but the UK is not a signatory to the 2012 Treaty on Stability, Coordination and Governance in the Economic and Monetary Union (EuroLex, 2012) with its mandated limits.

Box 7.3.   The State as an Entrepreneur

Long before Mazzucato's, 2013 book, *The Entrepreneurial State*, Elizabeth I, faced with a depleted State Treasury and a dilapidated navy but both needing to protect England's borders and control piracy in the English Channel and, a foreign policy imperative to be strong in the face of an assertive Spain, adopted a policy of licensing Pirates to become Privateers. Elizabeth I was an investor in some Privateering expeditions. We are told by Keynes (1930) that she so profited from Drake and the Golden Hind plundering the Spanish Main that she paid off the entire national debt and still had £40,000 available, which she invested in the Levant company which subsequently became the East India Company that later led the conquest of India (Price, 2010) — the entrepreneurial state at work.

A more controversial example can be taken from the financial engineering of Hjalmar Schacht in the period 1934–1936 through the Metallugische Forschungsgesellschaft, a dummy corporation with a private structure that sold its debt (mefo bills) to the Reichsbank for Marks. The proceeds from the sale of the 'Mefo Bills' were used to fund German Rearmament in contravention of the 1919 Treaty of Versailles limit on state borrowing. By 1939 bills from the company accounted for around 39 per cent of German Government debt, indicating its importance to both German Rearmament and Germany's exit from the Great Depression. Figure B7.3 shows the impact on German GDP.

As a footnote to this episode, although Schacht was tried and acquitted of War Crimes at the 1946 Nuremberg Trials rearmament. The Second World War and the evil of the Holocaust make an objective assessment of 'mefo bill' financing impossible. Many Holocaust scholars see mefo bills as the backdrop that forced the criminal Nazi expropriation of Jewish assets; whilst Schacht in his Nuremberg Testimony (Schacht, 1946) is somewhat unconvincing,

> *Mefo bills, of course, were a thoroughly risky operation, but they were absolutely not risky if they were connected with a reasonable financial procedure and to prove this I would say that if Herr Hitler, after 1937, had used the accruing funds to pay back the mefo bills, as had been intended — the money was available — then this system would have come to its end just as smoothly as I had put it in operation.*

The historical lesson in our context — such methods of financing must have a clear and preannounced and monitored repayment path. No 'fudge' can be allowed.

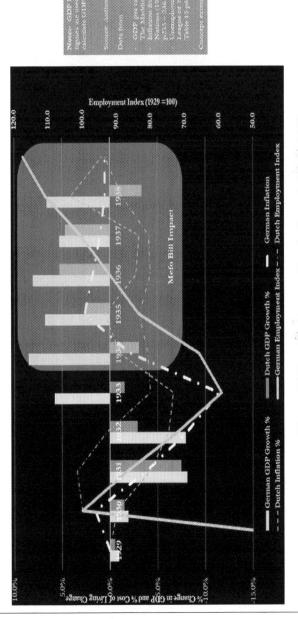

Figure B7.3.   German vs. Dutch Growth 1929–1938.

Box 7.4.   Block Chain and Payment

Much has been made of 'block chain' technology in the context of 'crypto-currencies' such as a 'Bit-Coin'. A more commonplace application has been under trial and development, which looks at using this technology to smooth and reduce the costs of international payments for MSMEs. Traditionally, an exporter needs to use some sort of internationally payment instrument such as a Documentary Letter of Credit, which assures payment from the importer's bank upon the presentation of the correct verified documents. These typically can include the Commercial Invoice, the Bill of Lading, the Certificate of Conformity and a copy of the original contract or order (although the document sets can change).

Payment is then instructed through the banking system in accordance with the instructions in the Letter of Credit. Overall the process is time consuming and costly to operate. Even without this process, relying on international bank transfers can be time-absorbing and more costly than a domestic sale. Enforcing payment in the case of delayed payment is also potentially costly and complex.

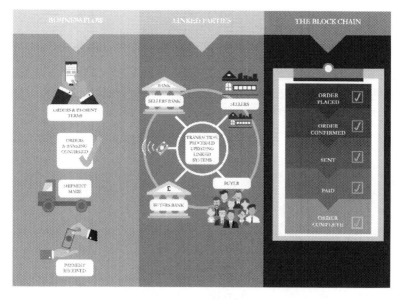

Figure B7.4.   Theoretical 'MSME Block Chain'.

Block chain, working on a distributed ledger system, can take a single supply chain event, such as shipment, and update the suppliers, customers, freight company, customs, banks and all other necessary parties in real time, thereby triggering a payment or delayed payment event. Every event in the business flow is validated against the systems of all the parties in the business relationship, upon confirmation all systems are updated as appropriate and a record added to the block chain to show the transaction was undertaken. In Figure B7.4 the authors have produced a very high-level concept example. In conception this is similar to a scheme suggested in the Breedon Review (BEIS, 2012, p. 28).

An order is placed by the customer on the seller and sets up the transaction in the customer, seller, seller's bank and buyer's bank. The order contains payment terms which are validated and confirmed by the buyer's bank, sending out a payment term confirmation message together with a delivery date confirmation message from the seller. A confirmation message is added to the block chain.

The shipment is made, validating the systems on the seller, customer and both buyer and seller banks. On successful validation, all systems are updated and a pending payment record set up in the seller and the seller's bank and a pending receivable set up in the seller and seller's bank (all records are maturity dated). A 'sent' message is added to the block chain. The Seller can still if it wishes "factor" the payment to improve its cash flow. Payment is received, validation made against all systems, the buyer bank debited, the seller bank credited, the customer payable cleared, the supplier receivable cleared and a block chain entry made. On completion of the order, all parties 'transaction records' are closed, and an order complete status added to the block chain.

Such a framework can operate nationally or internationally, provided all parties are accredited into the network. Being technical and commercial it benefits from not needing an international standard or treaty to enable early implementation, although in the long term undoubtedly a series of agreed technical standards and accreditation procedures will be developed.

a private community block chain[8] international payment system have been undertaken in 2016 by Belgian Lender KBC (KBC, 2016). This trial has now been extended to a consortium of seven banks (IBM Corporation, 2017). Government can speed the introduction of such a

---

[8]Private community blockchains are far more energy efficient than the more well known public ones, making them practical for commercial applications. (IBM, 2017)

private 'block chain' ledger system by requiring head contractors for government contracts to use the technology to pay their subcontractors.

Assuring payment is of course not something new, and we could view the letters from the members of the 'Merchant Adventurers' in sixteenth-century Antwerp as being the 'block chain' technology of the 1550s. Instead of computers, the Merchant Adventurers had accredited members and agents who relied on their network of trust and relationships to validate transactions and assure payment. For example, Thomas Stacey, a former warden of the London-based 'Mercers Company', was a well-respected Merchant Adventurer who based himself in Antwerp from 1544, so putting himself in the centre of the action to build the relationships and trust he needed to develop his business into Antwerp's continental hinterland. George Needham served as Stacey's apprentice and in about 1553 joined the Merchant Adventurers, able to trade English Cloth into Antwerp, on the basis of his relationship with Stacey. In block chain terms, validating him with Stacey allowed him to be authenticated by the Merchant Adventurers and to set up his own business and ledger system in Antwerp (historical detail from Ramsey, 1979).

7.1.3. Proposition 3: Create an MSME Banking Ombudsman Service

The sharp downturn in 2008 saw banks reduce lending and tighten loan terms to the MSME sector (BEIS, 2012a). Without the power of larger businesses to enter corporate bond markets, MSMEs face few banking options in the face of such changes. They can borrow from large customers, move from asset ownership to asset leasing, employ invoice factoring and they can reduce activity to deal with working capital losses. All such activities come at additional cost to the MSMEs and in some cases, apply additional barriers to opening export markets — for example when bid or performance bonds are required as the basis for contracting in specific markets. Equally there is hotly disputed evidence in reports such as the 'Tomlinson Report' (2013) about the alleged mis-selling of 'swaps to SMEs' and (now not contested following the January 2017 convictions) in the Lloyds/HBOS Reading Office MSME bank lending fraud. The disputed Tomlinson Report (2013) described how a clearing bank sought to move MSMEs with liquidatable assets into its restructuring operation, and then allegedly liquidated the business unnecessarily. Whilst hotly disputed, for an MSME it is unrealistic to assume that competition allows the MSME to easily switch lender when facing a cash crunch, wobbly bank support and a challenging economic situation. Power rests with the bank.

The current Financial Ombudsman Service allows investigation into complaints from micro business (below £2 million turnover and less than 10 employees). MSMEs would benefit from having a specialist Business Ombudsman Service, trained and attuned to MSME issues and capable of entering into dialogue with banks on disputed issue. An ideal 'home' for such a service would be within the UK Business Bank (which already has the detailed knowledge of existing UK MSME finance), with a covenant that would make the Ombudsman Office report independently into Parliament in the event the British Business Bank being privatised.

7.1.4. Proposition 4: 'Share the Problem and the Solutions'

Trouble never comes alone.

– Rusp (2017)

It seems to be an unwritten rule, that when things become challenging, everything seems to go wrong at once! Orders fall, customers delay payments, currencies change, banks go wobbly, suppliers press for payment and that is not to mention some R&D or product liability or litigation issue. Sometimes formally confident subordinates lose confidence and stop dealing with even the simplest of issues as they become unsure about the future of the business. Running a company in such a situation can sometimes feel like a daily 'near-death' experience (from the personal experience of one of the authors).

In 'near death' one always has the risk of two reactions: (i) *the ostrich* – head in the sand and hope it all goes away; (ii) *combine Atlas with a superhero* by taking the weight of the world on one's shoulders and trying to solve everything oneself. Large companies have non-executives to assist and usually some resources and market power to buy time to react. In a small company these are often missing, so at this point focus, teamwork, instilling confidence and both having a good idea of what is going wrong and a plan to solve it are crucial.

Dealing with crisis requires a different skill set from day to day chugging along. Many of the skills learned in chugging along can be adapted, which is why so many MSMEs survive Sudden Stop events. But adapting these skills can be challenging and painful, at a time when the learning by the 'trial-and-error' method is at its most risky. Even for a large company this can be very challenging. Failed mega-liths such as Polaroid, Kodak, Woolworths in the UK, Comet, etc.

demonstrate that even big companies will not always survive. Community and support which can provide important peer to peer support and shared learning in the face of shared challenges, can be delivered via local-themed networking events, perhaps facilitated by a local University. Such sessions should include both a formal presentation on a relevant issue and extensive informal networking. These types of event offer opportunities for two-way learning and communication, giving University Business Schools working with local Regional Development Agencies and Business Support Organisations together with MSME owners and managers gain the opportunity to come together, jointly learn and work corroboratively to overcome challenges. Adopting an 'Anchor Institution' to catalyse regional support and innovation networks (Culkin, 2016) would help focus a local gateway to facilitate this activity and to help channel and focus much-needed support resource.

Don't Forget the Need to Grow.

Near death inevitably takes the focus away from growth. Survival is not enough; there must be innovation and growth. There will always be some small practical things that can be done in the face of adversity. Competitor firms will not stop to wait for UK firms to catch up.

7.1.5. Proposition 5: 'Initiate an MSME-focused Exporting Program'

The Select Committee on Small and Medium Sized Enterprises was appointed by the House of Lords on 29 May 2012 with the terms of reference 'to consider the Government's assistance and promotion of the export of products and services by Small and Medium Sized Enterprises and to make recommendations' (Lords, 2012). Their findings were published in the first quarter of 2013 and their principal message was of positive opportunity, for two main reasons. First, the potential of British SMEs was huge; and, second, support for SMEs to help them export is extensive, with advice on how to begin exporting, exporting more effectively in known markets or entering new markets.

However, five years on such 'positive' words appear all the more important in the face of potential Brexit disruption to existing trading flows. New markets will need to be added, existing non EU market penetration will need to be deepened. Below are a few measures that may help.

1. *Build 'agent network' links in relevant markets.*
2. *Move MSME Export Guarantee Responsibility into the British Business Bank to allow a seamless set of products, whilst retaining 'functional' relationship with the Department of International Trade to ensure overall policy coherence.*
3. *Integrate export credit guarantees (including bid-and-bond guarantees) into proposed 'block chain' environment.*
4. *Decentralise export promotion initiatives into a regional framework (integrated into regional innovation hubs) that leverages national coordination and diplomatic resources.*
5. *Focus new industry export initiatives around building university, venture capital and scientific community links using British Council and Embassy facilitation, seeding with Development Aid where appropriate.*

One imagines that some of the Brexit challenges may be similar to those faced by English wool merchants selling in Antwerp in the 1550s. In the '1550s' context, a merchant needed to be connected to the market by means of a member of the Merchant Adventurers, a group that handled everything from making the sale through to arranging the finance (if required) and organising the shipping. Box 7.5 continues our narrative.

Box 7.5.   Plague in London, Closure of Antwerp and the 1564 Emden Adventure

Trade has historically depended upon building personal relationships; new trading locations and deals depend upon personal trust and mutual interest.

Turbulent relationships between England and Catholic Europe during the reigns of Hapsburg Phillip II and the English Queen Elizabeth I impacted the English wool trade through the port of Antwerp, a port located in the Catholic administered Netherlands, which in the early 1560s was being ruled by Margaret of Austria, Philip II's named Regent. Tension already existed between the Regent (Margaret of Parma) and the 'Burgers' of the Netherlands as Philip II had moved to centralise his power over that of the States General, extend the Catholic inquisition, direct tax levels. Antwerp as the main market for English wool was crucial to the Elizabethan economy, earning important foreign currency to fund England's appetite for especially luxury imports (for example, wine). In November 1563 Margaret closed Antwerp to English merchants on the pretext of a plague in London.

Faced with the closure of their gateway to Europe and the markets of the Hanseatic League, the English Privy Council were led to pick up an earlier proposal from Thomas Needham that trade be moved to Emden. Needham had for some years seen Emden as an alternative to Antwerp, and had already suggested this in a letter to the Queen in 1560. In 1563 Needham went to Emden and building personal relationships 'opened the door' for the English wool fleet to sail to Emden in 1564, thereby moving the wool market to Emden. The move was short-lived as Spain and England reached an accord to reopen the Antwerp market from January 1565. Emden had had its day as the sole English wool market, as when in December 1568 the Spanish Viceroy ordered the arrest of all English merchants in Antwerp the market subsequently moved to Hamburg, because Emden was judged to be too risky from a military viewpoint (Ramsey, 1979).

Perhaps a corollary to this fluctuating role for Antwerp (in the face of Hapsburg political and religious priorities) was the 'Dutch Revolt' and Eighty Years' War most commonly dated as starting in 1568.

Our example from Box 7.5 suggests that much can be done to grow trade by establishing effective trust and relationships, even in a world of political conflict. Personal relationships across boundaries can overcome political difficulty to make trade happen. Without these personal relationships, all the treaties in the world are unlikely to make trade grow, and building relationships does not need to work for Brexit day.

UK export support activities are run through UKTI,[9] including a website of potential opportunities, trade missions and local embassy functions supported by Export Credit Guarantees to the banking sector. It is easy to criticise initiatives in the export area, given the UK's large trade deficit and the somewhat limited listing of known export opportunities in some potential markets. Countries of the Gulf Cooperation Council (GCC) offer willing markets for UK goods yet there were only six opportunities for Saudi Arabia listed on the UKTI website (DOIT, 2017) on 23 July 2017 against 33 opportunities for the UAE despite Saudi Arabia being a far larger market. The Saudi opportunities were, in the main, suitable for larger end contractors. Access to the Saudi market for MSMEs (as in so many GCC markets) is normally through local agents

---

[9]UK Trade and Investments – part of the Department for International Trade.

being run by well-established local families. There is a network of local Saudi companies who specialise in taking agencies for foreign companies and developing the local market for their product. Perhaps facilitating connection to these agents would be more effective than a website listing.

This trust and relationship can already exist in the form of both educational and existing trading links along with the highly respected (globally outside the OECD) British Council. Business often comes through being introduced by trusted people with existing relationships.

Globally, there are significant gaps in building high intellectual content value-adding services and new media products. Each group of countries is different. For example, in the GCC there has been a huge investment in education with many people taking business, marketing or information technology degree-level courses in the West, especially in the United Kingdom. Equally as in the United Kingdom, high-quality job opportunities for new graduates are not as extensive as many would wish, yet there is opportunity to build licence and grow new business based upon the new skills these graduates acquire. This is fertile ground for post-graduation joint entrepreneurship projects sometimes using existing technology and selling it in new markets and sometimes developing new products and selling these in more than one market.

This is especially true in new media where, for example, Saudi Arabia has the highest YouTube usage in the world. For other countries with lower income per capita, huge agricultural sectors and widespread smart phone availability (East Africa, India, etc.), partnership opportunities exist to utilise local web technologies to facilitate technology transfer globally back to developed nations.

East Africa has, for example, a better smart phone payment system than much of the OECD with 'M-Pesa'. Equally GPS-linked crop management technologies and 'green power' technologies could have significant market possibility. In today's hyper-connected world, cross-border collaboration enabled by web infrastructure can flourish from targeted cooperation fostered by both universities and institutions such as the British Council, and indeed as a historic broadcasting 'gold standard', the BBC. This could be a great opportunity to use part of the foreign aid budget to foster cross-border trade and entrepreneurship.

Building links at all levels, professional, academic, development and trade and working in partnership with the British Council, enables far more localised information to become available on business opportunities, which can be integrated into the centralised UKTI, and can be shared regionally by the universities acting as local innovation hubs.

7.1.6.   Proposition 6: Kill Non-viable Firms

Additional access to finance, especially finance underpinned by state guarantee, carries both lender and borrower moral hazard. Building economic efficiency requires both building and growing new and existing firms and killing non-viable firms. Killing non-viable firms rapidly addresses the moral hazard issue.

The Weinstock GEC experience in Box 7.6 emphasises the importance of swift action in response to poor business performance. Many MSMEs do not have sophisticated in-house financial or business performance monitoring capability. As in GEC, a monitoring framework can

---

Box 7.6.   Lesson from a Master – Weinstock and GEC

By the 1990s one person who stood out in UK manufacturing was Lord Weinstock – who had taken GEC through a series of mergers and rationalisations to become an industrial giant in the defence and electronics industries. He made this journey in partnership with his Finance Director Sir Kenneth Bond (whom he insisted move with him to GEC in 1962). Together they evolved a simple set of management controls that allowed them to control over 100 diverse business units in a decentralised manner with minimal head office staff.

Using a series of simple ratios: return on capital, return on sales, sales as a multiple of capital employed, fixed assets and stocks, as well as sales and profit per employee reported on a monthly basis, operating units were controlled against the financial plan. Managers knew they had to be on top of their business as the knew that they could receive a probing phone call from Lord Weinstock on any day at any time. Legend amongst GEC employees in the early 1980s had it that failure to meet target for three months led to being 'on watch' and failure to deliver after a further three months meant almost certain intervention and probable management change.

The system which had a huge focus on cash generation was very successful and during the 1980s GEC became famous for its cash mountain. A key criticism at the time was that *'the external capital market was at least as efficient as internal allocation and that the centre did not add any value'* (Seal, 2010). In effect GEC head office in the Weinstock years had become the funder and behaved as an 'activist hands-on investor'.

Was Arnold Weinstock better at generating long terms operating returns than the market? His regime lasted over 30 years. How many activist funds can claim to have improved returns over such a long period without large-scale 'buying and reselling' businesses? Perhaps a good rival is the so-called 'sage of Omaha' – Warren Buffet. The last word goes to a former GEC employee and now financial director of a consultancy:

> *What was my focus as a senior manager? Daily cash performance and tight cost control. I have often wondered whether certain organisations no longer with us would still be here today if only they had benefited from Weinstock's approach to cash management, which helped the company prosper during the trials and tribulations of British industry in the 1970s and 1980s*
>
> – Morling (2011)

be injected by risk financiers in the form of non-executive directors and standardised regular reporting. Knowing there is divergence from agreed plan and knowing that this divergence is not being corrected become important warning signals to ask the question as to whether to 'kill the firm' and free resources for more productive activities. Ensuring that poorly performing firms face such consequence is key to limiting 'moral hazard' on both lender and borrower. Both lose when there is bad lending and both need to face their losses.

7.1.7. *Proposition 7: Accept that the Supply Chain Status Quo Must Change: UK Competitiveness Must Rise or UK Operations Risk Redundancy*

Challenged supply chains will require compensating rises in competitiveness; It is likely that Brexit will place cost pressures on complex supply chains as they face changes and possible non - tariff barriers. In the face of these challenges these challenged supply chains will require compensating rises in competitiveness. Some of this change in competitiveness may come from a fall in sterling but some will most likely need to come from a more effective and higher value-adding UK component. For this to happen overall UK Capital Investment and Innovation needs to rise.

The alternative? The Antwerp 1570s solution when faced with significant disruption to its markets and supply chains was to accept the changes that were happening around it.

The Port of Antwerp entered into decline as it lost its key international role of creating international markets and financing them (see Box 7.7). Post-Brexit faced with more customs formalities, tariffs, certificates of origin and proof of conformity, UK-sourced products will be less competitive (European Commission, 2017a).

Box 7.7.   Disrupted Supply Chains

Archaeological finds suggest that post-AD 410, Roman pottery supply chains progressively broke down (on a region-by-region basis) for all but the more luxurious items. Duggan (2016) examines the archaeological evidence for post-AD 410 pottery supply chains, and describes how following the breakdown of previous supply chains at around AD 410, new much more limited chains start to form in the mid-fifth century. These chains are new and different to previous ones, in that shipments come directly to the United Kingdom from the Eastern Mediterranean and not via North Africa or the European Atlantic Seaboard. Tintagel in Cornwall (the legendary supposed home of King Arthur!) has the highest number of finds for this trade, although other sites are scattered around the South West Coast with some limited evidence of inbound distribution.

What does this evidence tell us? The supply chains did not break because of a lack of latent demand, rather other evidence suggests that the combined loss of new Roman coinage plus the break down in markets broke the supply chains and associated trade. Supply chains can be broken and they can be broken catastrophically.

By contrast the English wool export trade survives the tribulations of Reformation and the Dutch Revolt even if its locus moves to a new location in response to evolving challenges. The difference?

In the sixteenth century the Merchant Adventurers (in the context of a supportive Queen and Privy Council) made it their business to develop and transform their relationships to maintain and grow trade through opening new market locations such as Emden and Hamburg. Supply chain continuity was maintained by removing the piece most prone to fail — in the context of the Dutch Revolt this was Antwerp.

As ever commercial self interest needs to align to broad market need before change can happen. George Needham tried to interest the English Wool Market in moving to Emden a number of times (not least to improve his own commercial position). With no success the first attempt; after a political scare that Antwerp may be shut in 1560, Needham recirculated a rewritten version of the 'Articles', this time written as a political tract addressed to Queen Elizabeth about the political dangers in Antwerp. Our entrepreneur was again out of step with the times, as Elizabeth was still an ally of the King of Spain then ruling Antwerp, and had no appetite to support moving the Wool Market at this time.

In consequence his suggestion fell on stony ground again but he was protected by friends at court (namely Cecil), so was able to live to fight another day. His time came in 1563 when Antwerp was closed to the English – now he had a solution to a real problem for his negotiating partners, and in 1564 the English Wool Market was held in Emden (detail from Ramsey, 1979).

Roll forward 450+ years and we see the same need for the entrepreneur to provide their negotiating partner with a solution not a problem. Bace (2013) describes how when she was a venture capitalist she met two entrepreneurs. They had a good product, and a good team; her VC was ready to invest – and then ... the entrepreneurs presented a huge unrealistic valuation, inflated sales numbers and presumably an equity split that was miles away from the VC's expectation. The deal had been killed by the entrepreneur. Personal experience (of one of the authors) has seen similar things on more than one occasion, where the entrepreneur presents an unrealistic deal. One trick can be (but not always!) to educate the entrepreneur how to signal that they want a deal that works for everyone. Maybe George Needham's friend helped educate him so he could finally taste success in 1563.

Tariff rises can be compensated by a fall in Sterling without matching increases in wages, pensions or other payments. 'Non-tariff barriers' are both more difficult to adapt for and likely to be more significant. Inventory levels will need to rise to mitigate customs clearance and associated potential port delay risks. Proving conformity is likely to require additional certification and Certificates of Origin may become more complex if they need to show accumulating local and

EU sourced content to enable access to preferential lower duty rates. Brexit implies uncertainty and operating margin pressures against a background of already internationally low levels of capital investment (OECD, 2015) threatening long-term competitiveness.

Could there be a way to transform the challenge into an opportunity? Could firms use the Brexit shock to raise investment and innovation levels, to produce next-generation products and leapfrog the competition? We suggest that Government can take three specific measures to encourage firms to 'leap frog' competition:

1. *Implement the 'access to finance' measures in Proposal 1.*
2. *Adapt the corporate tax system to raise tax incentives to invest and penalise companies that do not invest/use resources to fund share buybacks.* Aim to deliver the OECD-agreed 'floor' aggregate corporate tax rate of 15 per cent by blending a higher nominal rate of say 25 per cent with generous capital allowances, *reducing the effective tax rate on companies that invest* in plant, machinery, R&D and innovation *to an effective zero* for the 48 months after the date of investment.
3. *Adapt public procurement policies for innovative schemes/products to favour MSMEs by tendering MSME friendly packages rather than large prime contracts.*

7.1.8.   Proposition 8: Publicly Contract MSMEs to Build Block Chain-based Real-time Certificates of Origin[10] System

Comprehensive Certificates of Origin will likely be required as part of any 'standard' post-EU customs procedure and to prove local and EU content for duty calculation, especially where there is some claim to 'import preference' based upon either local or allowable cumulative EU content (assuming cumulation procedures are possible post-Brexit). Easy validation and proof of this content composition is likely to be essential. There is scope for procedural integration[11] into an

---

[10]DEXU (2017a) proposes something similar to one of its long-term customs arrangement options.

[11]An Authorised Operator Regime is a request in DEXU (2017a).

'Authorised Economic Operator'[12] regime that could offer considerable simplification and trust benefits. Shipment, declaration and origin validation could be enabled by combining ledger information with lot number tracking which is already in many cases, a global supply condition.[13] Private block chain technology allows such 'real-time' combination across customers, suppliers, logistics providers and customs authorities and can be combined with international electronic customs standards being developed under the UN/CEFACT umbrella.[14] Adopting a 'block chain' approach to generate a full electronic declaration, including origin validation based upon appropriately sealed containers using the 'TIR'-sealed transport procedure,[15] could then be linked to an inland customs clearance scheme allowing a 'wave through' at the ports unless (as is the case today) there is a specific reason to pull the shipment for inspection. Combining GPS container tracking could in addition to providing near real-time tracking trigger the customs transit entry at the point the container is detected as leaving the ship/plane.[16]

Such a system has potential for both commercial and trade flow benefits. Whilst taking time and investment to develop this could offer significant real-time information benefits, and could be adapted for resale worldwide.

Could this be an opportunity to use Public Procurement, as in our example in Box 7.8, to seed MSME innovation by assuring an end

---

[12]The Authorised Economic Operator regime originated from the 'World Customs Organisation' and has been available in the EU with associated 'security' amendments since 2008 under Regulation (EC) 648/2005 according to the European Commission (2017b). The EU Repeal Bill (Parliament, 2017) will not cover this as the regime requires 'Mutual Recognition' both to the EU and by implication to the United States, Japan, China, Switzerland and Norway where current recognition is accessed via the EU (EUOJ, 2012).

[13]For example, appropriate product traceability (in the context of managing product quality issues) is referenced in the latest standard: ISO/TS *16949:2016* − an industry-specific tailored version of ISO 9001 'Total Quality' management (AIAG, 2017). The degree of subcontractor enforcement on lot traceability is left to the contracting parties.

[14]See for example the Extension of Cross Industry Technical Artefacts Project (UNCEFACT, 2017).

[15]DEXU (2017a) makes reference to the TIR procedure, a procedure the United Kingdom is already signed into.

[16]An alternative to GPS is to use either 'Near Field Communication' as used in mobile phone contactless payment systems or 'Radio Frequency ID' (RFID) as currently used in Oyster Cards in London.

Box 7.8.   Innovation and Business from Government Contracts

US spy agency, the CIA, funded a small company named 'Keyhole Inc' in February 2003 from its non-profit Venture Capital Arm Q-Tel to develop cyber views online (The CIA, 2012). Keyhole created 'Earthview' that combined geographic data and satellite imagery into a 3D view that allowed users to 'fly' over and into terrain digitally. One minute in outer space, the next zoomed into a specific street location. Adoption was rapid, with TV stations being civil-use early adopters as they reported the 2nd Gulf War. Before long Keyhole was being more widely noticed, and in October 2004 Keyhole was acquired by Google. Its core technology became the base of Google Earth … and after this the history is well known.

---

market for such a system? A known end market helps enable confidence to bring in venture. Just as in our example, could the creator of the successful scalable system eventually be sold to one of the UK industry big players to help freshen their product range and gain global marketing reach whilst earning a health return for entrepreneurs and investors?

The benefits?

The entrepreneurial approach avoids the expensive and complex public procurement procedures, reduces State contracting risks (time, specification and overruns) often associated with huge government IT contracts by moving development risk to the venture capital-funded entrepreneur(s). In compensation for bearing the risk, the entrepreneur and their backers can market the system globally and so gain the 'super-rewards' success should bring. It is a new way to contract publicly to support and grow an innovative technology sector — a twenty-first-century 'Merchant Adventurers' approach.

7.1.9.   Proposition 9: Follow in the Footsteps of 'Economic Miracle' Countries to Establish 'Innovation Contracts' that Blend Public and Private Sectors

> *No one should be discouraged [....] who can make constant progress, even though it be slow.*
> *– Plato (Sophist 261b 360 BC from Fowler, 1921)*

Change is a constant feature in the modern world, products come and go and industries rise and die. Change is continual, with competitive advantage being built and shifting as new products and technologies emerge. David Hume (1742) is clear that competitive advantage changes and adapts to new circumstances:

> *There seems to be a happy concurrence of causes in human affairs, which checks the growth of trade and riches, and hinders them from being confined entirely to one people [...] Where one nation has gotten the start of another in trade, it is very difficult for the latter to regain the ground it has lost; [....] But these advantages are compensated, in some measure, by the low price of labour [...] Manufactures, therefore gradually shift their places*

Trade benefits flow from continual innovation and capital investment that builds and grows competitive advantage.

No product lasts forever. The move to electric cars where electric motors replace complex internal combustion engines implies significant component industry changes, as old components become obsolete and new ones are needed. Sherefkin (2009) reports that automotive manufacturers have faced challenges building electronic cars as new parts and in some cases new capabilities are required from parts suppliers. Early Brexit-induced loss of market has potential to 'kick start' innovation and adaption in impacted industries, so leapfrogging competing nations.

David Hume's description of the evolution of competitive advantage demonstrates we need to build competitive advantage rather than assume it permanently exists. R&D in universities is not enough on its own (especially when there is overstress on the R of basic research that is not matched by the D of Development and Application). Venture capital on its own is not enough. Knowing the market on its own is not enough. Top flight management on its own is not enough. 'Realised innovation' requires a complex and ever-evolving blend of these components. We turn to measures to support this. Measures that are additional to and not a substitute for the proposals we have already made, especially proposals on access to finance. Box 7.9 discusses how opportunities can fail to launch.

Brint (2017) talks of 'Academic Innovationism' as a component in new global products. He finds that for the top 50 global innovations[17] from 1955 to 2005, university researchers played a key[18] role in 40 per cent of these.

---

[17] The top 50 innovations are identified from a panel vote held by the magazine *Popular Mechanics*.

[18] *'Central figures of very important figures'* (Brint, 2017).

Box 7.9. '**Opportunity Knocks**'

History is full of missed opportunity, inventors who failed to connect to markets, and 'robber barons' who seized inventions from impoverished inventors (for example, Charles Goodyear, the inventor and patentee of vulcanised rubber, who died after having tried and failed to defend his 'vulcanising' patent in the United Kingdom against Thomas Hancock).

Inventions like the Linear Induction Motor, first conceived in the 1840s by Charles Wheatstone at Kings College, London), developed into a working model in 1935 by German engineer Herman Kempner and into a full-size working prototype during the 1940s by Eric Laithwaite (Imperial College London), gathered dust waiting to grow commercially. Whilst the linear induction motor has some limitations compared to conventional motors, it is well adapted for 'mag lev' travel – where the vehicle is propelled on a magnetic field – hovering over the ground. It is very silent, and because there is no contact with the rails, it is able to run in any weather conditions.

Commercialisation had by the 1960s been picked up by a German funding programme with an aim to implement a 'Maglev' rapid transit system train in Canada. By the mid-1970s the German funding stopped, the Canadians refused to replace the funding and the train became a rubber-wheeled contact train powered by a linear induction motor. The development was undertaken by a state-owned company and eventually sold to Bombardier who marketed the technology for metros and urban rapid transport systems especially in the far east. Which brings us into the current Millennium where the 'Maglev' dream of levitated trains with capability to achieve very high speeds and very low levels of maintenance have been launched in China, Japan and Korea. Work is under way for such a train in the United States.

Graphene, a ground-changing material discovered in a British University (Manchester 2004) by immigrants (Nobel laureates Geim and Novoselov), is a one-atom-thick carbon-based material capable of being manufactured for use in numerous applications. Novoselov et al. (2012) explain, its

> *mechanical stiffness, strength and elasticity, very high elec-*
> *trical and thermal conductivity, and many others – are*
> *supreme. […] that all these extreme properties are*
> *combined in one material means that graphene could also*
> *enable several disruptive technologies. The combination of*
> *transparency, conductivity and elasticity will find use in*

flexible electronics, whereas transparency, permeability and conductivity will find application in transparent protective coatings and barrier films and the list of such combinations is continuously growing.

Global excitement has grown since the 2004 discovery, with substantial development (application and research) efforts under way in China, the United States, and Japan. In 2013 it was reported that in respect of Graphene Patents China has 30 per cent of the total, the United States 23 per cent, South Korea 15 per cent and the United Kingdom with only 54 patents − less than 1 per cent. Of course, the 54 UK patents may be the crucial ones that enable commercial products. Geoffrey Clifton Brown (House of Commons, 2014) posed to Parliament that the United Kingdom *'put £50 million into developing the product, yet the South Koreans put £190 million in and the Europeans are putting in £1 billion. This invention will transform most electrical products and most people have never even heard of it'*.

Professor Jones (Graphene Council, 2014) emphasises that whilst the basic discovery is a scientific breakthrough, development through to product application is driven by market need. Jones sets out three possible commercialisation models (whilst acknowledging there can be more). A university can register the IP and then participate in a venture capital-funded spin out; it can license the technology or it can work collaboratively to develop the technology.

Crucially Brint (2017) finds:

Academic researchers were not highly concentrated at the top 50 world universities, but rather were spread over a wide range of universities. Nor were their contributions limited to early stage (or downstream) research, but instead were distributed throughout the early and refining stages of research, as well as in development activities.

Commercial success requires a process to blend and integrate diverse capabilities: *innovation, research, development, market vision, risk finance, management capability and practical routes to prototype and abilities to reach the market* into a working paradigm to drive the resulting commercialised product into one of the top two slots globally in each of the evolution of stages for specific market areas (Welch, 2001).

Germany, Japan, Taiwan, South Korea, China — all have at some time over the past 80 years been viewed as 'Economic Miracles'. One thing these models have in common is that state/quasi-state institutions and private sector work together collaboratively to drive growth. Public and quasi-public institutions act to support and facilitate growth that is driven and led by the private sector, albeit a private sector that may be driven by large firms who then drive change whilst providing financial stability in their sectors.

7.1.9.1. Fraunhofer and the German Mittlestand

Many German 'Mittlestand' companies sit within complex (especially within the automotive industry) supply chains, and innovate in partnership with their customers and the state through both geographical clustering and the Fraunhofer Institute programme. The Fraunhofer institutes, (founded in 1949), focus on 'applied research' — that is transforming basic research into usable technologies. This research can often be in partnership with SMEs, SMEs who have sometimes (especially in the automotive sector) been encouraged to undertake this research by their customers.

For example, Simboli, Raggi, and Rosica (2015) look at realised innovation in producing a motorcycle spindle and demonstrate how innovation depends upon working across all partners in the supply chain: *'geographical proximity and the presence of ties that enable the sharing of knowledge and facilitate the creation and the diffusion of innovative products and technologies'*. The innovation is also (they acknowledge) enabled by *'a different surface treatment that involves the PECVD'*, a technology championed by Fraunhofer FEP (FEP, 2017).[19] It is a whole ecosystem linked to both the university sector for research and to customers for market need.

There are 69 Fraunhofer institutes that are specialism focused, but that cluster into alliances to satisfy specific market needs. Over seventy percent of Fraunhofer funding comes in the form of contracts for public / private research. Defence projects at €127m are a minor part of the overall work. The balance of non-contract funding comes from EU and state grants. The €2 billion+ p.a. organisation employs over 24,000 people (Fraunhofer, 2015). By contrast Innovate UK has a wider focus and about 50 per cent of the budget (c. €940 million including

---

[19]It is unclear whether Fraunhofer was directly involved or licensed technology in this area (Simboli et al., 2015, credit help from Cometa Group S.p.a towards their article but they do not reference PECVD in their process). The connection is made to show relevance of technologies.

c. €280 million non-core budget funding). Unlike in Germany all this funding comes from the state – comparing like for like, German and EU state funding to the Fraunhofer institutes is around €1,200 million.

7.1.9.2. DARPA in the United States

By contrast, the US agency DARPA (founded in 1957 after the Sputnik launch to promote defence innovation) contracts private companies to develop new technologies across 250 programmes (DARPA, 2017). Two key elements in its success are its willingness to contract to SMEs (who may have the best innovation skills) whilst managing the programmes with programme managers rotated in from industry and research institutes on a 3- to 5-year cycle (long enough to be effective, short enough to have up-to-date knowledge). This cross-fertilisation not only brings government industry and research skills but also embeds innovation back into industry and research institutes. Its budget is about €2.5 billion. DARPA has had many successes including the precursor to the GPS (Global Positioning System). An example of innovation within this model is given in Box 7.8 regarding 'Keyhole Technologies'.

The Fraunhofer experience, DARPA and the dynamics of innovation within complex supply chains share a number of characteristics.

1. Innovation, especially MSME innovation (where the company's in-house resources are limited), requires on open approach to sharing between different partners. (This is reinforced in the findings in a compilation of studies on SME innovation; Spitzley, Rogowski, & Garibaldo, 2007.)
2. Needs come from the market, from the end customer or from the OEM customer in a complex supply chain and it is the needs that drive the scientific application.
3. Proximity, horizontal and vertical clustering make important contributions – informal contacts to firms in the geographical or virtual proximity – networking combine with contacts into players and institutions in similar spaces (horizontal clustering). Equally contacts across the supply chain, from end customer through to the base material suppliers (vertical clustering) all add value.
4. The state can play key 'trigger' and 'access to finance' roles, but the way in which it does depends upon local culture and tradition. Fraunhofer is very different from DARPA in organisational terms, but in their own way they are both very effective.

For the United Kingdom, with top flight global research universities, there is an opportunity to evolve a UK DARPA-type model led by Innovate UK (we will be expanding on the DARPA theme in a complimentary context in the next chapter). The model should copy the Fraunhofer model of part-state, part-industry funding. In funding the 'D' or development of R & D, don't forget the 'R', basic research – make sure this is fully funded via academic funding channels. Encourage companies to place innovation support contracts or funding with Innovate UK through a 200 per cent tax credit as an offset to taxable profit in the current tax year corporation tax bill. This (i) incentivises funding source diversity and binds innovation closer to market needs, (ii) increases innovation resources and (iii) provides a focus for commercialising great British research. Executing the innovation should be by Innovation Contracts awarded on merit only. Other gender-, age- or minority-related objectives need to be handled by additional grant and support schemes to give special help to these groups. Don't mix apples and pears.

Each innovation contract needs to carry deliverables and be tightly monitored for delivery. Where a contract is for a product enabler, the contract should allot shares to Innovation UK so the State (via Innovation UK) can participate in the value they enabled in any later roll out to market. Where it is to develop intellectual property, establish standard published clauses on intellectual property creation, licensing and ownership and allow no exceptions. A frequent complaint with Fraunhofer regards the delays in signing contracts. In many cases these delays are due to disputes on how generated intellectual property is to be owned. In a fast-moving world, being late to market is a serious threat to reaping the rewards of successful innovation. If negotiating and splitting the potential rewards from the intellectual property to be created proves highly contentious, pilot the split over the initial contracts and then evaluate the experience.

Managing the contracts needs to be grounded in the real world, so mimicking the DARPA technical staffing approach of seconding project managers/sector champions from universities, research charities and large manufacturers on a 3- to 5-year cycle should be affirmed. Encourage these secondments to be seen as career steps towards consideration for senior roles in their host organisations and super-reward delivery wherever possible. These staff are the 'catalysers' – they have the market feel, the technical feel and act to focus contracts onto growth areas. Contracts should carry an MSME preference, and matching MSME funding for the contracts should be facilitated by the British Business

Bank through its sponsored outlets such as venture capital and commercial banks. Equally, Innovate UK should 'up-skill' venture funds and other specialist capital providers by funding 'seconded' (possibly from universities, from charities such as the Welcome Trust or from large manufacturers such as GSK or Rolls Royce) research posts into UK-focused funds to build in-depth technical capability. For example, funds specialising in biotechnology need to understand developments and trends in the basic science and the product futures trends in manufacturers.

Innovate UK works in a 'Civil' space and should not cross into the defence area. Security, Prime Contractor, NATO interoperability and other considerations mean defence innovation should be handled under a separate stream, albeit if the need is felt, such an organisation could 'structurally' mirror Innovate UK and give MSME innovators access to funding via specific security-cleared venture funds supported by the Business Bank. Such a defence innovation framework should offer an effective opportunity to put UK 'offset' entitlements to innovative use. Subject to security considerations, there is every reason to have some form of informal liaison between the defence and civil innovation catalysers to see if areas of mutual interest exist.

7.1.10. Proposition 10: Build the Venture Capital Exit Chain

A great innovative MSME sector cannot sit on its own; it needs to support great global companies who have the scale, resources, market reach and inter-connection to drive innovations globally. Very few start-ups reach the IPO stage where they list on the stock market, and even fewer reach the global role of a Google, Apple or Facebook. Some innovative high-growth MSMEs do end up being acquired and then forming the backbone of further global business expansion.

For entrepreneurs, acquirers' and investors' exit can offer an attractive way forward (Box 7.10). Cumming and binti Johan (2008)

Box 7.10.   Lasik Eye Surgery from SME to Global Presence

For many, the late 1990s saw the introduction of a welcome innovation — Lasik eye surgery that (within medical limits) adjusts myopic vision in a simple procedure and absolves the person of the need to wear glasses or contact lenses. In 1991 Hansa Research and Development Inc, a small company based in Florida, had the FDA approve the enabling technology, an 'automatic corneal shaper'

(FDA, 1997). In 1992 this company entered an exclusive supply agreement with Chiron Vision, a supplier of surgical eye products (Bausch & Lomb, 1999). In 1997 the FDA approved the Hansa Research and Development Inc Keratome into the market (FDA, 1997), thereby enabling rapid expansion of Lasik Surgery. By 1999 when Chiron Vision was acquired, together with Hansa Research and Development Inc by global eye care giant Bausch and Lomb. At that time 8 out of 10 machines enabling refractive surgery worldwide had been made by Hansa Research and Development Inc (Bausch & Lomb, 1999).

A small company that grew first by an exclusive marketing agreement was then acquired into a global eye care giant.

examined 223 companies across 11 countries and found that in 31 per cent of cases the exit had been pre-planned; exit was identified before the investment was made and the bulk of these were trade sales. Quality Venture Capital is not only patient and long term, but also awake to the exit opportunities. Equally, for large companies sometimes it can be more productive and more cost-effective to buy companies with successful technologies that can be integrated into the overall corporate structure to strengthen its product portfolio and utilise its corporate global sales and distribution footprint. These links can be quite sophisticated, sometimes with large companies co-investing in promising technologies, sometimes with specialist funds looking to invest across competing technologies to treat a specific condition − so they can profit from whichever technology establishes itself in the market.

Entrepreneurs can be unrealistic in their expectations. Many of them believe that they will be (and tell whoever will listen) the next superstar. They have little understanding as to the time and resource commitment that each funding round can imply, and in almost all cases are paranoid about losing control. From experience, it takes enormous patience and commitment to mentor and teach the entrepreneur that a deal must work for all parties. A venture capitalist will most likely be more than happy that the entrepreneur run the company on a day-to-day basis, provided all is going reasonably closely to plan, but a venture capitalist will require 'step-in' rights whereby he or she can intervene if the business is going off the rails. To build understanding and venture capability, we suggest courses and workshops are held to help entrepreneurs understand the importance of exit, deal structures, and understand the financial return venture capitalists and the control venture capitalists need to protect their investments. Perhaps there is scope to develop 'best practice' principles for how the venture capital/entrepreneur relationship will be structured. Both entrepreneur and venture capitalist need each other, so this needs to be a win−win not a win−lose relationship.

7.1.11.   *Proposition 11: Make it Worthwhile Patenting*

> *Look inward. Don't let the true nature or value of anything elude you.*
> — Aurelius (AD 167)

Some claim that the rate of patenting demonstrates the rate of innovation whilst various studies suggest that (i) patenting is used for many reasons − competitive posturing (licensing and avoiding litigation), employee motivation, tax management and innovation protection amongst many (Holgersson, 2013) and (ii) SMEs can opt for secrecy rather patenting (Hughes & Mina, 2010). The great majority of patents are filed by large companies (Freitsch, Neuhäusler, & Rothengatter, 2013) who have a higher chance of their patents being accepted than MSMEs. Most MSMEs tend to patent domestically rather than globally and are adept at using alternative strategies such as secrecy to protect their innovations (Holgersson, 2013). There is a sectoral differentiation − High-Growth SMEs outside high-technology sectors seldom use patenting whereas High-Technology MSMEs make far more extensive use of patenting, not primarily to protect product innovation, but mainly to help raise venture capital. Financial markets and investors thereby valuing patents more than entrepreneurs (Holgersson, 2013).

Allison, Lemley, Moore, and Trunkey (2003) undertook a study of nearly 3 million patents granted between 1963 and 1999 to determine what the value of a patent is. They also studied every litigation case (4,247 cases involving 6,861 patents) across these patents. They found that there are two distinct segments to the patent universe. First, the great bulk of patents are made up of patents that are not litigated and tend to include fewer patent claims than the litigated ones. The second group is the litigated patents that tend to have different characteristics (more claims, more citations, and to be in specific industries such as bio pharma, medical device, computers − high-technology industries). Allison et al. assert that litigation indicates that the patent has significant financial value to a company, a view that corresponds with others who see the number of patent citations as indicative of their importance (litigated patents have, on average, more than double the number of non-litigated patent citations).

These 'litigated' patents look like some of the key product 'technology-enabling' patents. They litigate more, litigate earlier in the patent life, have more patent claims, are generally owned by individuals or smaller companies and they are classically in high-growth disruptive industries. Drawing patents up and defending patents are expensive activities.

In Box 7.11 we see how an MSME fought a major industry player, and although we do not know the legal fees we can be confident these

---

Box 7.11.   Hepatitis C Diagnostic Kit – Innogenetics N.V. vs. Abbott Labs

2005 saw Belgian-based SME Innogenetics N.V. launch a patent suit against Abbot Laboratories in respect of its patented Hepatitis C Diagnostic Kit. The suit ran for 3 years until 2008 when it was settled through a licensing deal between Abbot and Innogenetics. During this time there were a number of judgements. First in 2006 a District Court decision that ordered Abbot to pay Innogenetics US$7 million and found that Abbot had been 'wilful' in infringing the Innogenetics patent. Subsequently, the District Court issued an injunction against Abbot selling its detection kits, denied Abbot a retrial and reversed its finding that Abbot had been 'wilful' in infringing the Innogenetics patent. Innogenetics appealed this judgement that Abbot had not been 'wilful' in its infringement (US Appeal Court, 2008).

In 2008 the Appeal Court (i) found the patent had been infringed and (ii) set aside the Innogenetics argument that the US$7 million represented infringement for prior damages and therefore it needed an injunction to stop future sales. Rather it argued that the US$7 million was a payment for past and future sales and removed the injunction. The corollary was a US$9.5 settlement that covered the standing US$7 million fine plus additional unspecified costs (Reuters, 2008) – so we can only guess the legal costs, but they are likely to have been significant (Llobet & Suarez, 2012).

Subsequently in 2008 Innogenetics was purchased by Sandol, who were in turn purchased by Abbot Laboratories in 2009, and then Innogenetics was sold on to Japanese Diagnostic Company Fujirebio in 2010 for €83 million. Abbot Laboratories is now a major supplier of Hepatitis C diagnostic kits (Abbot Labs, 2017).

will have been substantial. Much has been written about the need to patent new inventions. Primary focus in the EU has been on having a 'Community Patent' that is easy to apply for, but rather less has been written about the need to have an easy way for MSMEs to enforce patents or to defend against spurious infringement patent suits. The whole area is fraught with difficulty along with the normal moral hazard issues associated with any insurance product. Patenting by its very nature is highly technical and highly specialised, especially when drawing up a patent that is rightly innovative, but that is close to other patents with competing claims (part of the legal argument in the case cited in Box 7.11).

For an MSME to be able to meet (potentially) millions of pounds in legal fees to defend a patent is unrealistic. When the EU Commission studied this area, they found that (i) due to patent due diligence costs and too small a risk pool, there is no effective commercial market in Patent Litigation Insurance; (ii) any practical scheme would require compulsion (to increase the risk pool) and involve premiums of just over €800 per patent per year for €500,000 of cover with an excess of €10,000 Euro (CJA Consultants, 2006). Even at €0.5 million this is not sufficient to underwrite patent suits that may cost maybe 2 or 3 million Euro. Equally the average cost of drawing an average patent was nearly €30,000 (EU Internal Market 2006) and no doubt substantially more if one is dealing with one of the complex 'High Tech Entrepreneurial SME Patents' that is most likely to be litigated.

But ... venture capital, acquiring large companies and investors often see well-drawn and defendable patents as fundamental elements in establishing a business's value.

Clearly, it is a market failure (there is no market), with the opportunity for a measured public intervention that will support the relatively few high-technology patents that are likely to be litigated whilst avoiding cost penalties on MSMEs involved in patenting the overriding volume of less critical patents and avoiding the moral hazard of giving large well-resourced a free ride into litigating their patent portfolios.

We propose:

1. Link patent assistance to Innovation UK innovation contracts, with each contract including a contract allowance of up to £100,000 to pay for the best possible drafting of the patent(s). To avoid price gouging the patent could only be drawn up by a firm already participating in a 'pre-agreed discount fee schedule' with Innovate UK. Thereby MSMEs benefit from access to Innovate UK consolidated

bulk buying power to create a patent that supports venture capital investment. In return, the MSME will be required to grant some notional amount of its equity to Innovate UK so Innovate UK can participate in any value generation.

2. For patents drawn under Innovate UK innovation contracts, support these with access to a £250 million litigation fund.[20] In return for paying 100 per cent of the (uncapped) fees on defending these patents over the first 5 years of their life, the fund should receive 90 per cent of the proceeds of any court damages and 100 per cent of court-awarded fees along with 25 per cent of the proceeds of the first 5 years of licensing deals related to defending these patents.

3. For litigation outside the United Kingdom, Innovate UK should retain a minimum of two top litigation firms (maybe more) in each relevant jurisdiction (especially the United States) on a retainer and shared profit basis to minimise overseas legal costs.

4. Long-term proceeds from Innovate UK liquidated shareholdings are to be credited to the UK Treasury.

With no historical data the £250 million should be written off on injection, although it is highly unlikely that this will represent a 'real' loss. Most likely (i) knowing there will be fully resourced litigation will act as a deterrent to potential infringers (who will look for a license deal instead) and (ii) proceeds from litigation and licensing should more than recover the fund.

7.1.12.   Proposition 12: Raise Management Competence

Next week there can't be any crisis. My schedule is already full.

— Henry Kissinger (1969)

Growing globally competitive businesses requires appropriately skilled management. Entrepreneurial management skills are not the same as big business management skills. Larger organisations have much more substantial support structures, with a much higher level of functional specialisation. By its nature entrepreneurship is about 'Leaping the Chasm' and avoiding the gap in the middle, and high-growth

---

[20]In practice, the existence of such a large litigation fund should put off all but the most serious litigator.

entrepreneurship is about catching the 'tiger by the tail'. Chaos threatens at every turn. 'Hands-on' operational control needs to be combined with strategic excellence, and most likely consultants, advisers, retired businessmen acting as 'hobby non-executive directors' will be ill equipped to help. Days are never long enough and keeping appropriate focus is one of the greatest challenges.

Negotiating skills and understanding venture capitalist needs would, from experience, be great components for a training program for entrepreneurs who want to approach venture capital markets for the first time. Box 7.12 shows the need for a 'win−win' approach to raising venture capital. Bace (2013) rightly refers to a relationship with a venture capitalist as being necessarily long term, built on trust and mutual respect, a fair sharing of risk and reward and a commitment to working together to make the business work. Equally surprisingly many budding entrepreneurs are amazingly financially illiterate and financially naïve. Understanding the financial consequences of operating decisions, making plans and making sure there is enough cash in the bank to keep the business running is another great candidate for training.

It's amazing how many business plans are presented for a venture capital raise without a basic forward cash flow. Some venture capitalists remedy this by requiring an authenticated 'feasibility study' from a top accounting practice. An expensive process that obviates the entrepreneur from the responsibility of knowing and owning their own forecast. Linked to this are weaknesses in understanding the market dynamics

---

Box 7.12.   Win−Win and Venture Capitalists

Experience can be a cruel leveller and experience can demonstrate how different communities have different expectations when it comes to establishing a business partnership. Cliff edges exist in all negotiations − make-or-break points − where overcoming them requires three enablers: trust, flexibility and a desire to make it easy for the other party to agree to terms that you yourself would find acceptable. Many try the 'caveman' negotiating strategy that seeks to find who can find a bigger piece of rock to beat the other party to submission. Civilisation has, one hopes, moved on from the 'caveman' strategy. Negotiation skills can be learnt and are, from experience on both sides of the funding table, a skill that budding entrepreneurs need to learn.

and how to demonstrate the products' features, its route to market and its price positioning/revenue model make sense – more opportunities for training.

One key challenge in a new rapidly growing business is knowing when to say, *'Help I don't know what to do'*. Training about when to call for the fire brigade is as important as knowing how to put out a small fire. Leave it too late and what is a fairly minor concern can mushroom into something altogether more challenging. These few examples are the tip of a very large iceberg containing an extensive range of subjects ripe for entrepreneurial 'up-skilling'. Regulation, quality management, international trade, human relations and many more are ripe for training programmes tailored to fit entrepreneurial needs and that it is not 'one size fits all'.

Entrepreneurs have very tight time constraints so every support needs to add value in their busy lives. Those around entrepreneurs such as non-executive directors need to adapt their skills to an MSME setting. MSMEs need sympathetic wise ears from people who have hands-on experience with the challenges they face. Some organisations have tried to cover this gap by employing an 'Entrepreneur in Residence', but for the potential superstars a non-executive team needs to complement the entrepreneur and their support team, helping discern focus, providing a repository of experience and wisdom, opening doors, fielding some of the investor concerns. The MSME non-executive needs to be strong enough to say 'stop and think' to some very headstrong entrepreneurs when it's needed, which can be far more challenging than in some public quoted companies! This role also needs training and support.

7.1.13.   Proposition 13: Give Control of Immigration to the Market and Up-skill the Indigenous Workforce through Vocational Training

Immigration has been at the heart of the debate concerning Brexit. Why?

Immigration levels have been a top issue with over 75 per cent of the UK population wanting to see immigration reduced. Concerns are slightly higher about non-EU migrants than with EU migrants. Migrants looking to unify with spouses are marginally more unpopular than economic migrants but all classes are unpopular, although there has been a shift over recent years to seeing migrants as helpful to the economy. Data is skewed so that migration is relatively more unpopular in places with few migrants compared to multi-cultural metropolises such as London. Personal relationships with migrants can change opinions. Opinions seem polarised and split on the cultural value of migrants; about 40 per cent are strongly negative or positive with the balance of about 20 per cent undecided (from Blinder & Allen, 2016). Confusing in the Blinder and Allen data is the inherent contradiction between the strong negative view on economic migrants and the majority that see them giving a benefit to the economy. Ruhs and Vargas-Silva (2015) find that although migrants do not have a significant overall effect on wages, there is a significant impact amongst the lowest paid. They cite a 2013 study that found the lowest 5 per cent of wage earners experience a 0.6 per cent fall in wages for each 1 per cent rise in immigrants. This finding aligns to a number of specific interviews undertaken in the food industry in 2008 reported in Scott (2013; Box 7.13).

Box 7.13. Salads, Supermarkets and Packhouses

Scott's study (2013) in the salad item preparation industry found an industry that had undergone significant change since the 1980s, as food retailing centralised into the major food retailers, and they in turn forced their supply chain processes back on their suppliers.

Consumer trends that demand prepacked and ready foods coupled while requiring low (falling real) prices have driven market expectations. Retailers have responded by passing what risk they can down the supply chain through imposing supply chain changes that force producers to have their own 'pack house' operations. Operations are required to scale up or scale down production at a moment's notice in accordance with supermarket orders, non-supply based not being a feasible option.

In the face of these pressures farmers moved to using agency workforces (recruited from mainly East European countries at first under the now discontinued Special Agricultural Workers Scheme that allowed migrant 6-month work visas, and then later with more general EU migration). East Europeans were in many cases using these jobs as 'stepping stones' to 'polish' their English and enter other employment for which they were qualified (some had MAs, others were doctors, etc.). Others were remitting money to their home country to give them seed capital to buy a house or start their own business when they returned. Their ability to see their next step meant they were highly reliable, intelligent hard-working workers. A stark comparison to local UK (or long-established migrant) workers who knew how to 'play the system', being unreliable, inflexible and as one interviewee said about one group of long-established migrants — lazy.

It is no surprise that lower quartile earners voted for Brexit. Migration has been a visible sign as to why their real wages have not risen, a visible sign of lost opportunity and a visible reason why they find it so hard to pay for the essentials of life such as affordable housing (based on author 2016 informal research amongst this group). Older voters have both fantasised invasions of Turkish (a non-EU member) migrants overwhelming every market town and village and expressed fear of groups speaking foreign languages in public areas such as bus stations!

Employers in low-wage industries such as hospitality have become dependent upon migrants. Some estimates suggest nearly 25 per cent of the hospitality workforce is made up of EU migrants (BHA & KPMG, 2017) and this industry cannot see how it could replace these workers with locals. Other lower-wage employers such as social care and agricultural picking are indeed mirrored by concerns on potential future difficulties in finding staff. This suggests that these industries will be challenged if EU migration is restricted, with cries from some that there will be skill shortages in certain professions such as engineering; and that high-technology entrepreneurs will locate elsewhere.

How are fear and frustration at economic exclusion blamed upon immigration to be reconciled with employers' needs for staff? A conundrum nicely reflecting the Brexit Referendum voting dynamics. A broad brush (so by definition open to criticism at a micro level) 'Leavers over 60' fearful of immigrant hordes destroying 'Englishness', nostalgic of some previous golden age (and this age differs according to region) and 'Leavers' under 60 feeling culturally and economically threatened.

Older people want state triple-locked pension increases, higher interest on savings, zero inflation, cheap foreign holidays and low prices; younger people want rising real wages, no tuition fees, career opportunities, cheaper house prices, low interest rates, zero inflation, cheap foreign holidays and low prices. These goals are not compatible and this inter-generational conflict cannot be resolved by Brexit, but it will form the backdrop to Brexit.

So how can migration, the issue that has become the focus of so many of these frustrations, be handled? Studying the US economy over more than 100 years – from 1869 to 1999, Marquetti (2004) demonstrates how rises in real wages led to employers making capital investments that raise productivity and thereby improve competitiveness. Such experience differs from industry to industry. The hospitality industry is keen to make clear that whilst investing in technology is an accepted method to deal with labour shortages (and by implication wage impacts from shortages) it has only very limited scope to do this (KPMG, 2017).

Economic theory tells us that in a world of 'perfect competition', wages would adjust in the hospitality industry to suck in quality UK nationals; and that assuming companies wanted to maintain their profit levels, prices would rise, demands would fall and a new equilibrium will be reached where uneconomic hospitality businesses are driven out of business. The invisible hand at work. Tourism is a key export industry, with important regional diversity and employment generation, and an industry that can grow post-Brexit. One way of handling this dilemma is to have a *'ministry of visas and work permits'* that second guesses market needs and negotiates and establishes sector visa work permit quotas.

Second, more flexible, method is to establish a market price for visas and work permits where the price is driven by three variables: (i) salary (charge the work permit as a percentage of the annual salary — an employer paid migrant tax); (ii) a sectoral credit of a per cent of the visa cost based upon that sector's contribution to UK exports and/or the sector's contribution to the national security; and (iii) a transitional relief giving 100 per cent credit for business training spend on 'up-skilling' UK nationals to fill the posts.

Our GCC example in Box 7.14 shows that work permit restrictions alone are not sufficient to move unemployed nationals into currently

---

Box 7.14.   Guest Workers — The Gulf Co-Operation Council (GCC) Kafala System

The GCC states operate a strict 'guest worker' work permit system — the Kafala system, where the work permit is requested by the employer and when issued is *unique to the employer*. Employees cannot leave their jobs without employer authorisation, cannot leave the country without an exit visa arranged by their employers, cannot change employer in the country without a new work permit and approval of the employer (or a special ministry action or amnesty). The work permit generates a residence payment and this is required to access banking and money transfers, to book travel tickets (train or plane). Employers have to provide a work contract plus proof of health insurance for the work permit to be issued. Work permits are forbidden for professions and industries reserved for locals. For example, only nationals can work in a mobile phone shop in one GCC country. Each private sector employer is required to have a percentage of local employees and if they fail they cannot have any more work permits or access crucial ministry services. In some countries expatriates have to pay a 'monthly access' fee to have their dependants with them.

Even a system as strict as this has not ensured full employment amongst the local population, not least as expatriate jobs are often unskilled low-wage occupations, and so unsuitable for university graduates.

Al Dosary (2004) highlights four concerns in having an expatriate workforce: (i) economic; (ii) social; (iii) workplace psychological tensions between expatriates and nationals; and (iv) security. All seem relevant Brexit concerns. Al-Asfour and Khan (2014), reviewing progress, highlight the need to train the indigenous workforce with skills that match labour market needs, and that part of this training process is to understand what skills are needed. One size does not fit all and there needs to be an emphasis on raising workforce quality and not just looking at quantities of expatriates who have been replaced. Equally there is a social pressure that sees government jobs as safer and more prestigious. Salary and career expectations are key in an area of the world with so many young people, many of whom now hold first or second degrees.

Other countries have followed strict Indigenisation programs such as Zambia with its Zambianisation program in the 1970's and early 1980's. Anecdotally results echo the findings above.

migrant held positions. It needs to be combined with a 'needs-based' workforce up-skilling.

This should partly be handled by the UK's newly introduced Apprenticeship Scheme, but learning from Germany, perhaps career progression and self-esteem can benefit from vocational and continuing vocational training. Hippach-Schneider, Krause, and Woll (2007) detail the workings of the German Vocational System (Box 7.15). Leaving aside

Box 7.15.   Chambers of Commerce

Chambers of Commerce have a 'special' role in countries such as Germany, France, Japan and the GCC countries. In addition to the lobbying role, in other countries state industry responsibilities are devolved to the Chambers in respect of Business Name and Registration Administration, Vocational Training, Export Trade Promotion (in some cases), document legalisation for international trade (GCC) and being the 'social partner' for government in developing business appropriate regulations. Membership is compulsory, governance managed by industry but dependant on country with a watchful government eye, and the organisations can provide a business driven first point of contact for business support information. They operate in parallel to other sector focused groups, so do not have an exclusive industry voice. In addition to approving company naming, in Germany these organisations can create and issue their own vocational qualifications that complement more formal institutions, something conceptually close to the UK City and Guilds institution.

qualifications and teaching methods which need adaptation, a key aspect of the German system is partnership between the state, educational structures, business support and organisations and companies. In particular, both the German Handleskammer (Chambers of Commerce) and educational institutions play key roles.

Formal training in German comes through the specialist *Fachhochschule* (University of Applied Science), something that combines practical and academic to improve workforce skills. Clear non-academic career routes are visible through the vocational training framework; enhancing student motivation to acquire the basic skills needed to access the opportunities and arguably student motivation is an important factor in improving skills. The United Kingdom should establish a vocational training framework to mirror the German one, with industry input led by a single specialised organisation (City and Guilds?) having compulsory business membership to ensure the voice from all strands of business is represented and heard. Up-skilling the workforce is a necessary requirement to replace migrant skills.

Society as a whole has made a decision to restrict migration through Brexit; society as a whole benefits from economic growth resulting from up-skilling across all age groups so society as a whole will need to pay the training costs. This cost can be paid via *either* (i) higher product prices through forcing industry to pay for schemes such as the compulsory apprenticeship levy, *or* (ii) general taxation, *or* (iii) student fees. 2017 is the first year where aspiring nurses have to pay for nurse training with the cancellation of NHS bursaries. UCAS (2017) reports a 23 per cent fall in applicants for nursing courses from England. The Royal College of Nursing commented, 'It casts doubt on the ability to train enough nurses to fill the 40,000 vacant nurse posts in England' (RCN, 2017). Could visa and work permit fees be used to fund this training, with a financial incentive being given to organisations who train a UK national to replace a migrant in the form of a visa fee rebate for the previous post occupant after the UK national has been in the post for 9 calendar months?

7.1.14. Proposition 14: New Trade Agreements

The avid Brexiteer will challenge why this is proposal 14 and not proposal 1. Our approach to trade agreements is pragmatic, believing that whatever is achieved or cannot be achieved will most likely be within the context of other international Free Trade Agreements, so new Trade Agreements are unlikely to unlock a golden future.

The *immediate challenges* will be to:

(i) Replace critical EU third-country bilateral treaties with appropriate grandfathered UK third-country bilateral treaties before Brexit day (critical areas include mutual recognition of regulators, air safety, peaceful use of nuclear materials, data safe harbour, and the mutual recognition of court judgements for enforcements). Legally, this is a complex area as some agreements are unique to the European Commission and some are 'Mixed', including Member State ratification. A legislative research paper on these treaties (House of Commons, 2017a) states:

> *Where the EU has concluded an external agreement in an area in which it has exclusive competence, the UK will not have ratified that agreement separately. Brexit will mean, therefore, that the UK is no longer bound by that agreement. Most EU external agreements include a 'territorial application' clause, which restricts the application of the agreement to the territories in which the TEU and TFEU are applied. With Brexit, these will therefore no longer cover the UK and its Overseas Territories.*

The position on 'Mixed Agreements' (defined by the European Commission where there is a mix of European Commission competences and Member State competences, and sometimes signed by each and every EU Member State. (EUPAR, 2016)) is less clear and subject to more debate.[21] Our narrative will therefore focus on the 'Exclusive Bilateral EU Third-Country Treaties'.

There are questions as to whether there are available legal devices to speed and simplify the transition process. For example, the Vienna Convention on the Law of Treaties 23 May 1969 allows the treaty parties to invite a third country to benefit from the treaty provisions. One hundred and fourteen countries have ratified this convention, but one of the non-ratifiers is the United States of America, casting doubt on whether this process could be used to address this issue on agreements with the United States.

The United States has a complex relationship between Congress and the President regarding treaties. There are three domestic categories that sum up to the word 'Treaty' internationally.

- Sole-Executive Agreements − The US president can make these alone but only as an Executive Order that can then be later revoked by a new president.
- 'Congressional Executive Agreements' − 50 per cent majority in both houses of Congress.
- Full treaties requiring Senate 'Advice and Consent' − two-third majority in the senate under Article II section II of the US Constitution.

It is unclear which category a new UK−US bilateral treaty would fall into.

(ii) Minimise incremental costs/damage from the Free Trade Agreement that replaces the current UK−EU Single Market arrangements.

(iii) Obtain public buy-in to some areas not having the time to be negotiated by Brexit Day.

Negotiating trade agreements is time consuming and complex. Much emphasis has been placed on negotiating new Free Trade deals with non-EU countries as the justification for Brexit. Box 7.16 shares overall experiences regarding this type of agreement, perhaps emphasising that

---

[21]It is argued by some that the 'Mixed Agreements' will continue in force after Brexit day as the United Kingdom is an independent signatory. Others argue that where there are quotas or other such provisions these will need revision to take account of the UK's new status outside the EU. Others argue that *in extremis* were these to be re-signed then *'all that would be needed would be a statement by the UK that it intended after Brexit to continue to operate the terms of the FTA between itself and Korea, and an acknowledgement by Korea that it would likewise continue to do so'* (House of Commons, 2017a).

Box 7.16.   Experience in Negotiating Preferential Trade Agreements

Preferential trade agreements, that is 'Free Trade Agreements', have been negotiated by many nations. Four-hundred and forty-seven agreements involving 202 contracting parties have been registered with the World Trade Organisation between 1948 and 2015, and 60 per cent are in force. Most of these agreements are in English, and drafting lawyers have ensured that wording is reasonably common between them. Alschner, Seiermann, and Skougarevskiy (2017) used automated textual analysis to analyse these and found some key trends.

First, if one of the contracting parties is demonstrably more powerful, then a disproportionate amount of the treaty text (and hence operation) can be traced back to that party. *Second*, treaties have grown in length over the years – in 1988 about 5,000 words was considered sufficient which had morphed into about 50,000 words in 2015. *Third*, unsurprisingly a Goods and Services Treaty is much more complex than one governing just, say, goods or paradoxically a Customs Union (on reflection the Customs Union agreement is simpler as many of the tricky items are handled as separately negotiated supranational regulations). *Fourth*, these agreements tend to cluster into regions – a *modern global cluster* which includes most of the third-country agreements between the United States (including NAFTA), the EU and the agreements connecting these to South East Asia. Second and third are East Europe Clusters and Central Asian Clusters of Agreements negotiated after the fall of the Soviet Union (the Central Asian ones are less complex than the European ones), and finally there is a residual of 'other agreements' not fitting this classification. *Fifth*, powerful countries tailor trade agreements to meet their strategic political aims for each individual country, so they can be significantly different dependent on overall geopolitical aims. *Sixth*, chapters within agreements can display a higher degree of similarity dependent on the sector being handled. For example, transportation is typically very different between agreements (approximately 85 per cent different) whilst telecommunications show a much higher similarity (approximately 50 per cent the same). *Seventh*, the appetite for goods Free Trade Agreements has tailed off with more focus on either combined Goods and Service Agreements or Service Only Agreements. No doubt this reflects the importance of the service economy.

> One final point in a Customs Union, the issue of specific standards (say, food) is handled by regulation agreed by expert groups and supranational political structures; in a Free Trade Agreement the issue can be agreed in the treaty at a fairly detailed level (for example, the status of chlorine-washed chicken (Crouch, 2017)).

international focus has moved from the liberalisation of goods trade to the liberalisation of trade in services. As we see, recent Trade Agreements tend to be long, complex and dominated by the more powerful partner, although this more powerful party may make certain concessions to achieve their long-term strategic objectives.

Trade agreements can be an opportunity to drive structural change in an economy. Other countries have used trade policy as a means to restructure their economies into higher value-adding industries and thereby to significantly raise living standards. Indeed, Adam Smith (1776) whilst expressing his preference for Free Trade admits a role for trade protection, especially in a world where other countries aggressively protect their own trade. Box 7.17 gives one such case study.

Perhaps a final cautionary and pertinent comment can be found in Box 7.18.

Box 7.17.   Transformation in South Korea

Using a constant US$ value from 2010, South Korea had a 1960 GDP per capita of US$944 that rose to over US$24,000 by 2016 (The World Bank, 2017). In 1960 South Korea was in the bottom 25 per cent of countries in GDP per capita — below the Congo and Ghana. In 2016 it was in the top 25 per cent. A radical and rapid transformation. What was the policy mix?

From Seguino (1999) the first phase in the 1960s saw private business forced to re-establish companies to work in heavy industry, companies that included a government as well as a private stake. Capital controls were imposed, Foreign Direct Investment restricted to sectors where technology transfer could be obtained, the banking sector nationalised and then directed to make available subsidised funds to industry for Capital Investment in incrementally higher value-adding industries. Overseas loans to business were state guaranteed, giving the state control on overseas funding. Business was directed to raise output, exports and investment. Time-limited import restrictions were used to provide short-term protection whilst competitiveness was raised to international levels.

The second phase came in the 1980s as banks were privatised, and moves were made towards trade liberalisation. Government action moved from direct financing towards tax and grant incentives. A relaxation of state intervention as self-sustaining momentum had built up. It is notable that throughout the transformation government policy looked to raise real wages to ensure that industry drove up the value and productivity chain rather than relying on low wages to drive competitiveness.

Box 7.18. Wishful Thinking, 'Enemies of The State' and Prerogative

Governments often wish for two entirely understandable things: (i) that there could be simple solutions to complex problems; and (ii) people either in disagreement with, concerned about or critical of decisions could be silenced. Renegotiating core trade arrangements will be no exception. Last time negotiating Trade Agreements happened in volume, when with the fall of the Soviet Union, there was no choice, and all parties were keen to make the process as straightforward as possible. Brexit is different. People will remember how things were before Brexit and contrast experiences post-Brexit to earlier times. If some in Russia and East Europe can look back to Soviet times as a golden age, then it will be unsurprising if Brexit suffers similar critical review.

Bishop (2016) takes us on a fascinating journey as to how state and people interacted through the Great Debasement of 1544 to 1551. The state, short of money and unable to push for more tax having just quelled the Pilgrimage of Grace uprising, started to debase coins. At first gradually and then after Edward VI's accession much more rapidly. As the situation deteriorated, government resorted to the use of proclamation to control public concern; for example, in 1551, 49 per cent of issued proclamations were about coinage. Inflation rose with reports of merchants 'sodainely raysed the prises of all things to a mervaylouse rekening' and proclamations blamed inflation on 'rumour mongers' and 'naughty people'. People heard spreading rumours were to be fined, and if they did not pay the fine were pilloried and had an ear cut off! Instead of stopping dissent, rumours increased! Officials found finding the source of a rumour to be as challenging as trying to 'herd cats'. Eventually with Elizabeth I on the throne, the coinage was overhauled and over time public confidence was restored.

The Brexit lesson: no amount of spin or being named 'enemies of the people' will compensate for a clear and well-understood revision to international arrangements. People, as in the mid-sixteenth century, are too smart to ignore what is in front of their noses just because of a threat — even one to cut off an ear.

7.2.   How Did They Cope in Previous Brexits?

How well have our 14 proposals served those challenged with previous Brexits (Table 7.1)? To what extent are these new, and to what extent are these a rediscovery of the past?

Recapping on our earlier findings in Table 3.5, we identify five major issues from previous Brexits:

- *Monetary stops* when the financial system is disrupted or fails.
- *Legal/Regulatory impediments* when legal frameworks become unclear.
- *Operation disruption* as supply chains collapse and markets change.
- *Innovative disruption* as products change.
- *Regional issues* such as implementation of change need to be 'owned' and adapted to local circumstances.

We have identified 14 possible 'Action Themes' which we have then assessed against previous Brexit experience in Table 8.1. Notwithstanding the obvious difficulties in contrasting solutions across such different ages, we have found three overriding themes from previous experience:

1. **Private Enterprise took the lead** — earlier Ages saw the state working with commercial merchant organisations and guilds to secure and build trade relations rather than relying on treaties. Some of this model survives to the present day in other countries such as Germany, where the 21st successors of the Medieval Guilds — the Chambers of Commerce — play an active role in organising trade missions.

Table 7.1. Previous Brexit Experience.

No	Proposal	AD 410	1530s	1560s
1	**Access to Finance** – create new 'family silver' (to sell at a profit)	**Failure** The monetary economy failed as new coinage ceased to be imported, trade declined, supply chains broke down and urban centres depopulated	**Failure** Although the king was always short of money and looking to raise taxes; after 1544 the answer was debasing the coinage, with the inflation and unrest this caused	**Success** The currency was rebased, confidence restored, Privateers licensed to loot Spanish Treasure, the national debt repaid and trade credit accessed and extended by the Merchant Adventurers
2	**Link public procurement to MSME innovation** – Example: use 'block chain' to establish event-triggered payment system for SMEs	**Failure** The Roman Army which had been important to local economic engine – for example archaeology in Carlisle shows linked activities (McCarthy, 2005) – was not replaced as activity fragmented over individual estates	**Failure** In Pre-Reformation England monasteries were integrated into local communities as delivery mechanisms for the poor, law and economic development; for example, Sayer (2009) explaining the role of the Abbey in Ramsey in fen drainage and agricultural development at Burwell. The dissolution saw land sold off but no replacement for the economic role as shown by the grievances in the Pilgrimage of Grace (1536)	**Partial Success** Elizabethan policy stabilised a challenging landscape, partly through the use of royal charters (for example the Hull charter of 11 May 1577), investments in Privateers and support for the Merchant Adventurers. There is evidence of state intervention to drive local support for specific projects – for example a letter from the Lord High Admiral requesting financial support for a specific ship (Hull Archive, 1597)

3	**Create an MSME Banking Ombudsman Service**	Not Applicable	Not Applicable	**Not Applicable** The relationships between Privy Council Members such as Robert Cecil and the Merchant Adventurers helped align policy and merchant requirements, but this is not an ombudsman
4	**Business Networking – 'Share the Problem and the Solutions'**	Not Applicable	In so much as networking happened, it was centred on the Guilds and Merchant Adventurers or was informal between the Aldermen of Cities such as London or Hull	**Both the Merchant Adventurers and the Guilds plus informally between the Aldermen of Cities such as London or Hull**
5	**Initiate an MSME-focused exporting programme**	Not Applicable	The London (and to a lesser extent, York) Companies of the Merchant Adventurers played a key role in facilitating the wool trade through these years of turmoil	In addition to supporting Privateering and the role of the Merchant Adventurers in the wool trade there is evidence of efforts to open an Oriental Trade (Brotton, 2016). Support also came through the Guilds and local City administrations
6	**Kill non-viable firms**	Yes	Yes	Uneconomic ventures were killed but individual entrepreneurs with good connections (as ever) such as

Table 7.1. (*Continued*)

No	Proposal	AD 410	1530s	1560s
				George Needham helped to transition across businesses in the face of failure (Ramsey, 1979)
7	**Supply chain changes**	The pan-European supply chain collapsed as to some degree the internal supply chain as towns depopulated, use of money was restricted by lack of new coinage and activity refocused around rural estates/villas	**Not Applicable**	The English wool trade which was critical to UK export earnings was maintained by continual adaption in the face of European religious wars and in respect of what value was added in which location
8	**Credible certificates of origin and conformity**	**Not Applicable**	The Merchant Adventurers' control of the English wool trade gave some assurance as to origin and quality of the product	The Merchant Adventurers' control of the English wool trade gave some assurance as to origin and quality of the product
9	**Learn from both the United States and one-time 'Economic miracle' countries … to deliver number**	**Not Applicable**	Merchant interaction in the wool market provided input on customer demands	Merchant interaction in the wool market provided input on customer demands (Merchant Adventurers) plus Privateers and Explorers opened new markets and products (for

1 globally in selected emerging technologies and products			example tobacco and the potato)
10 **Build the venture capital exit chain**	**Not Applicable**	**Not Applicable**	**Not Applicable**
11 **Patenting**	**Not Applicable**	**Not Applicable**	Reductions in piracy by privateer licences (the state took control) and more central control of local port-based operations (for example Hull Archive correspondence from Lord High Admiral in 1570s (Stanewell, 1951))
12 **Raise management competence**	**Not Applicable**	**Not Applicable** Cromwell's administrative reorganisation impacted the Tudor Court by more devolved structures such as customs farms continued	**Not Applicable** Elizabethan reforms looked to raise competence of the administrative organs state – linked to defence and revenue raising needs
13 **Control of immigration**	The previous fortifications to stop Saxon invaders on the East Coast fell into disrepair and invasion became	**Not Applicable**	**Not Applicable** Following *Regnans in Excelsis* – the Papal Bull excommunicating Elizabeth I in 1570 and to a degree the

Table 7.1. (*Continued*)

No	Proposal	AD 410	1530s	1560s
		synonymous with some form of migration		Recusancy Act of 1593 emphasis was on using the Treason Laws against, for example, Jesuit missionaries (penalty execution)
14	New trade agreements	Not Applicable	Merchant and defence driven, lifting of the 1528 closure of Antwerp in 1529	Merchant-Driven Trade Expansion Letters of Patent granted to trading companies – the Levant Co, Barbary Co, the East India Co along with support and financing for privateers (using state-authorised piracy rather than a trade treaty[a])

Source: Authors.

[a]An anecdote relating to 'state'-supported piracy in our own age relates to a small state that supported the armed smuggling of gold to Asia and used the profits to fund its own economic development.

2. **The state was happy to license aggressive private activities** that had a mixture of military, foreign policy and enterprise dimensions such as privateers and the East India Company.
3. **Monetary collapse** meant trade collapse.

Over the long run, the Elizabethan Age set the foundations for the following centuries of growth and imperial development. The Henrician Reformation was the precursor to monetary and political chaos with the Great Debasement of Edward VI and the purges of Mary I, and the end of Roman Britain was the precursor to the collapse of supply chains and urban life as it had been known. Elizabeth I's genius was to engage right across the spectrum, from aristocracy to pirates, to refresh and renew. The close relationships between her Privy Councillors, especially Robert Cecil, and merchant interests meant that commercial interests were considered and remembered in the policy making process. The move of the English Wool Trade to Emden, even if short lived, was supported end endorsed by those around the Queen. The privateer licences were supported and endorsed again by those around the Queen, and the Queen herself invested in some missions and some of the commercial companies. Contrast this to her father Henry VIII's court where change was driven from a legal rather than commercial perspective by Thomas Cromwell; and where a factional court could lead to being in favour one day and headless having been executed the next. Those responsible for Brexit would be wise to reflect on the limitations of a legislator-driven strategy and the dangers of factional splits on how Brexit is to be executed. Previous Brexits suggest much more can be achieved through a pragmatic partnership with industry, trade and commerce than relying only on a legal and political strategy.

We close this chapter with an important warning from history on how political dislocation can impact global centres, especially global financial centres in Box 7.19.

Box 7.19. Shifting Sands — Banking Centres and Competitive Advantage

The closure of the Port of Antwerp after the Dutch Revolt, not only moved the wool trade, but also coupled with a number of sovereign defaults, led to Antwerp losing its status as a trading and banking hub long term.

The experience of Antwerp, and indeed before that the experiences of Venice and Florence, we can see that once a financial cluster starts to break up it is challenging for it to retain its former glory.

Spufford (2006) describes a process spanning five centuries in which European financial centres grew and declined as trade (and many of the key players) moved to a secondary but growing rival centre. Bruges to Antwerp, Antwerp to Amsterdam and Amsterdam to London. Spufford (2006) identifies clustering and critical mass as essential features in maintaining banking centres. He demonstrates how when centres start to fragment the trade moves with the key players. For example, the decline of Amsterdam as a banking centre and the growth of London towards the end of the eighteenth century (there is some dispute on the dating but the wars after 1680 seem to be a watershed that builds on a previous period of challenge from the 1650s to 1670s) was associated with the relocation of key banker assets from groups and individuals such as the Barings, the Hopes, Gerard De Neck and Abraham Ricardo, father of economist David Ricardo. By the early nineteenth century, London which had been the secondary financial centre is the world's financial sector.

Announcements confirming financial institutions are moving operations in response to Brexit to alternative EU locations started in Quarter 2, 2017, just as in the 1670s when operations moved from Amsterdam to a range of centres, and in the 1560s when operations moved to a range of centres. Austen et al. (2017) reports Frankfurt and Dublin as favoured locations, although there is some hint that other operations may move to the Far East of United States. The authors have raised their estimate on lost 'wholesale banking' jobs due to Brexit from 12,000 to 17,000 in 2016, to 35,000 to 40,000 in their latest forecast (Austen et al., 2017). This number is a quantum higher than the 2016 estimate which estimated a total financial system exodus of 35,000 to 40,000 jobs. Estimates are not fact and we do not know what the impact will be on London as a financial hub, but structural change looks likely. Such structural change will most likely lead to associated money flow changes with the possibility to bring the UK's trade balance into sharper focus and associated potential for downward movements in sterling.

In a historical context, the trigger event forcing change has been mainly warfare (civil or international) acting as a catalyst to long-standing changes in commercial trade, previous financial events such as defaults and rising operating costs. The previous centre continued to function in some reducing form for many decades after the trigger event. Finally, Spufford (2006) concludes that the survival of financial centres depends on the continued presence of the key international bankers and the associated retention of 'critical mass'.

Chapter 8

Epilogue: Unlocking Our Potential

Those who failed to realize that the phrase 'combining factors', when applied to a going concern, denoted little more than routine management; and the task of combining factors becomes a distinctive one only when applied not to the current administration of a going concern but to the organization of a new one.

— Schumpeter (1954/1986, p. 530)

We return to the theme we started with; how can we unlock the UK's innovation potential? Partly we need to listen to Schumpeter and focus on the Entrepreneur, partly we need to avoid confusing re-organisation for innovation (Schumpeter again) and partly we need to focus on working together to share and coordinate resources in the most effective way. Charlton Ogburn in 1957 writes (although sometimes wrongly attributed to a fictional Gaius Petronius Arbiter in Nero's Imperial court, conjuring up an impression of a disgruntled cynical legionnaire in a spoof example of c. AD 60 fake news)[1]:

We trained hard, but it seemed that every time we were beginning to form up into teams we would be reorganized. Presumably the plans for our employment were being changed. I was to learn later in life that, perhaps because we are so good at organizing, we tend as a nation to meet any new situation by reorganizing; and a wonderful method it can be for creating the illusion of progress while producing confusion, inefficiency and demoralization.

— Ogburn (1957)

---

[1]It appears that this quote is oft mis-attributed to Pertonius, comes from a 1957 edition of *Harper's* magazine and was made by Charlton Ogburn in an article entitled 'Merrill's Marauders'. Our intrepid first-century courtier becomes a twentieth-century writer.

An alternative paradigm may be to equate the challenges in public innovation policy (so varying are the different actors and components) to the difficulty one would have if one wished to 'herd cats'.

At the end of Roman Britain, the Roman Army ceased to provide the necessary infrastructure (in our analogy to 'herd the cats') as it stopped providing the coinage, the security and purchasing power that was required to keep the previous supply chains and associated urban settlements in tact with a consequent falling apart of the urban business environment. Henry VIII mistakenly thought prerogative and the executioners axe could make 'the cats' point in the same direction. Fear does not unify, it divides; fear does not improve risk taking, it makes one run for the bunker. Bullies don't foster entrepreneurship and they don't foster innovation. In our story, the success comes from the Merchant Adventurers who play a critical role as the 'Cat Herders' of the sixteenth century, bringing people together in a chaotic fractious situation and building relationships and structure to facilitate business.

The Brexit narrative of fear and bullying (for example, the *Daily Mail* in 2016 branding judges 'Enemies of the People' for affirming the role of Parliament within the rule of law) is unlikely to bring people together. The narrative of jealousy that is often associated to tax, wealth and income distribution is also unlikely to bring people together as is the narrative of some that 'we won the war' when most people saying it were not even born when the Second World War ended.

The state capitalism narrative of big regulated and protected monopolies and oligopolies, the world of lobby groups, public relations and media consultants and of big business-driven restrictions is unlikely to unlock innovative potential. The demand by the old that they be protected from economic hurricanes through triple-locked pensions, social care, unrestricted access to health, occupational pensions and sky high house prices is unlikely to promote entrepreneurship. The desire of a financial system to provide returns well above interest rates through complex products and the emphasis of business and 'private equity' focus on cutting costs and growth through rationalizing mergers and acquisitions is unlikely to unlock risk taking linked to innovation and higher capital investment.

Can anyone reasonably suggest that short-term, Brexit is going to do anything other than add uncertainty and dislocation? The open question is if this dislocation and uncertainty can act as a spur into a new entrepreneurial age? So our story ends where it started – that the UK's future economic well-being requires a policy and resource (both private and public) focus on entrepreneurs and upon catalysing innovation. To do this we have to put the Entrepreneur in the driving seat and everyone else needs to take their place in the supporting cast.

8.1. Entrepreneurs Must Drive What Support They Need

In our MBA class, the authors have often posed the question, 'Who is the expert? The blender who created the tea? The brewer who brewed the tea? The customer who drinks the tea? The waiter who advised which tea blend to use?' At some relevant point in time each one is the expert, but there can only be one expert at a specific point in time. Although many may be expert in their own field, the expert in the MSME is the Entrepreneur − the person who matches their business to the market need. But as in our example above, not everyone has the skills of the 'tea blender' (without which there would be no tea), there are many who have differing knowledge and skills, all of which can support and help enable the Entrepreneur.

These organisations are classified in Table 8.1.

Table 8.1. Support Organisations.

Sector	Type	Driver
Public	Local Enterprise Partnerships	Regional Development
	Overseas Promotion (UKTI)	Exports and Inward Investment
	Ministries	National Policy
	Bank of England	Economic Activity
Education	Universities	Enterprise and Entrepreneurship teaching
		Academic research
		Community catalysts
		Technical teaching and qualifications
	Schools & Colleges	Enterprise and entrepreneurship awareness
Professional Bodies	Institutes (Accountants, Law Society, etc.)	Professional standards
		Professional certification/register
		Curriculum development
		Regulatory oversight
		Continuing professional education

Table 8.1. (*Continued*)

Sector	Type	Driver
		Promoting awareness to change
		Informal network
		Lobbying on new legislation
Industry Bodies	Federations (i.e. EEF), prime contractors	Management education
		Promoting awareness to change
		Driving change through specification
		Lobbying
Business Support Organisations	Federations sometimes industry based, sometimes company size based, sometimes locality based, includes Chambers of Commerce	Lobbying and public input
		Member discounts such as insurance and compliance packs
		Promoting awareness to change
		Member advocate on local, regional and national issues
		Informal network
Incubators, Growth Accelerators	Public, non-profit or private	Service provision
		Networking support
		Management education
		Lobbying
Research Institutes (See Box 7.17)	Public, non-profit, industry funded or private	Research partnership
		Technical advice
Professional Advisers	Lawyers, accountants, etc.	Sub-contracted technical work
		Management education
		Consultancy
Standards Bodies	Notified bodies, research establishments and standards institutes (BSI, BRE, CAA, etc.)	Regulation
		Standards development input
		Management education
Service Providers	Outsource providers (e.g. payroll HR, etc.)	Service provision
		Management education
	Capital providers	Strategic business development

Table 8.1. (*Continued*)

Sector	Type	Driver
Venture Capitalists		Management education
		Non-executive input
		Capital
		Network links
Non-executive Board Members	Non-executive directors	Strategic development
		Management development
		Network links
		Review and advice
Consultants	Advisers	Management education
		Specific technical assignments (procedure writing, etc.)

Source: Authors.
Notable Omissions: Bank Managers (bank relationship managers largely extinct for SMEs with the exception of niche players such as Handelsbanken), Financial Advisors (boutique investment bank advice too expensive for SMEs), Friends and Family, Local Community.

8.2. MSMEs as Revenue Stream for Some Advisors

The complex network of advisers in Table 8.1 is illustrative of the coordination challenge. All have their raison d'être. For some their work is revenue generating (for example banking, lawyers, accounting, consultants). MSMEs can represent important revenue and profit streams. Brexit may be seen as an important potential revenue by many of these groups, yet given the scale of potential change the advisers may themselves be ill equipped to be 'experts' on the issues involved. In the face of these challenges we suggest a number of execution themes.

Execution Theme 1: Sharing the Challenge with Multiple Ways to Communicate Solutions

With so many groups, each with differing motivations, the opportunity for divisive messages and narrow advice is clear. The potential speed with which the landscape could change suggests that coordination to build 'common understanding' will be a key enabler. Building a coordinated common base of knowledge may be puzzling for some but it should not be a mystery. Wool and cloth merchants competed with each other for individual sales over 400 years ago, but worked together to maintain market access, safe transport, credit worthiness knowledge. They competed but equally they understood the benefits of a collaborative network. Professional Institutes bring together professionals (such as accounting, civil engineering, etc.) to share ideas, challenges, opportunities and to raise professional standards in their industry; the self-same professionals compete at a commercial level.

Brexit challenges will require coordination to share and solve issues that cut across professional boundaries, that helps 'up-skill' advisers and that complements fee-earning opportunities. MSMEs have a natural voice in their Not-for-Profit Lobby organisations that working together can help establish needs and priorities. Teasing out these issues and assigning priorities requires knowledge, analytical and professional skills that sit, partly in research and professional standards arms of the Institutes, and partly in Business Facing Academia.

Box 8.1 demonstrates that the United Kingdom already has, in some of its 'newer' more entrepreneurially facing universities, the ideal catalysing agents to pull together the disparate groups in their locality. This resource combination can facilitate flexible change support programmes to enable professionals to support MSME transformation through the Brexit process. Firmly rooted in a 'local' context, by embedding relevant universities in partnership with their Local Enterprise Partnerships (LEP) and combined with MSME Business Support Organisations, for national context, what we will now call the Entrepreneurial University can bring all the actors into the same collaboration space.

Box 8.1.   Academic vs. Entrepreneurial Universities

Culkin and Mallick (2011) highlight the need for Entrepreneurial Universities capable of producing graduates steeped in business and innovation, and an institution that can interact with innovative MSMEs as a source of innovation and management support, thereby focusing on transferrable skills such *'as creativity, leadership and research analysis'*. They highlight the practical value of the University of Hertfordshire's Graduate Consulting Unit as a bridge between business and academia. Brint (2005) talks of leading research universities — pure academia; and it is no surprise to find Harvard, Yale, Stamford and MIT in this list of institutions. If we were in the United Kingdom the names that would immediately spring to mind would be Oxford, Cambridge, Imperial College, University College London and maybe Manchester and Edinburgh. There are great intellectual paragons of ground-breaking basic research, linked through their science parks and licensing and venture capital links into commercial spin outs.

Both Brint (2005) and Culkin and Mallick (2011) lead us towards seeing as an alternative to a 'research university' a more multi-disciplinary mission-focused alternative – the entrepreneurial or innovation university – universities that act as unifying catalysts for change and innovation within their own geography, often partnered into local institutions (Culkin, 2016). By their very nature these universities bring a different, more 'vocational', 'entrepreneur friendly' and 'innovation friendly' focus, one that can, if properly orchestrated with other local institutions and business, be the catalyst to unlock latent business potential. An ideal catalyst, as these institutions have an academic mission and so can act as a neutral facilitating agent for business. Research universities by contrast are adept at finding new ways to 'split the atom' or 'edit the human genome' – basic research that they then help feed through to application.

Such action can start immediately, with government allocating an additional, small enabling budget (from the Brexit contingency budget) for each region through LEP or Innovate UK research contracts to seed and promote this cooperation. A seed cost of a few million pounds out of a Brexit transformation programme costing billions that could make a significant contribution to supporting MSME innovation efforts.

Execution Theme 2: Build the Regional Transformation Plans and Delivery Structures

Once the actors are engaged, the deliverable becomes our second theme. Each deliverable needs to be accompanied by a detailed needs statement that highlights what needs to be done with each target group with how they can be helped and the budget cost and proposed funding. These deliverables need to be sensitive to the revenue-earning goals of MSME advisors, consultants and professional services.

8.3. MSME Characteristics

Each MSME is different, with different markets, at a different stage of development, and with different capabilities. It faces its own innovation challenge that is unique to its own context. Innovation among MSMEs

---

Box 8.2.   The Sailing-Ship Effect

This mechanism is often referred to as the 'sailing-ship effect', after Gilfillan's study on innovation in ships (Gilfillan, 1935). He showed how the then current product (sailing ship) was improved as the new product (steamer) surfaced in 1813. Almost all of the components and materials of the sailing ship were subject to incremental advances, transforming it from a wooden structure to basically a metallic one, whose carrying capability was hugely improved. Gilfillan wrote, 'it is paradoxical, but on examination logical, that [...] during her decline and just before extermination, [she] was partly vouchsafed by her supplanter, the steamer' (1935, p. 156).

---

lies at the heart of structural change and innovative discontinuous change is one of the driving forces of economic development.

Two salient features of western economies are product cycles (e.g. technological stability often favoured by incumbent firms) on the one hand and product disruptions (e.g. technological breakthroughs, more often favoured by new firms) on the other. A technological paradox in the process of competition between two technologies – one old, one new – arises from the observation that old out of date technologies often continue to be utilised despite having outlived their technological 'sell-by' date, despite being outperformed by new ones (Box 8.2).

Schumpeter's original concept of an entrepreneur was that of a 'heroic individual' who possessed supernormal qualities of intellect, carrying out new combinations, while powerful elements of society erected barriers in his way, intent on maintaining the status quo. Discontinuous and revolutionary change is the core of economic development, and breaks the economy out of its static mode (e.g. the circular flow) and sets it on a dynamic path of fits and starts (Sledzik, 2013, p. 89). Small firms and high-growth firms differ, but both undertake an essential role in a successful economy, despite being very different sorts of enterprises. One theme from a recent survey of MSMEs with 1,659 respondents was the importance MSMEs put on having access to business support. Fifty-eight per cent saw this as critical as opposed to 52 per cent naming access to Access to Finance (FSB, 2017). Unsurprisingly, these respondents want a simple system that works for them and is non-bureaucratic and flexible.

Equally there is a need to up-skill regional delivery and Local Economic Partnership MSME engagement. MSMEs are different from big companies.

Big company experience can be inappropriate to the challenges of MSMEs, which is why we see the 'catalyst' role of the Entrepreneurial University as key. It is an institution of sufficient size to work with and understand the challenges the Local Economic Partnerships face, but granular enough, in that it works with thousands of individual students to be able to tailor programmes to meet individual needs. Policy makers also need to acknowledge and respond to the growth and impact of home-based businesses on neighbourhoods and cities (Box 8.3). Assuming that entrepreneurial processes are predominantly resource-based, we need to think about the mobilisation and access to resources (Mason & Harrison, 2015, p. 275).

The programme requires: (i) setting potential scope by identifying key needs (like access to finance, importing/exporting); (ii) establishing a process for matching which module (or part of a module) is appropriate for which MSME; (iii) determining who is best to deliver this;

Box 8.3.   Home Alone: Innovation and sales growth intentions among the solo self-employed

According to a recent Policy Paper from the Enterprise Research Centre, around one in six of the UK labour force is self-employed (Gkypali & Roper, 2017). In addition, self-employment now accounts for 40 per cent of the increase in employment since 2010. Using the latest data set from the Longitudinal Small Business Survey, Gkypali and Roper provide new insights on the behaviour of this 'solo' group and the implications for national discussions about productivity. The group's diversity and varied growth aspirations imply that a combination of policy initiatives may have more effect in stimulating growth intentions, as opposed to a single policy measure. For example, evidence suggests a mix of social media and engagement with informal business networks is strongly related to growth intentions, for the 'solo' firm's growth comes through increased sales and profitability. Some 46 per cent of Gkypali and Roper's respondents intended to introduce a new product or service over the next three years and on average they aimed to grow sales by 18.6 per cent over the same period. Public support for open learning networks around social media, and targeted at the solo self-employed, would have a combined effect on growth ambitions. Similarly, business networks, which stimulate collaborative or open innovation, would have similar effects.

(iv) deciding whether there are any compulsory elements; (v) using the support process to build longer term self-help sharing networks; (vi) establishing policy feedback networks to policy makers, regulators and vocational training programme creators.

Execution Theme 3: Implementation

Implementation should be undertaken in phases:

- **MSME Cohort Recruitment** – providing MSMEs with the opportunity to self-select into the parts of the programme that are most relevant for them. For example, any companies crossing international boundaries will face a revised declaration and logistics system – could there be benefit in running a series of sessions that combine with being networking events to explain the changes?
- **Feedback** – feedback will be a key component in identifying new support needs and in continually improving the programmes.
- **On-going Networking** – building informal networks so that MSMEs can help each other.

8.4.   New Structures Will Be Required Before Brexit Day

New structures need to be 'road tested' and proven well before Brexit day. Brexit day will result in many changes, some planned and foreseen and some not planned and not foreseen. Customers, the market and business need something that is working day one and they will not wait for grand IT projects, new unknown regulators, gaps in supply chains or gaps in access to finance. Ideally, new arrangements need to be clear maybe 15 months before the exit day. This will give business some certainty with which to start adapting their businesses to be ready for Brexit day.

Execution Theme 4: Government 'Programme Office'

At a national level, partnership between Ministries, Parliament, Business Support Organisations and Entrepreneurial Universities will require fastidious coordination. State-of-the-art project and programme management techniques need to be utilised to ensure, working back from the delivery date, that Brexit delivery elements are in place in good time. Both public accountability and ease of operation will be greatly aided by publishing (i) a list of roles and responsibilities for the heads of each and every UK replacement function for an EU function 12 months before

Brexit day, (ii) the names and contact details of transition programme and project managers, (iii) a schedule of the main goals by responsibility set out on a quarter-by-quarter basis so that these goals are monitored and any slippage identified and remedied.

8.5. The Real Brexit Challenge

Brexit has become synonymous with division. There are divisions between Leavers and Remainers, divisions between young and old, divisions between rich and poor, divisions between free-market ideologues and social market advocates; in reality, there are divisions, anger and bitterness all around.

Our journey has shown us that such divisions have occurred before; for example, the fissures opened by the Henrician Reformation took centuries to resolve. Equally, our journey has shown how pragmatists and reality-grounded entrepreneurs can drive stability in even the most challenging of times (such as the 1563 closure of Antwerp).

The real Brexit challenge is not today's unfolding drama, rather it is to deliver a result, whatever the shape of that may be, that allows the historian in 50 years' time, to describe the Brexit transformation, not the Brexit disaster. The jury is out until some future historian seals the prognosis.

The one certainty is that the Brexit is too important and too risky to be left to the politicians. Instead, let us learn from over 2,000 years of history and put the Entrepreneur centre stage; empowered, affirmed, supported and able to drive a twenty-first-century Britain. It does beg the question: why do we need the risk and upheaval of Brexit if all we need to do is to 'Take Back Control' from the politicians and empower the Entrepreneur?

Appendix: Simple Glossary

Adverse Selection

Adverse selection occurs when one party in a negotiation has relevant information the other party lacks. The asymmetry of information often leads to making bad decisions.

Big Bang Disruptions

Products or services that restructure and disrupt entire industries. For example, the digital camera vs. the film-based camera.

Business Catalyst/ Incubator

Offers a spectrum of advice, marketing support, facilities and where appropriate translational research and development activities and opportunities, enabling access to equipment and facilities that would otherwise be beyond the reach of start-ups and small- or medium-sized companies.

Crowding Out

The crowding-out effect is an economic theory stipulating that rises in public sector spending drive down or even eliminate private sector spending. Though the 'crowding-out effect' is a general term, it is often used in reference to the stifling of private spending in areas where government purchasing is high. The term is used in this context in this book.

Dynamic Stochastic General Equilibrium Models

A form of mathematical computable economic model that integrates Equilibrium Theory, Rational Expectations and specific econometric research into historical economic behaviour to define modelling functions to predict future economic trends.

Firm

A firm is a business organization, such as a corporation, limited liability company or partnership, that sells goods or services to make a profit.

Innovation	Product or services change to embed new technologies, features or designs.
Internal Rate of Return (IRR)	You can think of IRR as the rate of growth a project is expected to generate. While the actual rate of return that a given project ends up generating will often differ from its estimated IRR rate, a project with a substantially higher IRR value than other available options would still provide a much better chance of strong growth. www.investopedia.com
Internet of Things	A term used to describe items (for example here is a non-exclusive list: consumer products such as refrigerators, or industrial products such as plant sensors or cars or heating/cooling systems) where the product has embedded sensors that send monitoring data to a controlling host, that then adjusts how the device performs or calls for maintenance based upon data received.
Market Facing Innovation	Where the market, customer and potential customer drive the 'needs statement' to innovate a new product or service as opposed to where the innovation idea *either* is a product idea that comes from within the firm and looks for a customer to need it rather than *or* is an idea that improves firm internal efficiency and does not touch the customer. Otherwise defined by Von Hippel as a *Customer Active Paradigm* or a *Manufacturer Active Paradigm*.
Natural Rate of Interest	Wicksell (1898) based his theory on a comparison of the marginal product of capital with the cost of borrowing money. If the money rate of interest were below the natural rate of return on capital, entrepreneurs would borrow at the money rate to purchase capital (equipment and buildings), thereby increasing demand for all types of resources and their prices; the converse would be true if the money rate was greater than the natural rate of return on capital.

Sunset Clause	An automatic binding provision to finish and arrangement on a pre-agreed date.
Total Factor Productivity	Measure of the efficiency of all inputs to a production process, so this includes labour and capital.
Zambianization	The process of replacing expatriate workers with the local population especially during the 1970's and early 1980's

Bibliography

Abbot Labs. (2017). Hepatitis C is testing us: We will not fail. Retrieved from http://www.abbott.com/corpnewsroom/product-and-innovation/hepatitis-c-is-testing-us.html

Abrams, E. (2014). The Tinker bell effect. *Weekly Standard, 19*(30). Retrieved from http://www.weeklystandard.com/the-tinkerbell-effect/article/786759

Accominotti, O., & Flandreau, M. (2008). Bilateral treaties and the most-favored-nation clause: The myth of trade liberalization in the nineteenth century. *World Politics, 60*(2), 147–188.

Afme. (2017). Bridging to Brexit: Insights from European SMEs, corporates and investors, Association for Financial Markets in Europe, July. Retrieved from https://www.afme.eu/globalassets/downloads/publications/afme-bcg-cc-bridging-to-brexit-2017.pdf

Afme. (2017). Bridging to Brexit: Insights from European SMEs, Corporates and Investors, Association for Financial Markets in Europe, July 2017. Retrieved from https://www.afme.eu/globalassets/downloads/publications/afme-bcg-cc-bridging-to-brexit-2017.pdf. Accessed on September 10, 2017.

AIAG. (2017). ISO/TS 16949. Retrieved from http://www.aiag.org/quality/iatf16949/iatf-16949-2016

Al-Asfour, A., & Khan, S. A. (2014). Workforce localization in the Kingdom of Saudi Arabia: Issues and challenges. *Human Resource Development International, 17*(2), 243–253.

Al Dosary, A. S. (2004). HRD or manpower policy? Options for government intervention in the local labor market that depends upon a foreign labor force: The Saudi Arabian perspective. *Human Resource Development International, 7*(1), 123–135.

Allen, A. M. (2006). Occupational mapping of 1635 Edinburgh: An introduction. In *Proceedings of the Society of Antiquaries of Scotland* (Vol. 136, pp. 259–296). National Museum of Antiquities of Scotland.

Allen Green, D. (2017). Brexit: The ballad of Digby Jones. Retrieved from https://www.ft.com/content/ed21472f-0432-358b-94de-adef0a01fef4

Allison, J. R., Lemley, M. A., Moore, K. A., & Trunkey, R. D. (2003). Valuable patents. *Georgetown Law Journal, 92*, 435. Retrieved from http://heinonline.org/HOL/LandingPage?handle=hein.journals/glj92&div=21&id=&page=

Alschner, W., Seiermann, J., & Skougarevskiy, D. (2017). Text-as-data analysis of preferential trade agreements: Mapping the PTA landscape. Retrieved from http://unctad.org/en/pages/PublicationWebflyer.aspx?publicationid=1838

Anderson, C. (2004). *The long tail*. New York, NY: Hyperion.

Andrews, K. R. (Ed.). (1959). English privateering voyages to the West Indies: Documents relating to English voyages to the West Indies from the defeat of the

Armada to the Last Voyage of Sir Francis Drake, including Spanish documents contributed by Irene A. Wright. Cambridge: Cambridge University Press.

Apostolides, A., Broadberry, S., Campbell, B., Overton, M., & van Leeuwen, B. (2008). *English gross domestic product, 1300−1700: Some preliminary estimates.* Coventry: University of Warwick. Retrieved from http://www2.warwick.ac.uk/fac/soc/economics/staff/sbroadberry/wp/pre1700v2.pdf

Aurelius, M. (AD167). *Meditations book VI, 3 Hay Translation.* New York Modern Library. Retrieved from http://seinfeld.co/library/meditations.pdf

Austen, M., Naylor, L., Davis, J., Darbyshire, N., Allchin, C., & Hunt, P. (2017). One year on from a briefing for wholesale banks. Retrieved from http://www.oliverwyman.com/content/dam/oliver-wyman/v2/publications/2017/aug/OW-Wholesale-Banking-Brexit-Briefing.pdf

Automotive Council UK. (2014). *Growing the automotive supply chain: Assessing the up stream potential sourcing* (Davies, Holweg, Hugget, Schramm, Trans.). Retrieved from http://www.automotivecouncil.co.uk/wp-content/uploads/sites/13/2014/11/Growing-the-Automotive-Supply-Chain-2014−0411141.pdf

Babwin, D. (2006). Independent bookstores fighting chains: Internet to stay open. *USA Today,* 9 October. Retrieved from https://usatoday30.usatoday.com/tech/news/2006-10-09-independent-bookstores_x.htm

Bace, R. (2013). Pain management for entrepreneurs: Working with venture capital. *IEEE Security & Privacy, 11*(4), 78−81.

Bacon, R., & Eltis, W. (1979). The measurement of the growth of the non-market sector and its influence: A reply to Hadjimatheou and Skouras. *The Economic Journal, 89*(354), 402−415.

Bahmani, M., Harvey, H., & Hegerty, S. W. (2013). Empirical tests of the Marshall−Lerner condition: A literature review. *Journal of Economic Studies, 40*(3), 411−443.

Bairoch, P. (1976). *Commerce extérieur et développement économique de l'Europe au XIXe siècle* (Vol. 53). Mouton: École des hautes études en sciences sociales.

Bank of England. (2014). Money creation in the modern economy. *Quarterly Bulletin* Q1. Retrieved from http://www.bankofengland.co.uk/publications/Documents/quarterlybulletin/2014/qb14q1prereleasemoneycreation.pdf

Barrie, J. M. (1911). *Peter and Wendy.* London: Hodder and Stoughtonnd.

Barro, R. J. (2001). Economic growth in East Asia before and after the financial crisis (No. w8330). National Bureau of Economic Research. Retrieved from http://www.nber.org/papers/w8330

Bartrum, P. (2013). Escape the zombie trap. The Director, February, p. 59. Retrieved from http://unpan1.un.org/intradoc/groups/public/documents/APCITY/UNPAN014330.pdf

Bausch & Lomb. (1999). Bausch & Lomb acquires Hansa Research & Development. Press Release. Retrieved from http://www.evaluategroup.com/Universal/View.aspx?type=Story&id=268360

Becker, S. O., Pfaff, S., & Rubin, J. (2016). Causes and consequences of the Protestant reformation. *Explorations in Economic History, 62,* 1−25.

BEIS. (2012). *Boosting finance options for business.* London: Department for Business Energy and Industrial Strategy. Retrieved from https://www.gov.uk/government/publications/improving-business-access-to-finance

BEIS. (2012a). *The impact of the financial crisis on bank lending to SMEs.* London: Department for Business Energy and Industrial Strategy. Retrieved from https://www.gov.uk/government/uploads/system/uploads/attachment_data/file/34739/12-949-impact-financial-crisis-on-bank-lending-to-smes.pdf

BEIS. (2017). *Business population estimates for the UK and regions 2017.* London: Department of Business Energy and Industrial Strategy. Retrieved from https://www.gov.uk/government/uploads/system/uploads/attachment_data/file/663235/bpe_2017_statistical_release.pdf

Bernard, G. W. (2011). The dissolution of the monasteries. *History, 96*(324), 390−409.

BHA, KPMG. (2017). *Labour migration in the hospitality sector.* Report for BHA by KPMG, March. Retrieved from http://www.bha.org.uk/labour-migration-hospitality-sector/

Bibby. (2016). Subcontracting growth. Retrieved from https://www.construction-line.co.uk/media/1435/16-11-18-subcontracting-growth-final.pdf

Bishop, J. (2016). Currency, conversation, and control: Political discourse and the coinage in mid-Tudor England. *The English Historical Review, 131*(551), 763−792.

Blackburn, R. (2012). Segmenting the SME market and implications for service provision. Retrieved from http://www.acas.org.uk/media/pdf/i/0/0912_Segmenting_the_SME_market_-_Literature_review_v2.pdf

Blackstone. (2011). Response to misleading UK news story about former portfolio company Southern Cross. Retrieved from https://www.blackstone.com/media/press-releases/article/response-to-misleading-uk-news-story-about-former-portfolio-company-southern-cross

Blinder, S., & Allen, W. (2016). Briefing UK public opinion toward immigration: Overall attitudes and level of concern. Retrieved from http://www.migrationobservatory.ox.ac.uk/wp-content/uploads/2016/04/Briefing-Public_Opinion_Immigration_Attitudes_Concern.pdf

Bloomberg. (2017a). Barclays picks Dublin as post-Brexit EU headquarters. Retrieved from https://www.bloomberg.com/news/articles/2017-01-26/barclays-said-to-pick-dublin-as-eu-headquarters-after-brexit

Bloomberg. (2017b). Trump says U.S. working on 'Big and Exciting' U.K. trade deal. Retrieved from https://www.bloomberg.com/news/articles/2017-07-25/trump-says-fox-visit-marks-even-better-u-s-u-k-relations

Bloy, M. (2017). Victorian census occupations compiled from parliamentary papers 1852-3, 1863 and 1873. Retrieved from http://www.victorianweb.org/history/census.html

Bolt, J., & Zanden, J. L. (2014). The Maddison project: Collaborative research on historical national accounts. *The Economic History Review, 67*(3), 627−651.

Borders Group. (2000). Annual report. Retrieved from http://media.corporate-ir.net/media_files/NYS/BGP/bgp_ar2000/index.html

Borio, C., James, H., & Song Shin, H. (2014). The International Monetary and Financial system: A capital account historical perspective. Retrieved from http://www.bis.org/publ/work457.htm

Bossone, B., Cattaneo, M., Gallino, L., Grazzini, E., & Sylos Labini, S. (2015). Free fiscal money: Exiting austerity without breaking up the Euro. Retrieved from http://www.syloslabini.info/online/wp-content/uploads/2014/11/Appello-Inglese-rivisto_9-03-2015.pdf

Boston.com. (2012). History of polaroid and Edwin Land. Retrieved from https://www.boston.com/uncategorized/noprimarytagmatch/2012/10/03/history-of-polar-oid-and-edwin-land?pg=1&t=100&cp=1

Bourlot, G. (2015). Alitalia and Etihad merger. Retrieved from http://tesi.eprints.luiss.it/15267/1/178241.pdf

Bowker. (2017). Books in print. Retrieved from http://www.bowker.com/products/Books-In-Print.html

Brint, S. (2005). Creating the future: 'New directions' in American research universities. *Minerva*, *43* (1), 23–50.

Brint, S. (2017). The role of university researchers in 50 top inventions, 1955–2005. Retrieved from http://www.education.ox.ac.uk/about-us/events/events-archive/

Broadberry, S., & Leunig, T. (2013). The impact of government policies on UK manufacturing since 1945. Future of manufacturing project: Evidence paper, 2.

Brotton, J. (2016). *This orient isle Elizabethan England and the Islamic world.* London: Allan Lane.

Brue, S. L. (1993). *The evolution of economic thought.* San Diego, CA: Harcourt, Brace & Co.

Buchmann, T., & Pyka, A. (2012). The evolution of innovation networks: The case of the German automotive industry. *Economics and Management*, 2012.

Bucholz, R., & Key, N. (2009). *Early modern England 1485–1714: A narrative history.* Chichester: John Wiley & Sons.

Burke, E. (1868). Reflections on the Revolution in France and on the proceedings in certain societies in London relative to that event: 1790. Risingtens.

Bush, M. L. (1991). 'Up for the commonweal': The significance of tax grievances in the English rebellions of 1536. *The English Historical Review*, *106*(CCCCXIX), 299–318.

Bush, M. L. (2007). The Tudor polity and the pilgrimage of grace. *Historical Research*, *80*(207), 47–72.

BVCA. (2017). Private equity and venture capital performance measurement survey. Retrieved from https://www.bvca.co.uk/LinkClick.aspx?fileticket=8T8PP5aPouw%3D&portalid=0

CAA. (2017). UKTiE: Brexit and aviation. Retrieved from https://www.caa.co.uk/uploadedFiles/CAA/Content/News/Speeches_files/UKTiE%20-%20Andrew%20Haines.pdf

Cambridge Associates. (2016). US venture capital index and selected benchmark statistics. Retrieved from https://www.cambridgeassociates.com/benchmark/global-ex-us-pe%e2%80%8a%e2%80%8avc-benchmark-commentary-fourth-quarter-2016/

Campbell, P. (2017). Investment in UK car industry plummets amid Brexit uncertainty. Retrieved from https://www.ft.com/content/0c3427b2-5ce1-11e7-9bc8-8055f264aa8b

Campos, E. V. (2002). Jews, Spaniards, and Portingales: Ambiguous identities of Portuguese Marranos in Elizabethan England. *ELH, 69*(3), 599−616.

Cantoni, D. (2015). The economic effects of the Protestant reformation: Testing the Weber hypothesis in the German lands. *Journal of the European Economic Association, 13*, 561−598.

Carlyle, T. (1849). Occasional discourse on the Negro question. *Fraser's Magazine for Town and Country, XL,* 670−767.

Carney, M. (2017). A fine balance. Retrieved from http://www.bankofengland.co.uk/publications/Documents/speeches/2017/speech983.pdf

Census Data For 2001. (2017). Office of National Statistics. Retrieved from https://www.ons.gov.uk/employmentandlabourmarket/peopleinwork/employmentandemployeetypes/adhocs/0069984digitoccupationsocand4digitindustrysicbyagebands

Cerretano, V. (2009). The Treasury, Britain's postwar reconstruction, and the industrial intervention of the Bank of England, 1921−91. *The Economic History Review, 62*(s1), 80−100.

Chamberlain, J. (1914). *Mr Chamberlain's speeches* (Vol. 2). New York, NY: Houghton Mifflin Company.

Chepurenko, A., & Vilenski, A. (2016). SME policy of the Russian State (1990−2015): From a 'generalist' to a 'paternalist' approach. Retrieved from https://wp.hse.ru/data/2016/09/15/1120501326/WP1_2016_02_____.pdf

CJA Consultants. (2006). Patent litigation insurance. A study for the European Commission on the feasibility of possible insurance schemes against patent litigation risks. Retrieved from http://ec.europa.eu/internal_market/indprop/docs/patent/studies/pli_report_en.pdf

Clark, G. (2007). The long march of history: Farm wages, population, and economic growth, England 1209−1869. *The Economic History Review, 60*(1), 97−135.

CNBC. (2017). BlackBerry financials: Toronto Stock Exchange. Retrieved from https://www.cnbc.com/quotes/?symbol=BB-CA

Company Watch. (2016). More Zombie firms more risk, 16 November. Retrieved from https://www.companywatch.net/article/2016/11/more-zombie-firms-more-risk

Cooper, A., & Cooper, S. (2015). The Council of the North. Retrieved from http://www.historytoday.com/stephen-cooper/council-north

Crouch, C. (2017). Riddle: When is a chlorinated chicken better than a regulated banana? Social Europe? Retrieved from https://www.socialeurope.eu/riddle-chlorinated-chicken-better-regulated-banana

Culkin, N. (2016). Anchor institutions and regional innovation systems for supporting micro and small businesses, e-organisations and people.

Culkin, N., & Mallick, S. (2011). Producing work-ready graduates: The role of the entrepreneurial university. *International Journal of Market Research, 53,* 347−368.

Cumming, D., & binti Johan, S. A. (2008). Preplanned exit strategies in venture capital. *European Economic Review, 52*(7), 1209−1241.

Cuomo, O. (2002). Employee participation in privatisation transactions, policies and performance: The Italian experience. In Presentation to OECD/Turkish Privatisation Administration Conference on Privatisation, Employment and Employees, Istanbul.

Damodaran. (2017). Profit margins (net, operating and EBITDA) data sets prepared by Prof. Aswath Damodaran Stern Business School (NYU). Retrieved from http://pages.stern.nyu.edu/~adamodar/

DARPA. (2017). About us. Retrieved from https://www.darpa.mil/about-us/about-darpa

Detzer, D. (2005). *Donnybrook: The battle of bull run, 1861*. Orlando, FL: Harcourt.

DEXU. (2017a). Future customs arrangements. Retrieved from https://www.gov.uk/government/publications/future-customs-arrangements-a-future-partnership-paper

DEXU. (2017b). Nuclear materials and safeguards issues: Position paper. Retrieved from https://www.gov.uk/government/publications/nuclear-materials-and-safeguards-issues-position-paper

DEXU. (2017c). Continuity in the availability of goods for the EU and the UK. Retrieved from https://www.gov.uk/government/publications/continuity-in-the-availability-of-goods-for-the-eu-and-the-uk-position-paper

Dimot, M. (1962). *Jews, God and history*. New York, NY: Penguin.

DOIT. (2017). Exporting is great opportunities in Saudi Arabia. Retrieved from https://opportunities.export.great.gov.uk/opportunities?utf8=%E2%9C%93&isSearchAndFilter=true&filterOpen=false&s=&countries%5B%5D=saudi-arabia&commit=Find+opportunities

Downes, L., & Nunes, P. (2013). Big-bang disruption. *Harvard Business Review*, (March), 45−56.

Dubois, A., Hulthén, K., & Pedersen, A. C. (2004). Supply chains and interdependence: A theoretical analysis. *Journal of Purchasing and Supply management*, *10*(1), 3−9.

Duggan, M. (2016). Ceramic imports to Britain and the Atlantic Seaboard in the fifth century and beyond. *Internet Archaeology*, (41).

Dyer, W. (2017). Success stories. Retrieved from http://www.drwaynedyer.com/blog/success-secrets/

Eichengreen, B., & Gupta, P. (2016). Managing sudden stops. Retrieved from http://documents.worldbank.org/curated/en/877591468186563349/Managing-sudden-stops

Elledge, J. (2017). The Tinker bell theory. Retrieved from http://www.newstatesman.com/politics/staggers/2017/03/tinkerbell-theory-politics-failures-my-lack-belief

Elton, G. R. (1953). *The Tudor revolution in government: Administrative changes under Henry VIII*. Cambridge: Cambridge University Press.

Elton, G. R. (1975). Taxation for war and peace in early Tudor England. *War and Economic Development: Essays in Memory of David Joslin* (pp. 33−48). Winter, J. M., ed.: New York: Cambridge University Press, ., Publication Date: April 25, 1975

Esmonde Cleary, S. (1989). *The ending of Roman Britain*. London: Batsford.

EUOJ. (2012). 2012/290/EU decision of the US-EU Joint Customs Cooperation Committee of 4 May. Published in OJ L 144 of 5 of June 2012, p. 44. Retrieved from http://eur-lex.europa.eu/legal-content/EN/TXT/?uri=OJ:L:2012:144:TOC

EUPAR. (2016). *A guide to EU procedures for the conclusion of international trade agreements.* Brussels: EU Parliament. Retrieved from http://www.europarl. europa.eu/RegData/etudes/BRIE/2016/593489/EPRS_BRI(2016)593489_EN.pdf

EuroLex. (2012). Treaty on stability coordination and governance in the economic and monetary union. Retrieved from: http://eur-lex.europa.eu/legal-content/EN/ TXT/?uri=LEGISSUM:1403_3

EuroLex. (2014). General state aid exemption. Retrieved from http://eur-lex.europa. eu/legal-content/EN/TXT/?qid=1404295693570&uri=CELEX:32014R0651

EuroLex. (2017). General state aid amendment. Retrieved from http://eur-lex. europa.eu/legal-content/EN/ALL/?uri=CELEX:32017R1084

EU Commission. (2017a). Administrative formalities and costs involved in accessing markets cross-border for provisions of accountancy, engineering and architecture. Retrieved from http://publications.europa.eu/en/publication-detail/-/publication/5c8a6c62-44e3-11e7-aea8-01aa75ed71a1/language-en

FDA. (1997). Hansa Research and Development Inc. Hansatome Microkeratome 510k Premarket Notification. US FDA, October 24. Retrieved from https:// www.accessdata.fda.gov/cdrh_docs/pdf/K972808.pdf. Accessed on 5 August 2017.

European Commission. (2017b). Authorised economic operator. Retrieved from http://ec.europa.eu/taxation_customs/general-information-customs/customs-security/authorised-economic-operator-aeo/authorised-economic-operator-aeo_ en#benefits

European Commission. (2017c). User guide to SME definition. Retrieved from https://ec.europa.eu/digital-single-market/en/news/new-sme-definition-user-guide-and-model-declaration

European Commission. (2017d). New approach directives. Retrieved from http:// www.newapproach.org/Directives/

EU Commission. (2017). Administrative formalities and costs involved in accessing markets cross-border for provisions of accountancy, engineering and architecture services — Final Report, May, Ecorys Netherlands B.V. Retrieved from http:// publications.europa.eu/en/publication-detail/-/publication/5c8a6c62-44e3-11e7-aea8-01aa75ed71a1/language-en

EU Internal Market. (2006). *Patent Litigation Insurance.* A Study for the European Commission on the feasibility of possible insurance schemes against patent litigation risks, CJA Consultants Ltd, Final Report June, Retrieved from http://ec. europa.eu/internal_market/indprop/docs/patent/studies/pli_report_en.pdf

Eurostat. (1991). *Rapid reports: Regions.* Luxembourg: Eurostat.

EUUSA. (1998). Agreement on mutual recognition between the European community and the United States of America. Retrieved from http://ec.europa.eu/ world/agreements/prepareCreateTreatiesWorkspace/treatiesGeneralData.do? step=0&redirect=true&treatyId=313

EUUSA. (2011). *USA – EU Air Safety Treaty*. Brussels: European Commission. Retrieved from http://ec.europa.eu/world/agreements/downloadFile.do? fullText=yes&treatyTransId=14841

FDA. (1997). Hansa Research and Development Inc. Hansatome Microkeratome 510k Premarket Notification. US FDA, October 24. Retrieved from https://www.accessdata.fda.gov/cdrh_docs/pdf/K972808.pdf. Accessed on 5 August 2017.

FAA. (2017). FAA boss outlines Brexit safety concerns for UK aviation. Retrieved from https://skift.com/2017/06/20/faa-boss-outlines-brexit-safety-concerns-for-uk-aviation/

Facebook. (2017). Facebook newsroom. Retrieved from https://newsroom.fb.com/company-info/

Fairweather, N. (1932). Hitler and Hitlerism: Germany under the Nazis. *The Atlantic*. Retrieved from https://www.theatlantic.com/magazine/archive/1932/04/hitler-and-hitlerism-germany-under-the-nazis/308961/

Farrell, M. (1986). The Boeing 767 program: A case study of issues related to success in managing an international co-operative project. Retrieved from http://www.dtic.mil/dtic/tr/fulltext/u2/a188848.pdf

FEP. (2017). High rate PECVD. Retrieved from https://www.fep.fraunhofer.de/en/Leistungsangebot/technologien/Hochrate-PECVD.html

Forbes, K. (2014). The economic impact of sterling's recent moves: More than a midsummer night's dream. Retrieved from http://www.bankofengland.co.uk/publications/Documents/speeches/2014/speech760.pdf

Fowler, H. (1921). Plato in twelve volumes, Vol. 12 (Harold N. Fowler, Trans.). Cambridge, MA: Harvard University Press.

Fraunhofer. (2015). Annual report. Retrieved from https://www.fraunhofer.de/content/dam/zv/en/Publications/Annual-Report/2015/Annual-Report-2015.pdf

Freeman, C. (1982). *The economics of industrial innovation*. London, UK: Pinter.

Freitsch, R., Neuhäusler, P., & Rothengatter, O. (2013). SME patenting – An empirical analysis in nine countries. Retrieved from http://www.isi.fraunhofer.de/isi-wAssets/docs/p/de/diskpap_innosysteme_policyanalyse/discussionpaper_36_2013.pdf

Friedman, M. (1962). *Capitalism and freedom*. Chicago, IL: Chicago University Press.

Frost, R. (1949). Quote attributed to Robert Frost but not confirmed. Retrieved from https://quoteinvestigator.com/2011/04/07/banker-umbrella/

FSB. (2017). Reformed business funding: What small firms want from Brexit. Retrieved from https://www.fsb.org.uk/docs/default-source/fsb-org-uk/reformed-business-funding.pdf

Gates, W. (1995). The importance of making mistake. Retrieved from http://izquotes.com/quote/69085

Gates, W., Myhrvold, N., & Rinearson, P. (1995). *The road ahead*. New York, NY: Viking.

Genberg, H., & Martinez, A. (2014). On the accuracy and efficiency of IMF forecasts: A survey and some extensions. Retrieved from http://www.ieo-imf.org/ieo/files/completedevaluations/BP-14-04.pdf

Gerrard, J. (2013). *The ruin of Roman Britain: An archaeological perspective*. Cambridge: Cambridge University Press.

Gilfillan, S. C. (1935). *Inventing the ship*. Chicago, IL: Follett Publishing Co.

Gkypali, A., & Roper, S. (2017). Home alone: Innovation and sales growth intentions among the sole self-employed. Research Paper No. 59. Retrieved from https://www.enterpriseresearch.ac.uk/our-work/publications/

Glazier, A. (1980). Review of Commerce extérieur et développement économique de l'Europe au XIXe siecle by P Bairoch. *The Journal of Modern History*, *52*(3), 489–491. (Sep., 1980).

Gomez, A., Shi, K., Quintana, C., Sato, M., Faulkner, G., Thomsen, B. C., & O'Brien, D. (2015). Beyond 100-Gb/s indoor wide field-of-view optical wireless communications. *IEEE Photonics Technology Letters*, *27*(4), 367–370.

Goodridge, P., Haskel, J., & Wallis, G. (2012). UK innovation index: Productivity and growth in UK industries. Nesta Working Paper 12/09. Retrieved from www.nesta.org.uk/wp12-09

Goolsbee, A. (1999). Evidence on the high-income Laffer curve from six decades of Tax Reform Brookings Institution. Retrieved from https://www.brookings.edu/bpea-articles/evidence-on-the-high-income-laffer-curve-from-six-decades-of-tax-reform/

Gove, M. (2016). Britain has had enough of experts. Retrieved from http://www.telegraph.co.uk/news/2016/06/10/michael-goves-guide-to-britains-greatest-enemy-the-experts/

Graphene Council. (2014). Professor Richard Jones, Vice Chancellor of Research and Innovation at Sheffield University talks about graphene commercialization. *Graphene Council Newsletter*. Retrieved from http://www.thegraphenecouncil.org/?page=JonesGrapheneComm&hhSearchTerms=%22richard+and+jones%22

Green Alliance. (2016). The UK's infrastructure pipeline. Retrieved from http://www.green-alliance.org.uk/resources/UK_infrastructure_pipeline_2016.pdf

Guitteau, J. (1942). Influence of the Huguenot Refugees on English manufactures. *Social Studies*, *33*(October 1), 6.

H.M. Government. (2017a). Building our industrial strategy. Green Paper. Retrieved from https://beisgovuk.citizenspace.com/strategy/industrial-strategy/supporting_documents/buildingourindustrialstrategygreenpaper.pdf

H.M. Government. (2017b). The United Kingdom's exit from and new partnership with the European Union. White Paper Cm 9417. Retrieved from https://www.gov.uk/government/publications/the-united-kingdoms-exit-from-and-new-partnership-with-the-european-union-white-paper

H.M. Government. (2017c). Legislating for the United Kingdom's withdrawal from the European Union. White Paper Cm 9446. Retrieved from https://www.gov.uk/government/uploads/system/uploads/attachment_data/file/604516/Great_repeal_bill_white_paper_accessible.pdf

HM Government. (2017d). *Enforcement and dispute resolution A future partnership paper*. London: DEXU. Retrieved from https://www.gov.uk/government/publications/enforcement-and-dispute-resolution-a-future-partnership-paper

H.M. Treasury. (2016a). Analysis: The immediate economic impact of leaving the EU. Cm 9292. Retrieved from https://www.gov.uk/government/uploads/system/

uploads/attachment_data/file/524967/hm_treasury_analysis_the_immediate_economic_impact_of_leaving_the_eu_web.pdf

H.M. Treasury. (2016b). Analysis: The long-term economic impact of EU membership and the alternatives. Cm 9250. Retrieved from https://www.gov.uk/government/uploads/system/uploads/attachment_data/file/517415/treasury_analysis_economic_impact_of_eu_membership_web.pdf

Hahn, L. A. (1920). *Economic theory of bank credit* (1st ed.). Oxford: Oxford University Press.

Haldane, A. (2017). Productivity puzzles. Speech at London School of Economics. Retrieved from http://www.bankofengland.co.uk/publications/Pages/speeches/2017/968.aspx

Hall, T. W., & Elliott, J. E. (1999). Poland and Russia one decade after shock therapy. *Journal of Economic Issues*, *33*(2), 305–314.

Hansard. (2000). Debate on South Yorkshire. Retrieved from https://www.publications.parliament.uk/pa/cm199900/cmhansrd/vo000726/halltext/00726h01.htm

Hanush, H., & Pyka, A. (2007). *Elgar companion to neo-Schumpeterian economics*. Cheltenham: Edward Elgar.

Harari, D. (2016). Regional and local economic growth statistics. House of Commons Library Briefing Paper 05795. Retrieved from http://researchbriefings.parliament.uk/ResearchBriefing/Summary/SN05795

Harra, J. (2017). Letter to Chairman House of Commons Treasury Select Committee, 21 February 2017 from J Harra Director General Customer Strategy & Tax Design. Retrieved from https://www.parliament.uk/documents/commons-committees/treasury/Correspondence/Jim-Harra-response-to-Tyrie-21-02-17.pdf

Herbert, I. (2006). Still Brassed Off: Mining village used in film reveals grim reality of closed pits. Retrieved from http://www.independent.co.uk/news/uk/this-britain/still-brassed-off-mining-village-used-in-film-reveals-grim-reality-of-closed-pits-351375.html

Heywood, J., & Powell, P. (1842). Statistics of the universities of Oxford and Cambridge. *Journal of the Statistical Society of London*, *5*(3), 235–244. doi:10.2307/2337921

Hillmann, H., & Gathmann, C. (2011). Overseas trade and the decline of privateering. *The Journal of Economic History*, *71*(3), 730–761.

Hippach-Schneider, U., Krause, M., & Woll, C.. (2007). Vocational education and training in Germany: Short description. In Cedelfop (Ed.), Cedefop Panorama series 138. Retrieved from www.cedefop.europa.eu/files/5173_en.pdf

Hodgson, G. M. (1988). *Economics and institutions*. Cambridge: Polity Press.

Holgersson, M. (2013). Patent management in entrepreneurial SMEs: A literature review and an empirical study of innovation appropriation, patent propensity, and motives. *R&D Management*, *43*(1), 21–36.

Holmes, P. (2016). A special deal for the car industry: How could it work? Retrieved from https://blogs.sussex.ac.uk/uktpo/2016/11/16/a-special-deal-for-the-car-industry-how-could-it-work/

Hook, L. (2017). Uber struggles for grip on the road to profit. Retrieved from https://www.ft.com/content/aabe4fe4-4bab-11e7-a3f4-c742b9791d43

House of Commons. (1922). Mr Young (Treasury Minister) answering question from Sir W. de Frece. Retrieved from http://hansard.millbanksystems.com/written_answers/1922/mar/29/trade-facilities-act

House of Commons. (2014). Debate on the address (Queen's speech). Retrieved from https://publications.parliament.uk/pa/cm201415/cmhansrd/cm140604/debtext/140604-0003.htm

House of Commons. (2017a). Legislating for Brexit: EU external agreements, Miller V, House of Commons Briefing Paper Number 7850. Retrieved from http://researchbriefings.files.parliament.uk/documents/CBP-7850/CBP-7850.pdf

House of Commons International Trade Committee. (2017). Oral evidence from Nissan re Brexit assurances from Government. Colin Lawther, Senior Vice President, Manufacturing, Supply Chain Management and Purchasing, Nissan. Retrieved from http://data.parliament.uk/writtenevidence/committeeevidence.svc/evidencedocument/international-trade-committee/uk-trade-options-beyond-2019/oral/48155.html

Hoyle, R. W. (1994). Crown, parliament and taxation in sixteenth-century England. *The English Historical Review*, *109*(434), 1174–1196.

Hoyle, R. W. (2001). *The pilgrimage of grace and the politics of the 1530s*. Oxford: Oxford University Press.

Hughes, A., & Mina, A. (2010). *The impact of the patent system on SMEs*. Centre for Business Research, University of Cambridge.

Hughes, J. (1986). *The vital few: The entrepreneur and American economic progress* (Vol. 819). Oxford University Press on Demand.

Hull Archive. (1597). C BRL/48 'Letter from Dr. Richard Hudson to the Mayor and Aldermen, applying for the appointment of deputy to Mr. Thweinge, the Assessor of the Admiralty Court', Hull City Archives at the Hull History Centre.

Hume, D. (1742). Of Money, Included in 'Essays, Moral, Political, and Literary' 1742. II.III.3. In E. F. Miller (Ed.), Indianapolis, IN: Liberty Fund, Inc. 1987. Liberty. Retrieved from http://www.econlib.org/library/LFBooks/Hume/hmMPL26.html

IBM. (2017). The difference between public and private blockchain. IBM. Retrieved from https://www.ibm.com/blogs/blockchain/2017/05/the-difference-between-public-and-private-blockchain/

IBM Corporation. (2017). Seven major European banks select IBM to bring blockchain-based trade finance to small and medium enterprises. Retrieved from http://www-03.ibm.com/press/us/en/pressrelease/52706.wss

Imai, K. (2016). A panel study of zombie SMEs in Japan: Identification, borrowing and investment behavior. *Journal of the Japanese and International Economies*, *39*, 91–107.

Jacobs, T. B. (2000). *Eisenhower at Columbia*. New Brunswick, NJ: Transaction Publishers.

Jobling, P. (2005). 'Virility in design': Advertising Austin Reed and the 'New Tailoring' during the interwar period in Britain. *Fashion Theory*, *9*(1), 57–83.

Kaldor, N. (1977). The nemesis of free trade. *Further Essays in Applied Economics* (pp. 234–241). London: Duckworth.

Kaldor, N., & Kaldor, N. (1978). Further essays on economic theory (No. 04; HB171, K3).

KBC. (2016). KBC and Cegeka trial ground-breaking blockchain application for SMEs. Retrieved from www.kbc.com/en/press-releases

Keeley, L., Walters, H., Pikkel, R., & Quinn, B. (2013). *Ten types of innovation: The discipline of building breakthroughs*. Hoboken, NJ: John Wiley & Sons.

Keen, S. (2015). The deliberate blindness of our central planners (Podcast). Transcript retrieved from https://www.peakprosperity.com/podcast/92208/steve-keen-deliberate-blindness-our-central-planners

Keen, S. (2017). Can opener quotes. Retrieved from: http://www.morefamous-quotes.com/topics/can-opener-quotes/

Keynes, J. M. (1920). *The economic consequences of the peace*. London: MacMillan and Co., Ltd.

Keynes, J. M. (1930). The economic possibilities of our grandchildren, printed in Vol. IX of the Collected Writings of J M Keynes (1973).

Keynes, J. M. (1936). *The general theory of employment interest and money*. London: Macmillan.

Kilpatrick, A. (2001). *Of permanent value: The story of Warren Buffett*. New York, NY: McGraw-Hill.

Kissinger, H. (1969). The only power Kissinger has is the confidence of the President, *New York Times Magazine*, June 1 1969.

Knibb, Gormezano and Partners. (2009). Mapping of the East Midlands automotive industry and identifying the main innovation drivers. Retrieved from https://doc-uri.com/download/mapping-automotive_59c1ea9cf581710b286dd86a_pdf

Knibbe, M. (2012). Macro-economic policy and votes in the thirties: Germany (and The Netherlands) during the Great Depression. Retrieved from https://rwer.wordpress.com/2012/06/29/macro-economic-policy-and-votes-in-the-thirties-ger-many-and-the-netherlands-during-the-great-depression/

KPMG. (2017). Labour migration in the hospitality sector. A KPMG report for the British Hospitality Association. Retrieved from http://www.bha.org.uk/hospital-ity-tourism-industry-announces-rst-post-brexit-sector-skills-strategy-2/

Krippner, G. R. (2005). The financialization of the American economy. *Socio-Economic Review*, *3*(2), 173–208.

Krueger, A. O. (2016). A tale of two crises: Greece and Iceland, Stanford Centre for International Development. Working Paper 574. Retrieved from http://scid.stan-ford.edu/sites/default/files/publications/574wp_0.pdf

Laffer, A. (2007). Overheating is not dangerous, *Morgunblai*, 17 November 2007 from Sigurgeirsdóttir & Wade (2015).

Lampe, M. (2011). Explaining nineteenth-century bilateralism: Economic and politi-cal determinants of the Cobden–Chevalier network. *The Economic History Review*, *64*(2), 644–668.

Landes, D. S. (2003). *The unbound Prometheus: Technological change and industrial development in Western Europe from 1750 to the present*. Cambridge: Cambridge University Press.

Lee, E. J., & Rhee, E. Y. (2008). Conceptual framework of within-category brand personality based on consumers' perception (WCBP-CP): The case of men's apparel category in South Korea. *Journal of Brand Management, 15*(6), 465–489.

Leemans, W. F. (1950). *The Old-Babylonian merchant: His business and his social position* (Vol. 3). Brill.

Leng, T. (2016). Interlopers and disorderly brethren at the Stade Mart: Commercial regulations and practices amongst the Merchant Adventurers of England in the late Elizabethan period. *The Economic History Review, 69*(3), 823–843.

Levie, J. (2014). State of small business Britain conference: The ambition gap. Enterprise Research Centre. Retrieved from http://strathprints.strath.ac.uk/59371/

Lewis, L., & Noonan, L. (2017). Nomura and Daiwa choose Frankfurt as post-Brexit EU base. Retrieved from https://www.ft.com/content/4586fe82-5740-11e7-9fed-c19e2700005f

Llobet, G., & Suarez, J. (2012). Patent litigation and the role of enforcement insurance. *Review of Law & Economics, 8*(3), 789–821.

Lords. (2012). House of Lords SME exports committee terms of reference. Retrieved from https://publications.parliament.uk/pa/ld201213/ldselect/ldsmall/131/13105.htm

Lucas, A. (1933). The bankers' industrial development company. *Harvard Business Review, 11*(3), 272–273.

Lucas, R. (1988). On the mechanisms of development planning. *Journal of Monetary Economics, 22*(1), 3–42.

Machin, S. (2015). Real wages and living standards: The latest UK evidence. Retrieved from http://blogs.lse.ac.uk/politicsandpolicy/real-wages-and-living-standards/

Macmillan, H. P. (1930). *Committee on finance and industry*. London: HMSO.

Malinvaud, E. (1981). Econometrics faced with the needs of macroeconomic policy. *Econometrica: Journal of the Econometric Society*, 1363–1375.

Marcuss, R. D., & Kane, R. E. (2007). US national income and product statistics. *Survey of Current Business, 87*, 2–32.

Marquetti, A. (2004). Do rising real wages increase the rate of labor-saving technical change? Some econometric evidence. *Metroeconomica, 55*(4), 432–441.

Marshall, A. (1890). *Principles of economics*. London: Macmillan.

Mason, C. M., & Harrison, R. T. (2015). Business angel investment activity in the financial crisis: UK evidence and policy implications. *Environment and Planning C: Government and Policy, 33*(1), 43–60.

Mason & Harrison. (2015). Business angel investment activity in the financial crisis: UK evidence and policy implications. *Environment and Planning C: Government and Policy*, 33.

May, T. (2016). Speech by Theresa May, launching her national campaign to become leader of the Conservative Party and Prime Minister of the United Kingdom. Retrieved from http://www.wlrk.com/docs/TheresaMayJuly11Speech.pdf

Mazzucato, M. (2013). *The entrepreneurial state*. London: Anthem Press.

Mazzucato, M. (2016). From market fixing to market-creating: A new framework for innovation policy. *Industry and Innovation, 23*(2), 140–156.

McCarthy, M. I. K. E. (2005). Social dynamics on the northern frontier of Roman Britain. *Oxford Journal of Archaeology, 24*(1), 47–71.

McGee, P. (2017). Volvo shakes up car market in pursuit of electric dream. Retrieved from https://www.ft.com/content/eda7aaca-618c-11e7-91a7-502f7ee26895

McLean, P. (2017). After Brexit the UK will need to renegotiate at least 759 treaties. Retrieved from https://www.ft.com/content/f1435a8e-372b-11e7-bce4-9023f8c0fd2e

McVeigh, K. (2015). Grimethorpe, the mining village that hit rock bottom — Then bounced back. Retrieved from https://www.theguardian.com/politics/2015/mar/03/grimethorpe-hit-rock-bottom-then-bounced-back

Media City. (2017). MediaCityUK marks 10 years since construction started. Retrieved from http://www.mediacityuk.co.uk/p/mediacityuk-marks-10-years-since-construction-started

Mehra, V. (2013). ARPA-E is here to stay. Retrieved from https://scienceprogress.org/wp-content/uploads/2013/01/ARPA-Ebrief.pdf

Merlin-Jones, D. (2010). The Industrial and Commercial Finance Corporation: Lessons from the past for the future. Retrieved from http://www.civitas.org.uk/pdf/ICFC.pdf

Miller, O. (1950). *The Forbes scrapbook of thoughts on the business of life*. New York, NY: Forbes.

Minford, P., Bootle, R., Bourne, R., Congdon, T., Lightfoot, W., Lyons, G., … Matthews, K. (2017). The economy after Brexit. Retrieved from https://www.economistsforfreetrade.com/publication/economy-after-brexit-publications/

Minsky, H. P. (1986). *Stabilizing an unstable economy*. New Haven, CT: Yale University Press.

Monkton Chambers. (2017). Aspects of post Brexit regulation in The Aviation Sector, Muttukumaru C. blog, 12 April. Retrieved from https://www.monckton.com/dfe-presentation-6-april-2017-aspects-of-post-brexit-regulation-in-the-aviation-sector-the-last-scene-that-ends-this-strange-and-eventful-history/

Morling, N. (2011). Behind the numbers the FD mentor: Arnold Weinstock. *Financial Director, January*, 48.

Moudud, J. K. (1999). Government spending in a growing economy: Fiscal policy and growth cycles. *Public Policy Brief//Jerome Levy Economics Institute of Bard College, 52*, 7−35.

Muellbauer, J. (2012). When is a housing market overheated enough to threaten stability? In A. Heath, F. Packer, & C. Windsor (Eds.), *Property markets and financial stability*. Reserve Bank of Australia.

Muellbauer, J., & Murphy, A. (1997). Booms and busts in the UK housing market. *The Economic Journal, 107*(445), 1701−1727.

Muller, T. (1989). Immigration policy and economic growth. *Yale Law & Policy Review, 7*(1), 101−136.

Murgia, M. (2016). How the Karhoo taxi app ended up running on empty. Retrieved from https://www.ft.com/content/0bb3cba0-a69b-11e6-8898-79a99-e2a4de6

Muttukumaru, C. (2017). Aspects of post Brexit regulation in the aviation sector. Retrieved from https://www.monckton.com/dfe-presentation-6-april-2017-aspects-of-post-brexit-regulation-in-the-aviation-sector-the-last-scene-that-ends-this-strange-and-eventful-history/

National Research Council. (2009). 21st Century innovation systems for Japan and the United States: Lessons from a decade of change. Retrieved from https://www.nap.edu/read/12194/chapter/15

NBER. (2012). US business cycle expansions and contractions. US National Bureau of Economic Research. Retrieved from http://www.nber.org/cycles/US_Business_Cycle_Expansions_and_Contractions_20120423.pdf

Nersisyan, Y., & Wray, L. R. (2010). Does excessive sovereign debt really hurt growth? A critique of 'This Time is Different', by Reinhart and Rogoff. Retrieved from http://www.levyinstitute.org/pubs/wp_603.pdf

New Policy Institute. (2014). Where does working tax credit go? Retrieved from http://www.npi.org.uk/files/1914/1261/8405/Where_does_working_tax_credit_go.pdf

Next. (2017). Our history Next Plc. Retrieved from http://www.nextplc.co.uk/about-next/our-history

NESTA. (2012). *UK innovation index: Productivity and growth in UK industries.* P. Goodridge, J. Haskel, & G. Wallis. Nesta Working Paper 12/09. Retrieved from http://www.nesta.org.uk/wp12-09. Data reproduced under https://creativecommons.org/licenses/by-nc-sa/4.0/

NIESR. (2016). The long and the short of it: What price UK exit from the EU? Blog Post by M. Ebell, R. Piggott, J. Warren, 12 May. Retrieved from https://www.niesr.ac.uk/blog/long-and-short-it-what-price-uk-exit-eu. Accessed on August 12, 2017.

Notcutts. (2017). History of Notcutts. Retrieved from http://www.notcutts.co.uk/a-complete-notcutts-history/content/fcp-content?#origins

Novoselov, K. S., Fal, V. I., Colombo, L., Gellert, P. R., Schwab, M. G., & Kim, K. (2012). A roadmap for graphene. *Nature, 490*(7419), 192−200.

Nunn, N., & Trefler, D. (2010). The structure of tariffs and long-term growth American. *Economic Journal: Macroeconomics, 2010*(4), 158−194.

O'Brien, P. K., & Pigman, G. A. (1992). Free trade, British hegemony and the international economic order in the nineteenth century. *Review of International Studies, 18*(2), 89−113.

OECD. (2002). High-growth SMEs and Employment, OECD, Paris. Retrieved from http://www.oecd.org/industry/smes/2493092.pdf

OECD/Eurostat. (2005). *Oslo manual: Guidelines for collecting and interpreting innovation data* (3rd ed.). Paris: OECD.

OECD. (2010a). Innovative SMEs and entrepreneurship for job creation and growth, Bologna + 10 high level review. Retrieved from https://www.oecd.org/cfe/smes/46404350.pdf

OECD. (2010b). High-growth enterprises: What governments can do to make a difference. Retrieved from http://www.oecd.org/industry/smes/high-growthenterpriseswhatgovernmentscandotomakeadifference.htm

OECD. (2010c). *SMEs, entrepreneurship and innovation.* Paris: OECD.

OECD. (2015). Lifting investment for higher sustainable growth, OECD economic outlook volume 2015/1. Retrieved from https://www.oecd.org/investment/Economic-Outlook-97-Lifting-investment-for-higher-sustainable-growth.pdf

Ogburn, C. (1957). Merrill's Marauders. *Harper's Magazine*, January.

ONS. (2017a). Count, employment and turnover for SME by broad industry group. Retrieved from https://www.ons.gov.uk/businessindustryandtrade/business/activitysizeandlocation/adhocs/006960countemploymentandturnoverforsmebybroadindustrygroup

ONS. (2017b). Analysis of real earnings: February. Retrieved from https://www.ons.gov.uk/employmentandlabourmarket/peopleinwork/earningsandworkinghours/articles/supplementaryanalysisofaverageweeklyearnings/feb2017

ONS. (2017c). Count, employment and turnover for SME by broad industry group, 26 April, dataset ah055. Retrieved from https://www.ons.gov.uk/businessindustryandtrade/business/activitysizeandlocation/adhocs/006960countemploymentandturnoverforsmebybroadindustrygroup

Parent, A. (2012). A critical note on 'This Time is Different'. *Cliometrica, 6*(2), 211−219.

Parliament. (2014). *British Business Bank: Written question - 54848.* London: UK Parliament. Retrieved from http://www.parliament.uk/business/publications/written-questions-answers-statements/written-question/

Parliament. (2014). "British Business Bank: Written question - 54848", UK Parliament: London, Retrieved from: http://www.parliament.uk/business/publications/written-questions-answers-statements/written-question/Commons/2016-11-24/54848

Parliament. (2017a). European Union (withdrawal) bill. Retrieved from https://publications.parliament.uk/pa/bills/cbill/2017−2019/0005/18005.pdf

Parliament. (2017b). Parliament's role in ratifying treaties: A Young, Briefing Paper 5855. Retrieved from http://researchbriefings.files.parliament.uk/documents/SN05855/SN05855.pdf

Penrose, E. T. (1959). *The theory of the growth of the firm.* New York, NY: Sharpe.

Peterson, V. (2017). Borders book history: The balance. Retrieved from https://www.thebalance.com/borders-group-history-the-creation-of-a-bookstore-chain-2800146

Piketty, T. (2017). *Capital in the twenty-first century.* Boston, MA: Harvard University Press.

Price, D. (2010). The queen's private navy region focus, Q4. Retrieved from https://www.richmondfed.org/~/media/richmondfedorg/publications/research/region_focus/2010/q4/pdf/economic_history.pdf

Prolink. (2016). France: Major overhaul of work permit rules brings new opportunities. Retrieved from http://blog.pro-linkglobal.com/immigration-alerts/france-major-overhaul-of-work-permit-rules-brings-new-opportunities

Puttevils, J. (2010). The international economy in the 'Age of the Discoveries', 1470−1570: Antwerp and the English merchants' world (288 pp). By BlanchardIan. Stuttgart: Franz Steiner Verlag. Tables, figures, maps, bibliography, notes. Paper, € 45.00. ISBN: 978-3-515−09329-3. *Business History Review, 84*(4), 853−855.

R3. (2013). Are zombies really attacking the UK economy? R3 Association of Business Recovery Professionals. Retrieved from https://www.r3.org.uk/media/documents/policy/research_reports/special_reports/R3_Zombie_Paper_JAN_2013.pdf

Ralph, O. (2017). Dublin was expected to be a big winner, but continental Europe has been more popular. Retrieved from https://www.ft.com/content/f79c8494-573f-11e7-9fed-c19e2700005f

Ramsey, G. (1979). *The politics of a Tudor merchant adventurer.* Manchester: Manchester University Press.

RCN. (2017). Nursing shortage may worsen. Retrieved from https://www.rcn.org.uk/news-and-events/news/nursing-shortage-may-worsen

Reinert, H., & Reinert, E. (2006). Creative destruction in economics: Nietzsche, Sombart, Schumpeter. *Friedrich Nietzsche (1844–1900)*, 55–85.

Reinhart, C. M., & Rogoff, K. S. (2009). *This time is different: Eight centuries of financial folly.* Pricetwon, PA: Princeton University Press.

Reuters. (2008). Innogenetics says resolves patent case with Abbott. Retrieved from http://www.reuters.com/article/pharmaceuticals-innogenetics-idUSL1474312220080414

Rhoades, D. (2014). *Evolution of international aviation: Phoenix rising.* Abingdon: Taylor and Francis.

Ricardo, D. (1815). An essay on the influence of a low price of corn on the profits of stock (Vol. 438). London.

Ricardo, D. (1817). *Principles of political economy and taxation. The works and correspondence of David Ricardo. Pamphlets and papers 1815–1823.* Volume I. P. Sraffa (Ed.), Indianapolis: Liberty Fund 2004.

Roaf, J., Atoyan, R., Joshi, B., & Krogulski, K. (2014). 25 years of transition post-communist Europe and the IMF. Retrieved from http://www.imf.org/external/region/bal/rr/2014/25_years_of_transition.pdf

Rogers-Davis, N. (2013). Angmering's post offices and postmen blog post. Retrieved from http://www.angmeringvillage.co.uk/history/Articles/Post.htm

Roper, S., & Hart, M. (2013). Supporting sustained growth among SMEs – Policy models and guidelines. ERC White Paper No. 7. Retrieved from https://www.enterpriseresearch.ac.uk/publications/supporting-sustained-growth-among-smes-policy-models-guidelines/

Ruhs, M., & Vargas-Silva, C. (2015). Briefing: The labour market effects of immigration. Retrieved from http://www.migrationobservatory.ox.ac.uk/resources/briefings/election-2015-briefing-immigration-and-jobs-the-labour-market-effects-of-immigration/

Rusp. (2017). Russian proverb. Retrieved from http://www.inspirationalstories.com/proverbs/russian-trouble-never-comes-alone/

Sachs, J. (2012). What I did in Russia. Retrieved from http://jeffsachs.org/2012/03/what-i-did-in-russia/

Sagan, C. (2007). *The varieties of scientific experience: A personal view of the search for God.* New York, NY: Penguin.

Sansom, C. J. (2008). The Wakefield conspiracy of 1541 and Henry VIII's progress to the North reconsidered. *Northern History*, *45*(2), 217–238.

Saridakis, G., Lai, Y., Muñoz Torres, R. I., & Mohammed, A.-M. (2017). Actual and intended growth in family firms and non-family owned firms: Are they different? Research Paper No 60. Retrieved from https://www.enterpriseresearch.ac.uk/publications/actual-intended-growth-family-firms-non-family-owned-firms-different-research-paper-no-60/

Sayer, D. (2009). Medieval waterways and hydraulic economics: Monasteries, towns and the East Anglian fen. *World Archaeology, 41*(1), 134–150.

Schacht, H. (1946). Statement in Nuremburg Trial proceedings, volume 12, Day 118. Retrieved from http://avalon.law.yale.edu/imt/05-01-46.asp

Schumpeter, J. A. (1934). *The theory of economic development: An inquiry into profits, capital, credit, interest, and the business cycle.* Cambridge, MA: Harvard University Press.

Schumpeter, J. A. (1950). *Capitalism, socialism, and democracy.* New York, NY: Harper and Brothers.

Schumpeter, J. (1954). *The history of economic analysis.* London: Allen & Unwin, Reprinted in Paperback 1986.

Scott, S. (2013). Labour, migration and the spatial fix: Evidence from the UK food industry. *Antipode, 45*(5), 1090–1109.

Scourfield, P. (2012). Caretelization revisited and the lessons of Southern Cross. *Critical Social Policy, 32*(1), 137–148.

Seal, W. (2010). Managerial discourse and the link between theory and practice: From ROI to value-based management. *Management Accounting Research, 21*(2), 95–109.

Seguino, S. (1999). The investment function revisited: Disciplining capital in South Korea. *Journal of Post Keynesian Economics, 22*(2), 313–338.

Shaw, G. B. (1907). Major Barbara – Preface to play. Retrieved from http://www.gutenberg.org/files/3789/3789-h/3789-h.htm

Sherefkin, R. (2009). EVs need new parts – And maybe new parts makers. *Automotive News, 84*(6383), 9 October.

Sigurgeirsdottir, S., & Wade, R. H. (2015). From control by capital to control of capital: Iceland's boom and bust, and the IMF's unorthodox rescue package. *Review of International Political Economy, 22*(1), 103–133.

Simboli, A., Raggi, A., & Rosica, P. (2015). Life cycle assessment of process eco-innovations in an SME automotive supply network. *Sustainability, 7*(10), 13761–13776.

Sledzik, K. (2013). Schumpeter's view on innovation and entrepreneurship management trends in theory and practice, Stefan Hittmar (Ed.), Faculty of Management Science and Informatics. University of Zilina and Institute of Management by University of Zilina.

Smith, A. (1776). An inquiry into the nature and causes of the wealth of nations. Retrieved from http://www.econlib.org/library/Smith/smWN13.html

Solow, R. M. (1956). A contribution to the theory of economic growth. *The Quarterly Journal of Economics, 70*(1), 65–94.

Solow, R. M. (1957). Technical change and the aggregate production function. *The Review of Economics and Statistics*, 312–320.

Sommerville, J. (2017). The decline of Roman Britain. Retrieved from https://faculty.history.wisc.edu/sommerville/123/123%2041%20FallRoman%20Br.htm

Southern Cross. (2006). Southern Cross announces IPO pricing at 225 pence per share. Retrieved from http://www.allipo.com/articles/1535/ipo-southern-cross-hc-gp-ipo-pricing%20%207

Southern Cross. (2008). Annual report. Retrieved from https://www.slideshare.net/canon99in/annual-report-2008—7472542?qid=5ac9afce-241f-4435-82d2-f2d24ac14249&v=&b=&from_search=9

Spitzley, A., Rogowski, T., & Garibaldo, F. (Eds.). (2007). Open innovation for small and medium sized enterprises: Ways to develop excellence. Retrieved from http://wiki.iao.fraunhofer.de/images/studien/open-innovation-for-small-and-medium-sized-enterprises.pdf

Spufford, P. (2006). From Antwerp and Amsterdam to London: The decline of financial centres in Europe. *De Economist, 154*(2), 143—175.

Spufford, P. (2010). 4th Ortelius Lecture from Antwerp to London, The Decline of Financial Centres in Europe, Netherlands Institute for Advanced Study in the Humanities and Social Sciences and University of Antwerp. Retrieved from www.nias.knaw.nl/Publications/Ortelius_Lecture/Ortelius_04_Spufford/at_download/file

Stanewell, L. (1951). Calendar of the Ancient Deeds, Letters, Miscellaneous Old Documents etc in the Archives of the Corporation, City & Country of Kingston upon Hull, available in Hull City Archives.

Start Business in France. (2017). Professional answers and advice on starting and running a small business in France. Retrieved from http://www.startbusinessin-france.com

Stiglitz, J. E. (1999). The World Bank at the millennium. *The Economic Journal, 109*(459), 577—597.

Stone, L. (1949). Elizabethan overseas trade. *The Economic History Review, New Series, 2*(1), 30—58.

Stuffins, C. (2012). Open public services: Experiences from the voluntary sector. Retrieved from https://www.ncvo.org.uk/images/documents/practical_support/public_services/open_public_services_experiences_from_the_voluntary_sector.pdf

Sufi, A., & Mian, A. (2014). *House of debt*. Chicago, IL: University of Chicago Press.

Summers, L. (1995). Ten lessons to learn. *The Economist, 23*, December, 46—48.

Tang, C. S., Zimmerman, J. D., & Nelson, J. I. (2009). Managing new product development and supply chain risks: The Boeing 787 case. *Supply Chain Forum: An International Journal, 10*(2), 74—86.

Tawney, R. (1926). *Religion and the rise of capitalism, Fifth Printing 2008*. New Brunswick, NJ: Transaction Publishers.

Tena-Junguito, A., Lampe, M., & Fernandes, F. T. (2012). How much trade liberalization was there in the world before and after Cobden-Chevalier? *The Journal of Economic History, 72*(3), 708—740.

The Boeing Corporation. (2013). Randy's journal, our supply chain. Retrieved from http://www.boeingblogs.com/randy/archives/2013/02/supply_chain.html

The Boston Consulting Group. (2017). Bridging to Brexit: Insights from European SMEs, corporates and investors. Retrieved from https://www.afme.eu/globalassets/downloads/publications/afme-bcg-cc-bridging-to-brexit-2017.pdf

The CIA. (2012). CIA's impact on technology. Retrieved from https://www.cia.gov/about-cia/cia-museum/experience-the-collection/text-version/stories/cias-impact-on-technology.html

The Daily Mail. (2016). Enemies of the people. Retrieved from http://www.dailymail.co.uk/news/article-3903436/Enemies-people-Fury-touch-judges-defied-17-4m-Brexit-voters-trigger-constitutional-crisis.html

The FCA. (2017a). Asset management market study final report: Market study. Retrieved from https://www.fca.org.uk/publication/market-studies/ms15-2-3.pdf

The FCA. (2017b). BIPRU 5 credit risk mitigation. Retrieved from https://www.handbook.fca.org.uk/handbook/BIPRU/5.pdf. Accessed 20 July 2017.

The HTA. (2017). Horticultural Trades Association: Garden industry statistics. Retrieved from https://hta.org.uk/learn-develop/market-information/garden-industry-statistics.html

The IFS. (2016). Brexit and the UK's public finances. Retrieved from https://www.ifs.org.uk/uploads/publications/comms/r116.pdf

The Investment Association. (2016). Asset management in the UK 2015–2016. Retrieved from https://www.theinvestmentassociation.org/assets/components/ima_filesecurity/secure.php?f=research/2016/20160929-amsfullreport.pdf

The Ipswich Star. (2007). Fifty years suits him. Retrieved from http://www.ipswich-star.co.uk/news/fifty-years-suits-him-1-115106

The League of Nations. (1938). Statistical year book of the League of Nations 1938/39. Retrieved from http://digital.library.northwestern.edu/league/stat.html#1938

The Maddison-Project. (2013). New Maddison Project database. Retrieved from http://www.ggdc.net/maddison/maddison-project/home.htm

The Scottish Parliament. (2017). SPICe briefing agriculture and Brexit in ten charts. Retrieved from http://www.parliament.scot/ResearchBriefingsAndFactsheets/S5/SB_17-12_Agriculture_and_Brexit_in_10_Charts.pdf

The Stratford Herald. (2017). Butterfly farm owner fearful of the impact of Brexit. The Stratford Herald. Retrieved from http://www.stratford-herald.com/72546-butterfly-farm-owner-fearful-impact-brexit.html

The Times. (1985). Tempus: J Hepworth & Son. The Times, 6 November, p. 19.

The Wall Street Journal. (2007). Alitalia holding pattern. *The Wall Street Journal*, 22 November. Retrieved from http://www.ascendworldwide.com/the_wall_street_journal_22-11-07.pdf

The World Bank. (2017). GDP per capita in 2010 constant US$ Data. Retrieved from http://data.worldbank.org/indicator/NY.GDP.PCAP.KD?locations=KR

Thornton, T. (2009). Henry VIII's progress through Yorkshire in 1541 and its implications for Northern identities. *Northern History*, *46*(2), 231–244.

Timmer, M. P., Dietzenbacher, E., Los, B., Stehrer, R., & Vries, G. J. (2015). An illustrated user guide to the world input–output database: The case of global automotive production. *Review of International Economics*, *23*(3), 575–605.

Toffler, A. (1970). *Future shock*. New York, NY: Random House.

Tomlinson. (2013). Banks' lending practices: Treatment of businesses in distress. Retrieved from http://www.tomlinsonreport.com/docs/tomlinsonReport.pdf

Tovar, C. (2008). DGSE models and central banks. BIS Working Papers No 256. Retrieved from http://www.bis.org/publ/work258.htm

Tubbs, G., & Gillett, T. (2011). *Harvesting the BlackBerry: An insider's perspective*. Tucson, AZ: Wheatmark, Inc.

Turvill, W. (2017). Japanese banks Nomura and Daiwa Securities Group to shift London resources to Frankfurt after Brexit. Retrieved from http://www.cityam.com/267158/japanese-banks-nomura-and-daiwa-securities-group-shift

Tyrie, A. (2017). Letter to Nick Lodge Director General, Transformation HM Revenue & Customs from Andrew Tyrie Chairman House of Commons Treasury Select Committee. Retrieved from https://www.parliament.uk/documents/commons-committees/treasury/Correspondence/Tyrie-to-Nick-Lodge-relating-to-CDS-30-03-17.pdf

UCAS. (2017). B7 applicants at the 30 June deadline (2017 cycle) IB.1 Nursing applicants for all courses by domicile group. Difference between cycle and 2016 cycle. Retrieved from https://www.ucas.com/file/115961/download?token=n9lk8cCN

Ugolini, L. (2000). Clothes and the modern man in 1930s Oxford. *Fashion Theory*, *4*(4), 427–446.

UNCEFACT. (2017). Cross industry technical artefacts deliverables. Retrieved from https://uncefact.unece.org/display/uncefactpublicreview/Public+Review%3A+Extension+of+Cross+Industry+Technical+Artefacts+Deliverables

US Appeal Court. (2008). Innogenetics, N.V., Plaintiff-Cross Appellant, v. Abbott Laboratories, Defendant-Appellant.Nos. 2007-1145, 2007-1161. Retrieved from http://caselaw.findlaw.com/us-federal-circuit/1063919.html

V & A. (2017). Style guide: Jacobean. Retrieved from http://www.vam.ac.uk/content/articles/s/style-guide-jacobean/

Vecteezy. (2017). Base handshake graphic for revectoring. Retrieved from https://www.vecteezy.com/vector-art/93907-handshake-gradation-icons

Verdoorn, P. J. (1980). Verdoorn's law in retrospect: A comment. *The Economic Journal*, *90*(358), 382–385.

Vise, D. A. (2005). *The Google story*. London: Pan Books.

Vision of Britain. (2017). Census report website. Retrieved from http://www.vision-ofbritain.org.uk/census/

Vlastos, G. (1956). *Plato, Protagoras*. Indianapolis, IN: Howard W. Sams & Co.

Viva. (2007). Open innovation for small and medium sized enterprises. In A. Spitzley, T. Rogowski, F. Garibaldo (Eds.). Retrieved from http://wiki.iao.fraunhofer.de/images/studien/open-innovation-for-small-and-medium-sized-enterprises.pdf. Accessed on August 5, 2017.

Von Moltke. (1871). "On Strategy" as translated in *Moltke on the Art of War: Selected Writings* (1995) by Daniel J. Hughes and Harry Bell, Presido Press (absorbed by Ballentine): New York p. 92

Ward, M., & Rhodes, C. (2014). Small businesses and the UK economy. House of Commons Library SN/EP/6078. Retrieved from http://researchbriefings.parliament.uk/ResearchBriefing/Summary/SN06078

Ward Perkins, B. (2013). A real economic meltdown: The end of Roman Britain. Retrieved from https://www.youtube.com/watch?v=iHduMbabjFM

Waymo. (2017). Fact Sheet: LiDAR, the 'eyes' of our self-driving car. Retrieved from https://storage.googleapis.com/sdc-prod/v1/press/Waymo_Lidar_Fact_Sheet.pdf

Weber, M. (1905). *The protestant work ethic and the spirit of capitalism*. London: Allen and Unwin, 1930.

Welch, J. (2001). *Straight from the gut*. New York, NY: Warner Books.

Westerndarp, J. (1968). *East Anglian window*. Ipswich: East Anglian Magazine Ltd.

White, R. (2016). The ruin of Roman Britain: An archaeological perspective, by James Gerrard.

Wicksell, K. (1898). Interest and prices (R. F. Kahn, Trans., 1936). London: Macmillan.

Wiesen Cook, B. (1981). *The de-classified Eisenhower: A divided legacy of peace and political warfare*. New York, NY: Doubleday.

Wolfers, J. (2014). Inequality and growth Brookings Institution from NBER. Retrieved from http://users.nber.org/~jwolfers/papers/Comments/Piketty.pdf

Woolf, C. (2016). Britain's first 'Brexit': 286 A.D. It didn't last long. Retrieved from https://www.pri.org/stories/2016-06-23/britain-s-first-brexit-286-ad

Index

Abbot Laboratories, 180
Academic university *vs*
    entrepreneurial universities,
    208−209
Act of Supremacy (1534), 31
Adam Smith's 'Invisible Hand',
    147−150
AIG, 101
Alitalia Spa, 59−60
Allocative or productive
    efficiency, 13
Amazon.com, 16, 66
Ambitious firms
    mission-based innovation
        driven by, 44−45
    role in innovation, 44
Amsterdam, 202
Ancient Civilisations, 22
Android alternatives, 15
Antwerp, 37, 161−162, 166−167,
    201−202
Apple, 113, 177
ARM Semiconductor Ltd, 15
Artificial intelligence self-drive
    component, 113
Asian Financial Crisis (1997), 20,
    104
Asset-based financing, 18
Austin Reed, 76−77
Automotive/Aerospace
    supply chains, 66−72,
    100
Automotive supply chain,
    complexity of, 66−72

Balance of Payments Sudden Stop
    Events, 104, 117
Barclays, 101
Basel Banking Capital Accords,
    106, 112, 150−151
Basel Capital Accords, 18
'Big Bang Disruptions', 16
'Bilateral Third Country' treaties
    with Third Nations, 27
Bio Technology research
    companies, 85
Bit-Coin, 156
BlackBerry, 15−16
Black Death, 31
Black swans and conspiracy
    theory, 128−129
Blockbuster disrupters, 16
Block chain international
    payment system, 153−158
Boeing Commercial Aerospace,
    68−69
Book market disruption, 64−66
Bookselling trade, 64−66
Borders, 65−66
Boston Consulting Group, 101
Brexit, 11, 26−27, 42
    Acts of Parliament and
        associated Proclamations,
        role of, 31
    AD 410 experience, 28−30, 78,
        166
    from adjustment and
        stabilisation, 36−39
    assumptions, 136−138

challenges, 40–41, 213
changes in purchasing power,
    99
debate, 122
definition, 27
EU impacts, 86–87
EU/UK negotiations, 39
implications, 85–92
induced supply chain
    dislocation, 70
1536–1541 insurrection and
    challenge, 34–35
issues emerging from, 28
issues from previous, 195–200
lessons from previous, 95–103
narrative of fear and bullying,
    204
new arrangements, 212
1530–1542 Reformation and
    English departure, 30, 33
reformation changes and,
    33–36
regional execution, 114–117
risks, 138
'Stones' and 'Ripples', 94–103
structural (1529–1540),
    31–32
'Take Back Control' and
    'Reclaim Our Sovereignty',
    121
UK preparation for, 38–39
Urban and Supply Chain
    Catastrophe (AD 410–AD
    420), 28–30
Brexit Day operational
    imperatives, 110–113
Business Accelerator Programme,
    43
Business Angels, 18
Business credit mechanisms,
    17–18

Capital investment funding, 18
Capital Requirements Directives,
    106
Carnegie, Andrew, 17
Carry trade, 20
Cell-based therapies, 14
Chamberlain, Joseph, 125
Chambers of Commerce, 188–189
Commercialisation, 172
Commercialisation process, 14
Common Agricultural Policy, 115
Community Care Act, 81
Comparative Advantage, theory
    of, 125
Complex supply chain players,
    66–72
    Automotive and Defence
        Contracting sectors, 67
    Automotive or Aerospace
        supply chains, 66–72
Coping with Brexit
    academic innovations, 171
    'access to finance' measures,
        168
    asset prices, managing, 150
    'block chain' approach,
        168–170
    building and growing new and
        existing firms and killing
        non-viable firms, 164
    building high intellectual
        content value-adding
        services, 163
    cost setting, 147–149
    credit model, 147–150
    developing negotiating skills,
        183
    efficient supply chains,
        165–168
    entrepreneurial 'up-skilling',
        182–184

establishing effective trust and relationships, 162
event-triggered payment system for MSMEs, 153–158
export support activities, 160–163
feasibility study, 183
financial ombudsman service, 159
innovation contracts, 170–177
lending support measures, 145–146
MSME funding gap, reducing, 144–147
new trade agreements, 190–195
patenting of innovations, 179–182
raising investment and innovation levels, 168
sharing of problems and solutions, 159–160
state as entrepreneur, 154–155
state funding, 172–175
structure to improve finance flows, 150
use of proclamation to control public concern, 194
venture capital funding, 177–179, 183
vocational training, 184–190
working with local Regional Development Agencies and Business Support Organisations, 160
work permit restrictions, 187–188
Corn Laws, repeal of, 123–125
Cost-effective human genome mapping, 14
Creative Destruction, 58
Cromwell, Thomas, 30, 201

"Crowding-out" of market sector investment, 133
Cryptocurrencies, 156
Customs Declaration Service, 112

Defence Advanced Research Projects Agency (DARPA), 13–14, 175–177
Devolution Settlement (1998), 114
Dismal Science, 128
Disruption events, 103
financial system, 104–106, 202
legal and regulatory risk, 106–110
ongoing market and technological innovation, 113
operational challenges, 110–113, 202
regional execution, 114–117
Dividend rents, 18
Dynamic efficiency, 13

E-commerce innovation, 48, 51
Economic models, 135
Economic Rent, 131–132
Efficiency of an economy, 13
allocative or productive, 13
dynamic, 13
English Industrial Revolution, 33, 62
English Taxation, 31
Enterprise mobility management (EMM), 15
Entrepreneurs, 17, 204–205
capitalism and, 18–21
Entrepreneurship, 21
Equipment leasing, 18
European Aviation and Safety Agency, 107
European Open Skies Treaty, 110

European Union
  'acquis communitaire', 106
  Brexit impacts, 86–87
  Directives, 106
  EU–UK academic research
      programmes, 114
  EU–UK Free Trade
      Agreement, 111
  EU/UK negotiations, 39
  EU/USA Air Safety Treaty,
      139
  EU/US Treaty, 108
  Free Trade Agreements, 111
  'Regulation 216-2008', 107
  Treaty provisions, 106
  UK contribution to, 106
EU/UK Brexit negotiations, 39
Event Cinema, 82–85

Facebook, 16, 177
Fashion retailing and brand
      identities, 76–78
Fast fashion, 14
Fast-growing firms, 44
Financialisation, effect of, 17–20
Financial services, 74–75
Food retailing, 185
Fraunhofer Institute programme,
      174–175
Free Trade to Chamberlain, 126
Frittered Debt, 132

German Automotive Sector,
      collaborative innovation in,
      71
German GDP *vs* Dutch GDP,
      154–155
German 'Mittlestand' companies,
      174–175
Good Friday Agreement (1999),
      114

Good Manufacturing Practice
      (GMP), 110
Google, 16, 62, 177
Google Self-Drive test car, 113
Graphene, 172–173
Great Debasement of 1544–1551,
      36, 194
Great Repeal Bill, 115
Grexit, 27
Grimethorpe, 102–103
Grimwades, 77–78
Gulf Cooperation Council (GCC),
      162, 186–187

Hague Documentary Convention,
      73
Hamburg, 37
'Hands-on' operational control,
      183
Hansa Research and
      Development Inc, 177–178
Hanseatic League, 37
Heinz, 17
Henrician Reformation, 32, 201
Hepworths, 78
High-growth enterprises, 44, 179
  role in innovation, 48
High-growth potential 'big'
      (or little!) bang disrupters,
      61–66
  annual returns, 63–64
  book market disruption,
      64–66
  definition, 63
  examples, 62–63
  internal rate of return
      thresholds on business
      plans, 64
  technology disrupters, 62–63
'High Tech Entrepreneurial SME
      Patents', 181

Hjalmar Schacht, 154
Huguenots' immigration, 39

Iceland's 2008 banking collapse,
    20–21, 103
Immigration concerns, 39,
    184–186
Information and data revolution,
    14
Innogenetics N.V., 18
Innovate UK, 174–175, 181–182
Innovation, 211
    in business processes, 16
    defined, 12–14
    E-commerce, 48, 51
    entrepreneurs *vs* professional
        managers, 17
    intangible, 48, 51
    product innovation and
        consumer expectations,
        14–17
    productivity *vs*, 12–14
    relationship between low pay
        and, 51–53
    technological examples, 14
Intangible investment, 48, 51
Internet of Things, 16
iPhone, 15

J Hepworth & Son, 78

Kafala system, 187–188
Kahoo, 63
Kendall & Sons, 78
Knowledge-driven innovators,
    82–85

Labour-intensive service MSMEs,
    80–82
Laffer, Arthur, 20
Laffer Curve, 129–130

Laithwaite, Eric, 172
Lasik eye surgery, 177–178
Librairie Nouvelle d'Orléans, 64
Library of Alexandria, 64
LIDAR (light-based technology),
    113
LIFI, 113, 114
Linear Induction Motor, 172
Lloyds, 101
London, 33, 202
    economy, 23
    role as a hub for financial
        flows, 23
    Thomas Cromwell's reforms
        and exit from, 33

Market and technological
    innovation, 113–114
Marshall/Lerner condition, 23,
    105
May, Prime Minister, 27, 94
Mazzucato, Mariana, 14
Medical Device Sector, 44
Merchant Adventurers, 87, 91,
    161
Merchant Adventurers Company,
    38
Micro, Small and Medium Sized
    Enterprises (MSMEs), 11,
    28, 88–90, 142
    birth of new firms, 58–61
    business ombudsman service,
        158–159
    by business stage segment sizes,
        47
    central role in innovation, 47
    characteristics, 209–212
    definitions, 45, 47
    employment rate, 48, 49
    equity return, 54
    financing costs, 54

high-growth, 47
importance to economy, 47−53
by industry, 46
in medical device sector, 48
needs and challenges, 43−44
opportunity segments, 54−58
pay rates, 51−53
pre-tax operating profit
    adjusted for leasing and
    R&D, 53
as revenue streams, 207−209
total factor productivity, 48, 50
Mission-based innovation, 19,
    44−45, 48
Mobile security, 15
Mobitex wireless packet-switched
    data communications
    networks, 15
Montague Burton, 77
MSME-focused Industrial and
    Commercial Finance
    Corporation (ICFC), 146
Multiplier effect, 101
    Grimethorpe case, 102
Mutual recognition treaty,
    137−138

Natural rate of interest, 132
Nissan Motor Manufacturing,
    Brexit-related issues in, 100
Non-Corporate Savings, 132
Northern Ireland, 114
Notcutt, Roger, 79−80
Notcutts Nurseries, 79−80

One size fits all approach,
    transformation challenges
    with, 60−85

Peace of Augsberg (1555), 32
Polaroid Corporation, 58−59

Poll Tax, 31
Post-Brexit barriers and impacts
    agriculture and horticulture, 80
    automotive supply chain,
        complexity of, 66−71
    book market disruption,
        64−66
    capital flows, 75
    contracting business, 72−73
    Euro-denominated
        transactions, 137
    EU−UK academic research
        programmes, 114
    farming and agriculture,
        115−117
    foreign trade patterns and
        restrictions, 135−136
    issue of financial services
        passporting, 74−75, 101
    issue of mutual recognition of
        professional qualifications,
        73
    knowledge-driven innovators,
        82−85
    labour-intensive small-scale
        local businesses, 80−82
    local retail, artisan products
        and local services, 75−80
    multiplier effects on London-
        based professional/business
        services, 75
    mutual recognition on air
        safety issues, 108
    small companies and micro
        exporters, 109
    structural view-point, 138, 141
    subsidies, 91
    transport access, 139
    treaty cover, 137
    UK-based Asset Management,
        75

UK-manufactured
pharmaceuticals and
medical devices, 139
UK suppliers, 72
Predatory entrepreneurship, 61
Private equity, 18
Productivity, 12–14
growth, 12
Professional managers, 17
Protestantism, 31

Ready-to-wear products and
supplies, 76
Reformation changes, effects of,
32, 35–36
Regional remoteness, 114–117
Relocation, 101
Research and development
programmes, 12
Research in Motion's (RIM)
Blackberry, 15
Residential mortgage markets, 18
Risk-weighted assets, 112
Roman Catholic Church, 30
Roman Coinage, 29
Roman pottery supply chains, 166
Russia, programme of shock
therapy, 60–61

Sailing-ship effect, 210
Schumpeter, J. A., 21, 54,
203, 210
Scotland, 114–116
Scotland Act (1998), 115
Self-driving car, 113–114
Self-employment, 211
50 Shilling Tailor, 77
Shock therapy, 60–61
Simple supply chain
subcontracting companies,
72

Small business sector, motivations
of, 43
Smart Phones, 14–16
Southern Cross Healthcare,
81–82, 92
Star businesses, 45
Starting business in France,
personal experiences, 77
Stratford Butterfly Farm, 109
'Style'-driven retailer, 78
Sunset clause, 153
Supply chains, 165–168
Automotive or Aerospace,
66–72, 100

'Tamkarum' (merchants), 22
Technology disrupters, 62–63
'Technology-enabling' patents,
180
Tesla, 113
Tinkerbell Effect, 129
Total Factor Productivity, 3
Trade policy, impact of, 37–38
Trailblazers, 16
Treason Act, 31
Treaty of Versailles (1919), 120,
154

Uber, 63, 113
UK Bi-Lateral Treaty (1995), 139
UK Civil Aviation Authority, 107
UK East Midlands Supply, 70
UK Film Council, 43
UK Professional Advice, 73
UK Zombie companies, 58–61,
92
United Kingdom
ageing society and pensioners,
24
'Ambition Gap' between UK
and US MSMEs, 44

balance of payments, 23
Conservative (2015−), 43
consumer spending, 22−23
contributions to the EU, 106
Current Trade Balance Deficit,
    104
GDP growth series
    (1300−1700), 32
international dependence,
    24−25
investment levels in, 22
Labour (1997−2010), 43
Liberal Democrat/Conservative
    coalition (2010−2015), 43
manufacturing sector, 24
regional dynamics, 23
services sector, 24
share of labour utilisation, 24
wage subsidies, 24
United Kingdom, post-Brexit
adoption of free trade, 122
government debt to GDP, 133
industrial change and tariffs,
    125−126
mainstream case examples,
    127−129

potential policy effectiveness,
    129−133
removal of bureaucratic
    barriers, 122
tariff liberalisation and
    protection, 122−126
unit labour cost reduction, 131
wealth distribution, 133
US−UK bilateral agreement
    (1995), 107

Venture Capital market, 18
Verdoorn's law, 62

Wales, 114
'Washington Consensus'
    approach, 61
Waymo, 113
Weinstock GEC experience,
    164−165
Western economies, 210
Westminster Parliament,
    114, 116
Work Programme, UK, 72−73

Zombification, 143